McDougal, Littell
SPELLING

Red Level

Dolores Boylston Bohen
Assistant Superintendent
Fairfax County Public Schools
Fairfax County, Virginia

McDougal, Littell & Company
Evanston, Illinois
New York Dallas Sacramento Raleigh

Objectives

- to teach the spelling of **words** as well as the spelling of sounds
- to stress the recognition of **structural** similarities as well as phonetic similarities
- to strengthen **associative** and **visual memory**
- to reinforce the **three modes of learning:** visual, auditory, and kinesthetic

Organization

Each lesson presents a word list that demonstrates one spelling pattern or generalization. The list is followed by three types of activities:

Practice the Words—three activities that require students to examine and write the words on the spelling list

Build Word Power—an activity that extends the application of words on the spelling list in a broader language arts context

Reach Out for New Words—two activities in which students work with new words that follow the spelling pattern

CONSULTANTS FOR THIS TEXT

Sandra Ausenbaugh Bauder, Teacher, Schertz-Cibolo-Universal City Independent School District, Schertz, Texas
Helen F. Bell, Teacher, Mercer County School District, Princeton, West Virginia
Catherine Berg, Teacher, Alachua County School District, Gainesville, Florida
Jewel Fleetwood, Department Chairman, Consolidated School Corporation, Columbus, Indiana
Jo Ann Frostad, Department Chairman, Medford School District 549C, Medford, Oregon
Linda S. Hindes, Teacher, DeKalb Community School District, DeKalb, Illinois
Carol J. Kelly, Department Chairman, Eugene School District 4, Eugene, Oregon
Beverly McDuffie, Teacher, Eugene School District 4, Eugene, Oregon
Frances M. Pinckley, Teacher, Lawrence County School System, Lawrenceburg, Tennessee
Lovette M. Rushing, Teacher, Medford School District 549C, Medford, Oregon
Jackie Vance, Teacher, Logan County School District, West Virginia
Michael Vanlandingham, Teacher, Roane County School System, Kingston, Tennessee

Acknowledgments
The Christian Science Monitor: For "Swift Things Are Beautiful," by Elizabeth Coatsworth; copyright © 1948, The Christian Science Publishing Society; all rights reserved. Random House, Inc.: For "Dreams" from *The Dream Keeper and Other Poems* by Langston Hughes; copyright © 1932 by Alfred A. Knopf, Inc. and renewed 1960 by Langston Hughes.

ISBN: 0-8123-5396-X

Copyright © 1990 by McDougal, Littell & Company
Box 1667, Evanston, Illinois 60204
All rights reserved. Printed in the United States of America

90 91 92 93 / 15 14 13 12 11 10 9 8 7 6 5 4 3 2

CONTENTS

A Writer's Journal

Spelling Is for Writing

Imagine that you are writing a sports column for the school newspaper. What would happen if you could not spell a single word? How would you communicate with others?

Knowing how to spell improves your ability to communicate important information and ideas. This book will provide you with the practice you need to become a better speller and, in turn, a better writer.

One fun way to practice your spelling and writing is to keep a journal. A journal is a notebook in which you write about your thoughts and feelings. A journal is for your own use and enjoyment.

Plan now to keep a journal throughout the year. Write in your journal often. On some days you might write only a sentence or two. On other days you might write several pages. Here are some ways you can use your journal:

- express how you are feeling
- keep a record of new ideas
- remember important events in your life
- react to a poem or story you have read
- try out ideas for stories or poems of your own
- describe something or someone you feel strongly about
- look at a problem you have and try to solve it
- think about what the future might be like

Spelling and Your Journal

When you write in your journal, you may want to use words that you do not know how to spell. If this happens, do not stop writing. Instead, write the words as you think they should be spelled. When you are finished, look up the correct spellings in the dictionary. Keep a personal list of the words that give you trouble. You can refer to this list when you need to write the words in the future.

Getting Started

If you need an idea for your first journal entry, try finishing one of these.

1. I feel _____ because . . .
2. I'm looking forward to . . .
3. Lately I've been thinking about . . .

Building a Personal Word List

What Is a Personal Word List

In your spelling book, you will learn to spell many words. You will also learn important information about how words in our language are spelled. In this way, the book will help you become a better writer. There will be times, however, when you misspell a word or need to write a word that you have not learned to spell. You can include these words in a special spelling list called a personal word list—a list of words *you* want to learn to spell and use. This list will be unique because *you* will decide which words you want to make your own.

Words for your personal word list can come from many different sources. Some of the words will come from your writing, but the words might also come from your reading or conversations. These are some other sources that might result in words for your personal list:

- your journal entries
- stories, poems, or reports you write
- readings in content areas such as social studies or science
- letters you write or receive

How to Keep a Personal Word List

You will need a special place to write your personal words, such as the back of your journal, a special notebook, or a card file. The most important thing is to keep your list handy so that you can add words to it and refer to the list easily.

As you collect words you have misspelled, examine them carefully. Notice the kinds of spelling mistakes you make. Are you making the same kinds of errors? Think about the words as you learn to spell them. Are any of them similar in spelling to words you already know? Are they comprised of spelling patterns you have studied?

Making Words Your Own

To make a word your own—that is, to make it one you can use correctly in your own writing—you will need to know the meaning and correct spelling of the word. A dictionary can provide you with this information. You will want to develop your own way of learning to spell the word, however. The strategy outlined on page 7 is one you might use.

How to Spell a Word

Each week you will be learning to spell a new list of words. You will also be learning words from your personal list. You will need a system—or strategy—for studying these words. One way to learn to spell a word is explained below. You can use it as you prepare for your weekly spelling test and as you learn to spell words on your personal list.

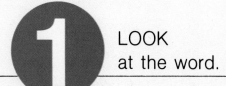 **LOOK**
at the word.

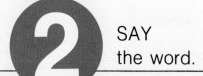 **SAY**
the word.

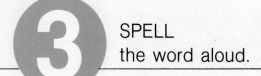 **SPELL**
the word aloud.

 **COPY**
the word.

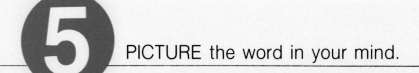 PICTURE the word in your mind.

 Cover the word and
WRITE it.

Check for mistakes.
If you have made a mistake, repeat steps 1 through 6.

Final silent e words and suffixes

use + age	= *usage*		store + age	= *storage*
create + ive	= *creative*		narrate + ive	= *narrative*
continue + ous	= *continuous*		ridicule + ous	= *ridiculous*
insure + ance	= *insurance*		ignore + ance	= *ignorance*
survive + al	= *survival*		refuse + al	= *refusal*
please + ure	= *pleasure*		literate + ure	= *literature*
mature + ity	= *maturity*		secure + ity	= *security*
believe + able	= *believable*		value + able	= *valuable*
televise + ion	= *television*		complete + ion	= *completion*
confuse + ion	= *confusion*		revise + ion	= *revision*

> A **suffix** is a word ending that changes the use of a word.

1. What nine different suffixes have been added to form spelling words?

   _____ _____ _____ _____ _____

   _____ _____ _____ _____

2. Does each suffix begin with a vowel or a consonant? _____

3. Before a suffix is added, each word ends with a letter that is not pronounced.

   What is that final silent letter? _____

4. What happens to the final silent letter when the suffix is added? _____

> When you add a suffix that begins with a vowel to a word that ends with a
> silent **e**, drop the final **e**.

PRACTICE THE WORDS

A Write the spelling word that matches each clue and fits in the boxes.

1. a corrected written work

2. disorder

3. delight

4. the condition of full development

5. lack of knowledge

6. story

7. going on without a break

8. foolish

9. easy to believe

What spelling word is
in the colored boxes? _____

A **base word** is a word before any changes have been made.
A **suffix** can be added to a base word to change the way it is used.

> Did my directions confuse you?
> Yes, your directions were confusing.
> I'm sorry my directions caused such confusion.

The underlined words are **related forms** of the base word **confuse**.
Related forms of the same base word may be different parts of speech. They
may be nouns, verbs, adjectives, or adverbs.

B Answer each question with a sentence that contains a spelling word. Use
a related form of the underlined base word.

1. Does that sculptor create art from old scraps of metal?

   _____

2. Did the hikers learn how to survive in the wilderness?

   _____

3. Do the new locks make you feel secure?

   _____

4. Is there room to store things in the basement?

   _____

5. Does the use of a word change when a suffix is added?

   _____

6. If they <u>refuse</u> to let Josh go, will he be upset?

   _____

7. Do those old coins have any great <u>value</u>?

   _____

8. When does Leah expect the project to be <u>complete</u>?

   _____

DICTIONARY

C Alphabetize the spelling words that would be listed between each pair of guide
   words on a dictionary page. Then use your spelling dictionary to write the abbreviation for the correct part of speech next to each word.

behave	**intact**	**limber**	**revival**	**rhythm**	**veto**
_____ _____	_____ _____		_____ _____	_____ _____	
_____ _____	_____ _____		_____ _____	_____ _____	
_____ _____	_____ _____		_____ _____	_____ _____	
_____ _____	_____ _____				
_____ _____	_____ _____				
_____ _____	_____ _____		_____ _____		
_____ _____	_____ _____		_____ _____		

BUILD WORD POWER

Write the base form of each of these spelling words. Then add one of the suffixes
from the box to each base word. Complete each of the phrases with one of the
new words. Use your dictionary to help you.

able   ion   al

1. usage   _____ + _____   1. the sculptor's _____

2. creative   _____ + _____   2. in _____ motion

3. narrative _____ + _____   3. not an _____ vehicle

4. continuous _____ + _____   4. not _____ anymore

5. insurance _____ + _____   5. the _____ of the tale

usage | survival | television | ridiculous | security
creative | pleasure | confusion | ignorance | valuable
continuous | maturity | storage | refusal | completion
insurance | believable | narrative | literature | revision

New Words
Discover new words below!

REACH OUT FOR NEW WORDS

A Find eight new final **e** words in this puzzle that fit the letters and spaces. Complete each word.

1. __ __ __ o __ __ __ __
2. __ __ s __ __ __
3. __ __ __ __ n __ __ __
4. __ __ h __ __ __ __ __
5. __ __ __ p __ __ __
6. __ __ __ t __
7. __ __ __ __ __ v __ __ __
8. __ __ v __ __ __

B Complete this story by adding the suffix shown after each blank to one of the eight new words. Write the new words.

The drama club, under Mr. Clark's __1__-ion, held a meeting to plan their spring play. Mr. Clark explained that a quick but thoughtful selection of a show was very __2__-able. The members all agreed that the play should __3__-ly be a comedy, one that would be both amusing and entertaining. Finally the club decided to do a __4__-al of an old musical that had all of the elements they wanted. It had music by a well-known __5__-er, __6__-able lines of dialogue, and __7__-ive scenery and costumes. The club got ready to begin __8__-al on what promised to be a wonderful production.

1. _____   5. _____

2. _____   6. _____

3. _____   7. _____

4. _____   8. _____

sincere	since**ri**ty	sincer**e**ly
secure	secu**ri**ty	secur**e**ly
active	activi**ty**	activ**e**ly
separate	separat**ing**	separat**e**ly
name	nam**ing**	nam**e**ly
close	clos**ing**	clos**e**ly
waste	wast**ing**	wast**e**ful
hope	hop**ing**	hop**e**ful
care	car**ing**	car**e**ful
forgive	forgiv**able**	forgiv**e**ness
like	lik**able**	lik**e**ness
move	mov**able**	mov**e**ment
require	requi**ring**	requir**e**ment
settle	settl**ing**	settl**e**ment
place	plac**ing**	plac**e**ment
measure	measur**ing**	measur**e**ment
involve	involv**ing**	involv**e**ment
amaze	amaz**ing**	amaz**e**ment
advance	advanc**ing**	advanc**e**ment
improve	improv**ing**	improv**e**ment

1. Why is the final **e** dropped from the words in the first column to form the words in the second column?

_____

2. What four suffixes have been added to form the words in the last column?

_____ _____ _____ _____

Does each suffix in the last column begin with a consonant or a vowel? _____

3. What happens to the final **e** when a suffix beginning with a consonant is added?

_____

> When you add a suffix that begins with a consonant to a word that ends in silent **e**, keep the final **e**.

PRACTICE THE WORDS

A Write the base form of each word. Then add the **ing** suffix to the base form.

Base Form | ing Form

1. separately _____ _____

2. involvement _____ _____

3. careful _____ _____

4. closely _____ _____

5. improvement _____ _____

6. requirement _____ _____

7. wasteful _____ _____

8. namely _____ _____

9. placement _____ _____

10. settlement _____ _____

11. advancement _____ _____

12. hopeful _____ _____

13. amazement _____ _____

14. measurement _____ _____

B Unscramble these groups of words to make complete sentences. Be sure to use correct capitalization and punctuation. Circle the spelling words.

1. two was amazing the between likeness the cousins.

_____

2. food forgivable good is never wasting.

_____

3. the careful was dancer to practice movement every.

_____

4. all securely the objects sailor fastened movable.

_____

5. pleased the sincerely is coach improvement by Lyle's.

_____

DICTIONARY

Suffixes may be listed as entries in a dictionary.	**-ly** (lē) [OE. *-lice* < *-lic*] *a suffix used to form adjectives or adverbs, meaning:* **1.** in a specified manner, to a specified extent or direction, in or at a specified time or place [*harshly, outwardly, hourly*] **2.** in the specified order [*secondly*] **3.** like or suitable to [*fatherly*]
Words formed by adding suffixes may also be entries.	**name·ly** (-lē) *adv.* that is to say [a choice of two desserts, *namely*, cake or pie]
Other words with suffixes may be found at the end of a base word entry. Each of these words is followed by an abbreviation that tells the part of speech.	**sin·cere** (sin sir′) *adj.* **-cer′er, -cer′est** [< MFr. < L. *sincerus*, clean] **1.** not pretending or fooling; truthful; honest [*sincere* in wanting to help] **2.** genuine; real [*sincere* grief] —**sin·cere′ly** *adv.*

C Look at the words in the third column of your spelling list. Then find each word in your spelling dictionary. The word may be listed as a separate entry, or it may appear at the end of an entry. Write it under the correct heading. Then write the abbreviation that tells the part of speech for each word.

Separate Entry   **End of Entry**

_____ ___ _____ ___ _____ ___

_____ ___ _____ ___ _____ ___

_____ ___ _____ ___ _____ ___

_____ ___ _____ ___ _____ ___

_____ ___ _____ ___ _____ ___

_____ ___ _____ ___ _____ ___

_____ ___ _____ ___

BUILD WORD POWER

The past tense ending **ed** begins with a vowel.
When it is added to a word that ends with silent **e**, drop the silent **e**.

The ending **ed** can be added to some of your spelling words to make the past tense form. Complete each phrase with the **ed** form of a spelling word.

1. _____ the book more than the movie

2. _____ the argument once and for all

3. _____ in an interesting discussion

4. _____ the yellow pieces from the red ones

5. _____ the distance correctly

6. _____ by the magician's tricks

14

sincerely naming careful requirement involving
securely closely forgivable settling amazement
activity wasting likeness placement advancing
separately hoping movable measurement improvement

New Words
Discover new words below!

REACH OUT FOR NEW WORDS

A Use the following code to find seven new words. Write each word.

S	I	K	M	O	B	N	V	T	A	X	G	R	L	Z	Q	C	W	E	H	P	D	U	Y	J	F
1	2	3	4	5	6	7	8	9	10	11	12	13	14	15	16	17	18	19	20	21	22	23	24	25	26

1. $\overline{1}\ \overline{17}\ \overline{10}\ \overline{13}\ \overline{17}\ \overline{19}\ \overline{14}\ \overline{24}$ _____

2. $\overline{9}\ \overline{13}\ \overline{2}\ \overline{6}\ \overline{19}\ \overline{1}$ _____

3. $\overline{8}\ \overline{19}\ \overline{7}\ \overline{9}\ \overline{23}\ \overline{13}\ \overline{19}\ \overline{1}\ \overline{5}\ \overline{4}\ \overline{19}$ _____

4. $\overline{2}\ \overline{4}\ \overline{21}\ \overline{23}\ \overline{14}\ \overline{1}\ \overline{19}\ \overline{1}$ _____

5. $\overline{13}\ \overline{10}\ \overline{13}\ \overline{19}\ \overline{14}\ \overline{24}$ _____

6. $\overline{9}\ \overline{13}\ \overline{5}\ \overline{23}\ \overline{6}\ \overline{14}\ \overline{19}\ \overline{1}\ \overline{5}\ \overline{4}\ \overline{19}$ _____

7. $\overline{19}\ \overline{11}\ \overline{21}\ \overline{19}\ \overline{7}\ \overline{1}\ \overline{19}\ \overline{1}$ _____

B Write the base form of each new word. Then make a new form of each word, using a suffix from the box. Use your spelling dictionary to help you.

ing	al	ity	ive

1. _____ _____

2. _____ _____

3. _____ _____

4. _____ _____

5. _____ _____

6. _____ _____

7. _____ _____

vacate + ion = *vacation*   locate + ion = *location*

educate + ion = *education*   punctuate + ion = *punctuation*

celebrate + ion = *celebration*   graduate + ion = *graduation*

hesitate + ion = *hesitation*   migrate + ion = *migration*

translate + ion = *translation*   complicate + ion = *complication*

operate + ion = *operation*   cooperate + ion = *cooperation*

investigate + ion = *investigation*   eliminate + ion = *elimination*

calculate + ion = *calculation*   circulate + ion = *circulation*

refrigerate + ion = *refrigeration*   regulate + ion = *regulation*

dictate + ion = *dictation*   duplicate + ion = *duplication*

A word that tells about an action is a **verb**: operate.
A word that names something is a **noun**: operation.
ate is a verb ending. **ion** is a noun ending.

1. All of the base words end with the same three letters. What are those letters? _____

   Is the final **e** pronounced or silent? _____

   Does the letter **t** have a hard sound (ra<u>t</u>e) or a soft sound (na<u>t</u>ion)? _____

2. What are the last four letters of each word after the **ion** suffix is added? _____

   What happens to the final silent **e**? _____

   Does the letter **t** have a hard or a soft sound? _____

The word ending pronounced **shun** is usually spelled **tion**.
Many verbs that end with **ate** can be changed to nouns by adding the suffix **ion**. The
hard **t** in **ate** becomes a soft **t** in **tion**.

A Complete these sentences with the **ion** forms of spelling words. Then find the
ate verb that appears in each sentence.

1. The detectives hoped everyone would cooperate with the _____ of the crime.

2. To eliminate the problem of overcrowding, the school's _____ ceremony is

   being moved to a new _____ .

3. A good secretary can take _____ and correctly punctuate letters and memos.

4. The surgeon says that this _____ can regulate the heartbeat and improve blood

   _____ .

5. I will not hesitate to try waterskiing when I am on _____ .

6. Are scientists able to calculate when the geese will begin their _____ from Canada?

7. Please duplicate your work on the board so the math class can see how the _____

   is done.

8. If you regulate the _____ carefully, none of the food will spoil.

9. Our class is planning a special _____ for the day we graduate.

10. You must learn some new _____ when you translate English into Spanish.

PROOFREADING

B Cross out the misspelled words that appear in Helpful Hannah's newspaper
column. Write the words correctly.

DEAR HELPFUL HANNAH: There is a complacation in my life,
and I need your advice. For months I have been planning a
surprise birthday celebration for my cousin Lucy. Her parents
promised me their cooperasion. Now I find out that they have
scheduled a graduashion party for Lucy's sister on the same
night. We would be inviting the same people. What should I do?

DOUBLEDATED

DEAR DD: Your sad problem calls for the eliminasion of this
duplicashun without hestation. I suggest you either move your
operation to a different night or hold both parties at the same
locashun. However it works out, let this experience be an
edukation.

HELPFUL HANNAH

1. _____   5. _____

2. _____   6. _____

3. _____   7. _____

4. _____   8. _____

C Each phrase in this chain should contain a verb and a noun. Complete the first phrase by finding the noun that fits in the boxes. Begin the next phrase with the verb form of the noun you just used. Complete the rest of the chain in the same way.

complicate _____ the ☐☐☐☐☐☐☐

_____ the ☐☐☐☐☐☐☐☐☐☐

_____ the ☐☐☐☐☐☐☐

_____ the ☐☐☐☐☐☐☐☐

_____ the ☐☐☐☐☐☐☐☐

_____ the ☐☐☐☐☐☐☐☐☐☐

WRITING

Add **'s** to form the possessive of most singular nouns.
Rya**n's** birthday   Bes**s's** house

Combine one word from the first list with one word from the second list to make possessive phrases. Add **'s** to make the first word show ownership. Use each phrase in a sentence.

| John | Sue | family | vacation | operation | graduation |
| camp | Chris | cousin | location | education | celebration |

1. _____

2. _____

3. _____

4. _____

5. _____

6. _____

vacation translation refrigeration graduation elimination
education operation dictation migration circulation
celebration investigation location complication regulation
hesitation calculation punctuation cooperation duplication

REACH OUT FOR NEW WORDS

A Find seven new **ate** words by following this code. Each letter in a word is represented by a capital letter and a number.

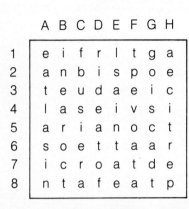

	A	B	C	D	E	F	G	H
1	e	i	f	r	l	t	g	a
2	a	n	b	i	s	p	o	e
3	t	e	u	d	a	e	i	c
4	l	a	s	e	i	v	s	i
5	a	r	i	a	n	o	c	t
6	s	o	e	t	t	a	a	r
7	i	c	r	o	a	t	d	e
8	n	t	a	f	e	a	t	p

1. $\overline{E4}$ $\overline{B2}$ $\overline{D6}$ $\overline{H7}$ $\overline{G1}$ $\overline{B5}$ $\overline{E3}$ $\overline{E6}$ $\overline{A1}$

2. $\overline{G7}$ $\overline{F3}$ $\overline{E1}$ $\overline{D4}$ $\overline{G1}$ $\overline{A5}$ $\overline{D6}$ $\overline{C6}$

3. $\overline{H8}$ $\overline{F3}$ $\overline{D1}$ $\overline{D8}$ $\overline{F5}$ $\overline{H6}$ $\overline{C8}$ $\overline{F7}$ $\overline{B3}$

4. $\overline{G3}$ $\overline{A8}$ $\overline{H3}$ $\overline{C3}$ $\overline{C2}$ $\overline{H1}$ $\overline{F7}$ $\overline{C6}$

5. $\overline{F2}$ $\overline{C7}$ $\overline{D7}$ $\overline{G5}$ $\overline{H6}$ $\overline{D5}$ $\overline{A6}$ $\overline{E6}$ $\overline{E4}$ $\overline{B2}$ $\overline{E7}$ $\overline{B8}$ $\overline{D4}$

6. $\overline{A2}$ $\overline{B7}$ $\overline{F1}$ $\overline{H4}$ $\overline{F4}$ $\overline{G6}$ $\overline{G8}$ $\overline{H2}$

7. $\overline{A5}$ $\overline{C4}$ $\overline{E2}$ $\overline{B6}$ $\overline{G5}$ $\overline{C5}$ $\overline{F6}$ $\overline{H5}$ $\overline{E8}$

B Unscramble each sentence, using the **ion** form of the underlined word.

1. is <u>procrastinate</u> bad a habit.

_____

2. baby studied <u>incubate</u> chickens of we the.

_____

3. has been with enjoyable them <u>associate</u> our.

_____

4. the went <u>delegate</u> Congress to.

_____

5. aided Act of <u>integrate</u> Civil 1964 Rights the.

_____

6. along <u>perforate</u> between tear the the stamps.

_____

7. robot us the startled <u>activate</u> the of.

_____

re	+	double	=	*redouble*	con	+	quest	=	*conquest*
re	+	commend	=	*recommend*	con	+	sequence	=	*consequence*
de	+	serve	=	*deserve*	sub	+	urban	=	*suburban*
de	+	part	=	*depart*	sub	+	division	=	*subdivision*
ad	+	join	=	*adjoin*	pre	+	diction	=	*prediction*
ad	+	minister	=	*administer*	pre	+	caution	=	*precaution*
ex	+	act	=	*exact*	per	+	cent	=	*percent*
ex	+	claim	=	*exclaim*	per	+	form	=	*perform*
in	+	dent	=	*indent*	pro	+	pose	=	*propose*
in	+	stall	=	*install*	pro	+	long	=	*prolong*

A **prefix** is a group of letters added to the beginning of a word to change its meaning.

1. What ten prefixes have been added to form spelling words? _____ _____

   _____ _____ _____ _____ _____ _____ _____ _____

2. Were the prefixes added to complete words? _____

3. Does the spelling of the base word change when the prefix is added? _____

4. Does the meaning of the word change when the prefix is added? _____

You can add a prefix directly to a base word to form a new word with a different meaning.
The spelling of the base word does not change when you add a prefix.

A Write the spelling words that match the definitions and fit in the puzzle.

Across

1. a foretelling
2. to offer advice
3. to attach to
4. precisely correct
7. to fix in position
9. result of an action
11. an area of land divided into smaller lots
12. to double again
13. move in from the margin

Down

1. to lengthen in time
3. to manage or direct
5. a victory
6. a part of one hundred
8. located in a suburb
10. to suggest

B Write the **ed** and **ing** forms of these spelling words. If a spelling word ends in a final silent **e**, drop the **e** before writing the related forms.

	ed form	**ing** form
1. perform	_____	_____
2. redouble	_____	_____
3. exclaim	_____	_____
4. recommend	_____	_____
5. prolong	_____	_____
6. deserve	_____	_____
7. propose	_____	_____
8. depart	_____	_____
9. install	_____	_____
10. indent	_____	_____

Prefixes are listed in the dictionary as separate entries. Each entry may give several meanings for a prefix.

C Read the entries for these prefixes in your spelling dictionary. Write the meanings. Then write the spelling words that match the definitions.

1. ad _____

2. de _____

3. re _____

4. per _____

5. ex _____

6. pre _____

7. pro _____

8. in _____

9. sub _____

10. con _____

1. be next <u>to</u> _____

2. cry <u>out</u> _____

3. go <u>away</u> _____

4. care taken
   beforehand _____

5. something told
   <u>before</u> it happens _____

6. area divided into <u>parts</u> _____

7. manage or give help <u>to</u> _____

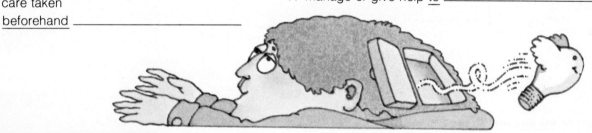

BUILD WORD POWER

Write the words formed by adding prefixes and suffixes to base words from your spelling list.

1. con + **form** + ity = _____

2. in + **cent** + ive = _____

3. in + **act** + ive + ity = _____

4. re + **act** + ive + ate + ed = _____

5. re + in + **stall** + ment = _____

6. pre + de + **part** + ure = _____

7. de + **part** + ment + al + ly = _____

8. in + **form** + al + ity = _____

redouble	adjoin	indent	suburban	percent	New Words
recommend	administer	install	subdivision	perform	Discover
deserve	exact	conquest	prediction	propose	new words
depart	exclaim	consequence	precaution	prolong	below!

REACH OUT FOR NEW WORDS

A Build a word pyramid by following the code. Use your spelling dictionary to find the four pyramid words that match the definitions.

The word **part** means "to divide or part."

1. something used to divide an area into parts

_____

2. not taking anyone's part

_____

3. a small part of

_____

4. person who takes one side or part

_____

P A R T

$\underset{3}{D}$ $\underset{4}{E}$ P A R T

P A R T $\overline{}_{5}$ $\overline{}_{2}$ $\overline{}_{6}$ $\overline{}_{4}$

P A R T $\overline{}_{5}$ $\overline{}_{10}$ $\overline{}_{1}$ $\overline{}_{8}$

P A R T $\overline{}_{5}$ $\overline{}_{11}$ $\overline{}_{5}$ $\overline{}_{9}$ $\overline{}_{8}$

$\overline{}_{1}$ P A R T $\overline{}_{7}$ $\overline{}_{4}$ $\overline{}_{8}$ $\overline{}_{11}$

$\overline{}_{5}$ $\overline{}_{7}$ P A R T $\overline{}_{5}$ $\overline{}_{1}$ $\overline{}_{6}$

A	C	D	E	I	L	M	N	O	S	T
1	2	3	4	5	6	7	8	9	10	11

B Build another word pyramid. Find the four pyramid words that match the definitions.

The word **form** means "to shape."

1. complete change of shape or form

_____

2. a rule for "shaping"

_____

3. all alike in shape or appearance

_____

4. the "shaping" of a group so that everyone is the same

_____

F O R M

$\underset{9}{P}$ $\underset{4}{E}$ $\underset{10}{R}$ F O R M

F O R M $\overline{}_{13}$ $\overline{}_{6}$ $\overline{}_{1}$

$\overline{}_{13}$ $\overline{}_{7}$ $\overline{}_{5}$ F O R M

$\overline{}_{10}$ $\overline{}_{4}$ F O R M $\overline{}_{4}$ $\overline{}_{3}$

$\overline{}_{2}$ $\overline{}_{8}$ $\overline{}_{7}$ F O R M $\overline{}_{5}$ $\overline{}_{12}$ $\overline{}_{14}$

$\overline{}_{12}$ $\overline{}_{10}$ $\overline{}_{1}$ $\overline{}_{7}$ $\overline{}_{11}$ F O R M $\overline{}_{1}$ $\overline{}_{12}$ $\overline{}_{5}$ $\overline{}_{8}$ $\overline{}_{7}$

A	C	D	E	I	L	N	O	P	R	S	T	U	Y
1	2	3	4	5	6	7	8	9	10	11	12	13	14

re + sist = *resist*   de + tain = *detain*

in + sist = *insist*   con + tain = *contain*

con + flict = *conflict*   pro + gress + ion = *progression*

in + flict = *inflict*   re + gress + ion = *regression*

de + script + ion = *description*   de + cis + ion = *decision*

in + script + ion = *inscription*   in + cis + ion = *incision*

pre + script + ion = *prescription*   pre + cis + ion = *precision*

in + vent + ion = *invention*   in + clude = *include*

con + vent + ion = *convention*   ex + clude = *exclude*

pre + vent + ion = *prevention*   con + clude = *conclude*

A **root** is a word part that cannot stand alone. It must be joined to other word parts to form a word.

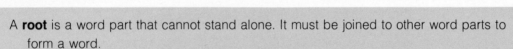

$$\frac{\text{Prefix}}{\text{in}} + \frac{\text{Root}}{\text{cis}} + \frac{\text{Suffix}}{\text{ion}} = \frac{\text{Word}}{\text{incision}}$$

1. Before the prefixes and suffixes are added, are the letter groups complete words? _____

2. A word part that must be joined to other word parts to form a complete word

   is called a _____.

3. How many different roots are used in the word list? _____

   How many different prefixes are used? _____

   What suffix has been added to some roots? _____

4. Do **resist** and **insist** have the same root? _____

   Do they have the same meaning? _____

A root can be joined with many different prefixes. Changing the prefix forms a new word with a different meaning.

The root **clude** means "to close."

    exclude = to close out or shut out   include = to close in

PRACTICE THE WORDS

A Find the spelling words that begin with the following prefixes. Write them in alphabetical order.

con

_____

_____

_____

_____

de

_____

_____

_____

ex

_____

in

_____

_____

_____

_____

pre

_____

_____

_____

pro

_____

re

_____

B Mrs. Mixit has the habit of using the wrong prefix with the right root. Help her say what she really means by changing the prefixes of the underlined words and writing the correct words.

Yesterday was not a good day. I was invited to be the guest speaker at a <u>prevention</u> of detectives. My topic was the <u>invention</u> of crime. I spoke for a half-hour and was about to <u>exclude</u> when I noticed that my purse was gone. "I've been robbed," I shouted.

Several of the detectives offered to help me. "What did your purse <u>detain</u>?" they asked. I gave them a <u>prescription</u> of the contents. They made an immediate <u>precision</u> to search everyone in the room. They conducted the search with great <u>incision</u>. They even decided to <u>conclude</u> me in their search.

One detective reached into my coat pocket and found my wallet. That's when I remembered that I had left my purse at home. I was embarrassed, but everyone was nice enough to <u>resist</u> that I really was a good detective. "After all," one said, "you did prevent a crime!"

1. _____   4. _____   7. _____

2. _____   5. _____   8. _____

3. _____   6. _____   9. _____

An **etymology**, or word history, may be shown as a special note in a word entry. It is often found before the definition. An etymology shows the languages a word comes from and gives the meanings of the word parts. A chart at the beginning of your dictionary gives abbreviations for the different languages.

symbol meaning "comes from"

abbreviation for *Latin*

ex·clude (iks klo͞od′) *v.* **-clud′ed, -clud′ing** [< L. *excludere* < *ex-*, out + *claudere*, close] to refuse to admit

Latin word

prefix and meaning

root and meaning

C Look up these words in your spelling dictionary. Write each word next to its etymology.

resist   insist   contain   detain   conflict   inflict

1. _____ [< OFr. < L. < *de-*, off + *tenere*, to hold]

2. _____ [< L.pp. of *infligere* < *in-*, against + *fligere*, to strike]

3. _____ [< MFr. < L. < *re-*, back + *sistere*, to set < *stare*, to stand]

4. _____ [< L.pp. of *confligere* < *com-*, together + *fligere*, to strike]

5. _____ [< OFr. < L. *continere* < *com-*, together + *tenere*, to hold]

6. _____ [< MFr. < L. *insistere* < *in-*, in + *sistere*, to stand]

BUILD WORD POWER

WRITING

Expand each phrase into a sentence. Then, on your own paper, use three of the sentences in a story that begins with the sentence: **Inspector Whodunit was baffled**.

1. the eyewitness's description _____

_____

2. could only conclude _____

_____

3. contain the missing jewels _____

_____

4. detain the suspect _____

_____

5. resist arrest _____

_____

6. prevention of crime _____

_____

resist   description   convention   progression   precision
insist   inscription   prevention   regression   include
conflict   prescription   detain   decision   exclude
inflict   invention   contain   incision   conclude

New Words
Discover new words below!

REACH OUT FOR NEW WORDS

A Build a word pyramid by following the code. Use your spelling dictionary to find the four pyramid words that match the definitions.

The root **tain** means "to hold."

1. used to hold something

_____

2. "held" or kept in good condition

_____

3. something held to amuse or interest

_____

4. being held in connection with

_____

TAIN

$\underline{D}_{4} \; \underline{E}_{5}$ TAIN

$\underline{\;}_{10} \underline{\;}_{2}$ TAIN $\underline{\;}_{5} \underline{\;}_{4}$

$\underline{\;}_{3} \underline{\;}_{10} \underline{\;}_{9}$ TAIN $\underline{\;}_{5} \underline{\;}_{12}$

$\underline{\;}_{11} \underline{\;}_{5} \underline{\;}_{12}$ TAIN $\underline{\;}_{7} \underline{\;}_{9} \underline{\;}_{6}$

$\underline{\;}_{8} \underline{\;}_{1} \underline{\;}_{7} \underline{\;}_{9}$ TAIN $\underline{\;}_{5} \underline{\;}_{4}$

$\underline{\;}_{5} \underline{\;}_{9} \underline{\;}_{13} \underline{\;}_{5} \underline{\;}_{12}$ TAIN $\underline{\;}_{8} \underline{\;}_{5} \underline{\;}_{9} \underline{\;}_{13}$

A	B	C	D	E	G	I	M	N	O	P	R	T
1	2	3	4	5	6	7	8	9	10	11	12	13

B Build another word pyramid. Find the four pyramid words that match the definitions.

The root **ven** means "come."

1. money coming in

_____

2. that which comes before to keep something else from happening

_____

3. to come or be between

_____

4. to come around an obstacle

_____

VEN

$\underline{\;}_{8} \underline{\;}_{2}$ VEN $\underline{\;}_{10} \underline{\;}_{2}$

VEN $\underline{\;}_{9} \underline{\;}_{10} \underline{\;}_{8} \underline{\;}_{2}$

$\underline{\;}_{7} \underline{\;}_{8} \underline{\;}_{2}$ VEN $\underline{\;}_{9} \underline{\;}_{3} \underline{\;}_{6} \underline{\;}_{5}$

$\underline{\;}_{3} \underline{\;}_{5} \underline{\;}_{9} \underline{\;}_{2} \underline{\;}_{8}$ VEN $\underline{\;}_{2}$

$\underline{C}_{1} \underline{O}_{6} \underline{N}_{5}$ VEN $\underline{T}_{9} \underline{I}_{3} \underline{O}_{6} \underline{N}_{5}$

$\underline{\;}_{1} \underline{\;}_{3} \underline{\;}_{8} \underline{\;}_{1} \underline{\;}_{10} \underline{\;}_{4}$ VEN $\underline{\;}_{9}$

C	E	I	M	N	O	P	R	T	U
1	2	3	4	5	6	7	8	9	10

proof + read = *proofread*

fire + proof = *fireproof*

time + table = *timetable*

life + time = *lifetime*

night + time = *nighttime*

some + one = *someone*

any + time = *anytime*

mean + while = *meanwhile*

every + where = *everywhere*

when + ever = *whenever*

blue + eyed = *blue-eyed*

one + half = *one-half*

ninety + four = *ninety-four*

self + addressed = *self-addressed*

great + aunt = *great-aunt*

does + not = *doesn't*

it + is = *it's*

there + is = *there's*

here + is = *here's*

would + have = *would've*

1. In the first column, are any changes made when the two smaller words are joined? _____

   Why does **nighttime** have two **t**'s?

   _____

2. In the second column, what punctuation is added to join the first five

   pairs of words? _____

   Does the spelling of either word change when the two are joined? _____

3. In the second column, what punctuation is added to join the second five

   pairs of words? _____

   What does the apostrophe replace in these words? _____

Complete words may be combined to form other words in several different ways.

When two words are simply connected with no change in either word, the word formed is
   called a **compound word**.

Words joined by a hyphen are another kind of compound word.

When an apostrophe is used to show that one or more letters have been omitted, the word
   is called a **contraction**.

A Write the spelling word that matches each clue and fits in the boxes.

1. as long as someone lives
2. at whatever time
3. not just anyone
4. non-flammable
5. at any moment
6. at the same time
7. after sunset
8. bus or train schedule
9. look for writing errors

What other spelling word do
you see in the colored boxes? _____

WRITING

B Write a sentence using each set of spelling words. You may use the words in any order.

1. there's, timetable, ninety-four _____

_____

_____

2. would've, lifetime, great-aunt _____

_____

_____

3. it's, whenever, self-addressed _____

_____

_____

4. doesn't, everywhere, blue-eyed _____

_____

_____

5. here's, proofread, one-half _____

_____

_____

PROOFREADING

C Proofread Martha's letter. Cross out each misspelled word. Then write the words correctly.

Dear Uncle Gene,

    I am writing an essay about my greataunt, Martha Calhoun. I know theres much you can tell me about her and what she did during her lifetime. Did she really help start onehalf of the hospitals in the county? Does'nt one of the hospitals have a portrait of her in the lobby? Is it true that she was still working at the age of ninetyfour?

    I hope its convenient for you to answer my questions soon. I have a timetable for writing my essay, and I'll also need time to proof-read the rough draft. Heres' a self-addressed envelope for you to use. I will appreciate any information you send.

Your niece,

Martha

_____   _____   _____

_____   _____   _____

_____   _____

BUILD WORD POWER

Two of the words in each group are related to one of the spelling words. One word in each group is not related in the same way. Cross out the word that does not fit. Write the spelling word that is related to the other two words.

1. short   blond   glasses   _____

2. compose   revise   recite   _____

3. morning   evening   midnight   _____

4. months   yesterday   years   _____

5. uncle   sister   grandmother   _____

6. everyone   anybody   she   _____

7. here   anywhere   somewhere   _____

8. schedule   menu   itinerary   _____

proofread	nighttime	everywhere	ninety-four	it's
fireproof	someone	whenever	self-addressed	there's
timetable	anytime	blue-eyed	great-aunt	here's
lifetime	meanwhile	one-half	doesn't	would've

New Words
Discover
new words
below!

REACH OUT FOR NEW WORDS

A All of these word parts have been joined incorrectly to make silly compounds.
Rematch the underlined parts to make real compound words and hyphenated
compounds. Cross out each part as you use it.

1. news<u>market</u> _____

2. north<u>natured</u> _____

3. super<u>place</u> _____

4. make<u>house</u> _____

5. paper<u>ache</u> _____

6. good<u>east</u> _____

7. back<u>self</u> _____

8. birth<u>up</u> _____

9. court<u>cast</u> _____

10. my<u>weight</u> _____

B Find the new word that fits each set of boxes. Count one space for hyphens.

1.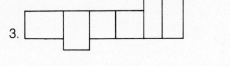

2.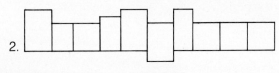

3.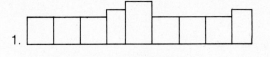

4.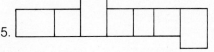

5.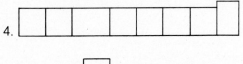

6.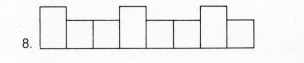

7.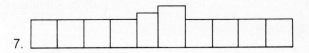

8.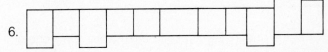

9.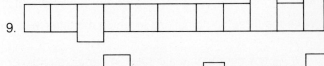

10.

31

sign   whose
resign   whole

reign   answer
foreign   sword

knives   written
knocked   wrapped

crumbs   raspberry
limbs   cupboard

palm   stalk
almond   folklore

Look at the underlined letters in each word. Only one of the two letters is pronounced. The other letter is a "silent partner." Say each word aloud.

1. Which letter is silent in each combination?

   gn _____   kn _____   mb _____   lm _____   wh _____

   sw _____   wr _____   pb _____   lk _____

2. Write the two combinations in which only the letter **m** is pronounced. _____ _____

3. Write the two combinations in which only the letter **n** is pronounced. _____ _____

4. Write the three combinations in which the letter **w** is silent. _____ _____ _____

> A few consonants are silent in certain combinations.
>   gn   kn   mb   lm   wh   sw   wr   pb   lk

A Follow these directions.

Write the spelling words that have a silent **w**. _____ _____

_____ _____ _____ _____

Write the words that have a silent **g**. _____ _____

_____ _____

Write the words that have a silent **l**. _____ _____

_____ _____

Write the words that have a silent **p**. _____ _____

Write the words that have a silent **k**. _____ _____

Write the words that have a silent **b**. _____ _____

Mnemonics (Cover the silent first letter and say *ne mon′ ics.*)
Mnemonics is a system of improving the memory.
A mnemonic device is a memory aid.

For example, the word **HOMES** can help you to remember the names of the five Great Lakes.

Huron
Ontario
Michigan
Erie
Superior

The word **FACE** tells you the four notes in the spaces of a musical staff.

	E	●
	C	●
	A	●
F	●	

Invent your own mnemonic devices for words that are difficult spelling problems.

B Look at the underlined letters in each phrase. Complete the phrase with a spelling word that uses those letters in a consonant combination. You will have to use the plural form of some of the spelling words.

My friend Norman . . .

makes bread _____,   paints big _____,

likes munching _____,   keeps no _____,

sends wacky _____,   wants halves _____,

gives no _____,   might break _____,

picks big _____,   swings wide _____,

may **n**eed **mn**emonics!

If you have trouble remembering how to spell any of these words, think of the phrases above. You will be using a mnemonic device!

Homonyms are words that sound the same but are spelled differently.

to–two–too   their–there

Homonyms do not have the same meaning.

C Choose the correct homonyms to complete the sentences.

whose   reign   wrapped   whole
who's   rain   rapped   hole

1. The _____ set of packages should be _____ in heavy paper.

2. The new queen _____ her scepter on the floor three times to mark the beginning of her

_____ .

3. The _____ poured through the _____ in the ceiling.

4. Anyone _____ in the art class can tell you _____ drawing this is.

5. _____ lunch is _____ in aluminum foil?

6. Leo _____ on the door so hard we thought he would put a _____ in it.

7. The weather forecast calls for _____ for the _____ day.

8. _____ going to report on the _____ of the Emperor Napoleon?

BUILD WORD POWER

WRITING

Write acrostic poems with two of your spelling words. Begin each line with a letter of the word. The poem should relate to the meaning of the word.

Raspberry

Red   _____

And   _____

Sweet for   _____

Pies, or jam on   _____

Bread when you want to   _____

Eat something   _____

Really   _____

Really   _____

Yummy.   _____

Stalk

Slender,   _____

Tall,   _____

And   _____

Laden with   _____

Kernels.   _____

sign	knives	palm	answer	raspberry
resign	knocked	almond	sword	cupboard
reign	crumbs	whose	written	stalk
foreign	limbs	whole	wrapped	folklore

New Words
Discover
new words
below!

REACH OUT FOR NEW WORDS

A Find nine new "silent partner" words. Begin with **sign** and find your way out of the maze. Write each new word.

R	E	A	T	H	C	A	M
W	D	W	R	O	U	G	P
T	E	E	A	D	K	H	A
H	L	N	**S**	**I**	N	T	I
G	R	K	**N**	**G**	O	W	G
I	A	N	G	L	L	R	N
R	W	Y	A	L	P	Y	C
			K	L	U	A	

sign

1. _____

2. _____

3. _____

4. _____

5. _____

6. _____

7. _____

8. _____

9. _____

B Complete each sentence with one of the new words. You will have to add **ed** to three of the words.

1. That author is known for her _____ sense of humor.

2. The mayor _____ tirelessly for re-election.

3. Shakespeare was a 16th century English _____.

4. Chris _____ the dough on a floured board.

5. Dwayne hung a holiday _____ on the door.

6. We _____ the tiles in the bathroom.

7. The old oak tree was knotted and _____.

8. We sat on a grassy _____ overlooking the river.

9. Tricia painted the _____ iron table.

35

1

please   pleasure
refuse   refusal
use   usage
continue continuous
believe   believable

2

sincere   sincerity   sincerely
separate separating separately
hope   hoping   hopeful
measure   measuring   measurement
improve   improving   improvement

3

celebrate   celebration
cooperate   cooperation
punctuate   punctuation
refrigerate refrigeration

4

precaution
percent
recommend
consequence

5

prescription
prevention
decision
insist

6

nighttime
ninety-four
doesn't
proofread

7

foreign
knives
whose
written

A An analogy is a special way of showing how words are related to each other. Complete each analogy with a spelling word that makes the second pair of words go together in the same way as the first pair of words.

1. **name** is to **namely** as **sincere** is to _____

2. **double** is to **redouble** as **commend** is to _____

3. **value** is to **believe** as **valuable** is to _____

4. **half** is to **halves** as **knife** is to _____

5. **sixty** is to **ninety** as **sixty-four** is to _____

6. **vent** is to **prevent** as **caution** is to _____

7. **usage** is to **use** as **percentage** is to _____

8. **hole** is to **whole** as **who's** is to _____

9. **close** is to **closely** as **separate** is to _____

10. **cent** is to **percentage** as **prove** is to _____

11. **useful** is to **using** as **hopeful** is to _____

12. **prescription** is to **precision** as **description** is to _____

13. **educate** is to **education** as **refrigerate** is to _____

14. **life** is to **lifetime** as **night** is to _____

15. **bite** is to **bitten** as **write** is to _____

B Complete these sentences with words from the spelling list.

1. I must _____ that everyone follow these safety _____.

2. Jane's stubborn _____ to _____ spoiled our plans for the

   big _____.

3. After taking Dr. Clark's _____, Leon saw a

   big _____ in his health.

4. A burglar alarm with a loud, _____ siren aids in crime _____.

5. Remember to _____ all of your written work for errors in spelling,

   _____, and word _____.

6. Margie's _____ to study a _____ language is a wise one.

7. Fifty _____ of the food supplies spoiled as a _____ of

   poor _____.

8. Jesse's obvious _____ when he apologized made me _____ that we

   could be good friends again.

PROOFREADING

C Improve this paragraph. Cross out each misspelled word and write it correctly. Then replace each underlined phrase with a spelling word. You may add word endings.

It was getting late, and we still hadn't completed preparations for that night's victory celebrashun. If everyone <u>worked together and helped each other</u>, I knew we could finish by <u>the time it got dark</u>. Mike reccomended that we separate into teams. Sean and Suzanne started refrigerating the drinks, while Greta and Paul put knifes and forks on the buffet table. As a <u>way to make sure that nothing happened</u>, Jorge steadied the ladder for Pat while she hung the banners. Finally, we taped up the signs we had writen, and hoped we had not forgotten anything. It was a <u>really nice feeling</u> to stand back and see how much the appearance of the room was <u>changed for the better</u> by all of our work.

Misspelled Words		Word Substitutions	
1. _____	1. _____	4. _____	
2. _____	2. _____	5. _____	
3. _____	3. _____		
4. _____			

USING MORE REVIEW WORDS

A Follow the directions to make other forms of spelling words.

1. pleasure	-ure + ant + un	=	_____
2. sincerely	-ly + ity + in	=	_____
3. continuous	-ous + ed + dis	=	_____
4. improve	-im + ed + dis	=	_____
5. precaution	-pre - ion + ious	=	_____
6. recommend	-re + able	=	_____
7. percent	-per + ury	=	_____
8. cooperate	-co + ion	=	_____
9. punctuate	-ate + al + ity	=	_____
10. graduate	-ate + al + ly	=	_____
11. prediction	-pre + ary	=	_____
12. forgiveness	-ness + able + un	=	_____
13. securely	-ly + in	=	_____
14. migrate	-ate + ant + im	=	_____
15. location	-ion + ed + dis	=	_____

B Three words in each row follow the same spelling pattern. Write the word that does not follow the pattern.

1. contain   televise   ridicule   ignore   _____

2. circulation   convention   hesitation   translation   _____

3. include   resist   detain   redouble   _____

4. almonds   folklore   conquest   foreign   _____

5. whenever   prevent   fireproof   anytime   _____

6. adjoin   recommend   insist   suburban   _____

7. forgivable   storage   activity   precaution   _____

8. lifetime   conflict   propose   translate   _____

C Complete each analogy with one word from the box.

duplicate	incision	refrigeration	likeness	complicate
raspberry	advance	one-half	almonds	punctuation
consequence	sword	stalk	graduation	nighttime

1. **fruit** is to **apples** as **nut** is to _____

2. **whole** is to **one** as **fraction** is to _____

3. **forget** is to **remember** as **simplify** is to _____

4. **car** is to **automobile** as **cut** is to _____

5. **color** is to **blue** as **flavor** is to _____

6. **sunlight** is to **daytime** as **moonlight** is to _____

7. **noise** is to **silence** as **cause** is to _____

8. **robin** is to **bird** as **comma** is to _____

9. **arrive** is to **depart** as **retreat** is to _____

10. **exact** is to **precise** as **copy** is to _____

11. **holster** is to **pistol** as **scabbard** is to _____

12. **response** is to **answer** as **resemblance** is to _____

13. **lettuce** is to **head** as **celery** is to _____

14. **light** is to **electricity** as **cold** is to _____

15. **award** is to **race** as **diploma** is to _____

sundae *ice cream* *walnuts* *spoonful*

dessert *marshmallow* *scoops* *carton*

whipped *caramel* *split* *sherbet*

topping *masterpiece* *heaping* *pecans*

pineapple *butterscotch* *mound* *method*

Prewriting. Prewriting is the thinking, planning, and organizing you do before you begin to write. In this lesson, you will plan and write an **explanatory paragraph**. Some explanatory paragraphs are used to explain a process. In this lesson, you will explain how to make a fabulous ice cream dessert.

USE PREWRITING SKILLS

A Begin the prewriting process by deciding what your ice cream creation will be. The names of ice cream desserts below may give you an idea. Complete each name with a spelling word. All words in each name begin with the same letter.

Super Special _____   _____ Bounty

_____ Paradise   _____ Concoction

Divine Dairy _____   _____ Mountain

Planning the ingredients is another important prewriting step. Use your spelling words to complete these prewriting notes about the things you might need to make a sundae.

_____ cream   ground _____

raspberry _____   chopped _____

vanilla _____ _____   chocolate _____

a banana, _____ in half

Besides the ingredients, list three utensils you might need.

_____

_____

B When you explain a process, you need to identify the steps to be followed. List these steps in your prewriting notes.

Use spelling words to complete the following sets of prewriting notes.

1. Chocolate Mint _____

    Cover ice cream with fudge _____ .

    Start with three _____ of mint _____ _____ .

    Finally, sprinkle with a _____ _____

    of chopped _____ .

    Add a _____ of _____ cream.

    Devour the _____ .

2. Butterscotch Sundae: The Easy _____

    Open a _____ of softened vanilla _____ _____ .

    Enjoy your _____ .

    Sprinkle ground _____ on top.

    Pour on butterscotch _____ .

C A logical order is important when you explain how to do something. Rewrite the details above. Put them in the correct order. Organize your notes using a time sequence, or step-by-step order.

1. _____

_____

_____

_____

_____

_____

2. _____

_____

_____

_____

_____

_____

NOW THINK   Make prewriting notes on how to make a great ice cream dessert. First, decide what your finished product will be. Then jot down the ingredients you will need. List the steps involved. Organize them in a logical order.

Writing. When you have finished your prewriting notes, you are ready to write a first draft. In a first draft, you put your ideas into sentence form for the first time. When you write your draft, try to make your ideas flow smoothly. Certain transitional words make directions easier to read and follow. Use transitional words such as **first**, **next**, and **then** to show the order of the steps in an explanatory paragraph.

USE WRITING SKILLS

Write the following steps in paragraph form. Use some of the transitional words from this list.

Next	First	At last	The first step
Then	Finally	Second	
Now	After that	Third	

Peaches and Cream Sundae

1. Peel and slice two peaches.

2. Line the ice cream dish with the peaches.

3. Put three big scoops of vanilla ice cream over the peaches.

4. Pour on as much marshmallow topping as you like.

5. Add generous mounds of whipped cream.

6. Sprinkle with chopped pecans.

7. If you are counting calories, share this dessert with a friend.

_____

_____

_____

_____

_____

_____

_____

_____

_____

_____

NOW WRITE   Use your prewriting notes to write a first draft of your instructions. Remember to use transitional words to make your directions clear and easy to follow.

Revising and Proofreading. When you revise your first draft, you make changes to improve your writing. First revise your ideas. Then proofread carefully to find mistakes in grammar, capitalization, punctuation, and spelling.

An important part of revising is checking to see if you have used pronouns consistently. For example, if you choose to write in the first person, use the pronoun **I** or **we**. If you begin with the pronoun **you**, continue to address the reader throughout your paragraph. Don't switch back and forth between **we**, **I**, and **you**.

USE REVISING AND PROOFREADING SKILLS

A The following paragraph begins by addressing the reader. Then it switches occasionally to first person. Rewrite the paragraph to remove the pronoun **we**.

    You need several ingredients to build the Rocky Mountain Masterpiece. Get a carton of chocolate chip ice cream, marshmallow topping, and cream. Then we use an electric beater to whip the cream. You will also need walnuts or pecans, whichever you like best. We should chop the nuts before we begin making the sundae.

_____

_____

_____

_____

_____

_____

_____

_____

B Proofread the following paragraph. Mark all mistakes in grammar, capitalization, punctuation, and spelling. Then rewrite the paragraph correctly on your own paper.

Remember
- The pronoun **you** is always used with a plural verb.
- Use commas after adverbs such as **first**, **second**, or **third** when these words begin a sentence.
- Do not divide a one-syllable word at the end of a line.

    Once you have all the ingredients, you is ready to make a sunday. First: put three sco–

ops of ice cream in a tall dish. Second you pours on the topping. Smother the ice cream in a

mound of whipped cream. Then add a spoonfull of walnuts. Finally, place a cherry on top?

This methid produces a masterpiece.

C Revise the following first draft. The directions below will help you. Then rewrite the paragraph correctly on your own paper.

1. Correct the capitalization errors in lines 2 and 6.

2. Reverse the order of two steps in lines 3 and 4.

3. Add a transitional word to the beginning of the first step.

4. Correct the punctuation errors in lines 6 and 7.

5. Correct the error in verb agreement in line 5.

6. Replace the first person pronoun in line 5.

7. Cross out the six misspelled words. Write them correctly on the lines below.

1   The Fabulous Fruit Fantasy is the freshest fruit creation since the banana splitt.

2 This sundae is easy to make, fun to eat, and Healthy, too. Put two scops of lemon

3 sherbert in a bowl. Next, pour a thin stream of raspberry sauce on the sherbet and

4 pineapple. After that, surround the sherbet with chunks of fresh pineapple. Then

5 you adds a heeping spoonful of whiped cream. We can be creative with the final

6 toping. try chocolate shavings, blueberries, or a single fresh strawberry? You will

7 add color as well as flavor with any of these toppings. Finally get a spoon and en-

8 joy your dessert. If you share this masterpiece with friends, expect them to ask for

9 seconds.

_____   _____   _____

_____   _____   _____

NOW REVISE

Revise your own explanatory paragraph. Are your directions in a logical order? Did you use transitional words? Are the pronouns consistent throughout the composition? Remember to proofread for errors in grammar, capitalization, punctuation, and spelling. For example, do the verbs agree with the pronouns? Then write your final copy.

You have used the process of writing to write a paragraph that gives directions. Share your paragraph in class. Ask other students if your directions would be easy to follow.

A Writer's Journal

SWIFT THINGS ARE BEAUTIFUL

Swift things are beautiful:
Swallows and deer,
And lightning that falls
Bright-veined and clear,
Rivers and meteors,
Wind in the wheat,
The strong-withered horse,
The runner's sure feet.

And slow things are beautiful:
The closing of day,
The pause of the wave
That curves downward to spray,
The ember that crumbles,
The opening flower,
And the ox that moves on
In the quiet of power.

—ELIZABETH COATSWORTH

Literature can give you ideas for your journal. A poem, for example, might deal with feelings or experiences that remind you of things in your own life. You can then write about these things in your journal.

Use this poem as a starting point for your next journal entry. Read the poem and think about what it means. Then discuss the questions with your class.

1. The poet finds beauty in two completely different types of things. What are they?

2. What kind of beauty do you think the poet finds in "the runner's sure feet" or "the ox that moves on in the quiet of power"?

If the poem or discussion has already given you an idea for your journal, start writing. If not, choose one of these ideas.

1. Describe a familiar sight that you think is beautiful. Create a vivid picture by using specific words to describe colors, shapes, sizes, and movements.

2. Write a listing poem called "Swift Is. . ." or "Slow Is. . ." Include other examples that the poet might have used.

3. Describe the feelings you have while experiencing a particularly fast or slow movement—for example, riding on a roller coaster, sledding down a steep hill, standing in line at the theater, or waiting for a school bus.

Building a Personal Word List

If you do not know how to spell a word you want to use in your journal entry, write the word as you think it should be spelled. After you have finished writing, check to see whether the word is on your personal word list. If the word is not there, look up the correct spelling in the dictionary, correct it in your writing, and add it to your personal word list. Finally, practice spelling the word several times.

spray	sprays	sprayed	spraying
display	displays	displayed	displaying
enjoy	enjoys	enjoyed	enjoying
survey	surveys	surveyed	surveying
delay	delays	delayed	delaying
holiday	holidays		
highway	highways		
valley	valleys		
essay	essays		
journey	journeys		
reply	replies	replied	replying
copy	copies	copied	copying
steady	steadies	steadied	steadying
empty	empties	emptied	emptying
multiply	multiplies	multiplied	multiplying
balcony	balconies		
society	societies		
cavity	cavities		
apology	apologies		
county	counties		

1. How many of the words in the first column have a vowel before the final **y**? _____

   What happens to the **y** when a suffix is added? _____

2. When the letter before the final **y** is a consonant, what happens to the **y**

   when the suffixes **es** and **ed** are added? _____

3. When **ing** is added to any final **y** word, what happens to the **y**? _____

> If the letter before a final **y** is a vowel, do not change the **y** when you add a suffix.
> If the letter before the final **y** is a consonant, change the **y** to **i** before you add any suffix
>   except **ing**. The **y** never changes before **ing**.

A Each group of letters below is contained in the base form of a spelling word. Find the base word, and write the **s**, **ed**, and **ing** forms. Do not repeat a word. The last nine words will have only the **s** form.

	s	ed	ing
1. joy			
2. tip			
3. tea			
4. play			
5. ply			
6. ray			
7. lay			

	s		s		s
8. say		11. our		14. count	
9. log		12. on		15. all	
10. way		13. day		16. it	

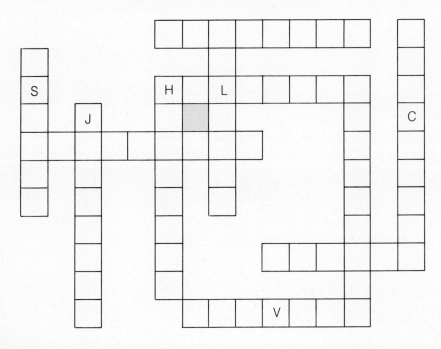

B Write the plural forms of eleven spelling words that fit in the puzzle.

47

Most verbs are listed in the dictionary in their base forms. The **ed** and **ing** forms may be included within the base word entry if the spelling of the base word changes when either of the endings is added.

cop·y (käp′ē) *n.*, *pl.* **cop′ies** [< OFr. < ML. *copia*, copious transcript < L. *copia*, plenty] a thing made just like another; imitation —*v.* **cop′ied, cop′y·ing 1.** to make a copy or copies of; reproduce **2.** to act or be the same as; imitate

en·joy (in joi′) *v.* [< OFr. *enjoir* < *en-*, in + *joir* < L. *gaudere*, to be glad] **1.** to get joy or pleasure from; relish [to *enjoy* family life, movies, etc.] **2.** to have the use or benefit of [the book *enjoyed* large sales]

(no word forms shown)

Plurals of final **y** nouns are shown in an entry if the **y** changes to **i** before **es** is added.

Note: Plural and verb forms may be shown in a shortened form if there is no change of spelling or stress in the first syllable(s).

bal·co·ny (bal′kə nē) *n.*, *pl.* **-nies** [< IT. < Gmc., akin to OHG. *balcho*, a beam] **1.** a platform projecting from a building and enclosed by a balustrade **2.** an upper floor of rows of seats in a theater, etc., often jutting out over the main floor

C Write the entry word you would look up to find the meaning of each word form shown below. Then tell whether the word form would be included in the base word entry.

1. multiplying _____ _____
2. delaying _____ _____
3. highways _____ _____
4. emptied _____ _____
5. displaying _____ _____

6. spraying _____ _____
7. cavities _____ _____
8. steadied _____ _____
9. surveying _____ _____
10. copied _____ _____

BUILD WORD POWER

Begin with each two-letter word and end with a spelling word. Add one letter from the spelling word at each step and rearrange the letters. There is more than one way to solve each puzzle.

A S	A T	I S
S E A	_ _ _	_ _ _
P E A S	_ _ _ _	_ _ _ _
S P E A R	_ _ _ _ _	_ _ _ _ _
R E P A Y S	S T E A D Y	_ _ _ _ _ _
S P R A Y E D		R E P L I E S

sprayed	delayed	essays	steadying	societies
displaying	holidays	journeys	emptying	cavities
enjoying	highways	replied	multiplied	apologies
surveyed	valleys	copied	balconies	counties

New Words
Discover new words below!

REACH OUT FOR NEW WORDS

A Eight new final **y** words are hidden in the sentences below. There may be punctuation marks or word spaces between the letters. Find and write the new words. The numbers in parentheses will tell you how many letters are in each word.

1. Every summer, cyclones endanger these islands. (5) _____

2. There were fifteen men vying for the regional championship. (4) _____

3. Nothing is as bad for a teacher as a laryngitis attack. (6) _____

4. We have reserved playing time at noon in Court E. Synchronize your watch with mine. (8) _____

5. You may join the class if your counselor gives you permission. (8) _____

6. Don't buy that shirt—not if yellow is a color you don't like. (6) _____

7. Please deliver the package addressed to "Larry Evans, 19 Army St.," if you will. (7) _____

8. The choral lyrics for that piece were hard to learn. (5) _____

B Write the eight new words in the order you found them above. Then add the endings.

1. _____ + ful = _____

2. _____ + ous = _____

3. _____ + es = _____

4. _____ + es = _____

5. _____ + cation = _____

6. _____ + ing = _____

7. _____ + cation = _____

8. _____ + es = _____

49

emotion + al =   emotion<u>al</u> + ly = *emotionally*

tradition + al =   tradition<u>al</u> + ly = *traditionally*

nation + al =   nation<u>al</u> + ly = *nationally*

accident + al =   accident<u>al</u> + ly = *accidentally*

incident + al =   incident<u>al</u> + ly = *incidentally*

temperament + al =   temperament<u>al</u> + ly = *temperamentally*

sentiment + al =   sentiment<u>al</u> + ly = *sentimentally*

historic + ally = *historically*

optimistic + ally = *optimistically*

periodic + ally = *periodically*

music + ally = *musically*

romantic + ally = *romantically*

academic + ally = *academically*

athletic + ally = *athletically*

frantic + ally = *frantically*

drastic + ally = *drastically*

sarcastic + ally = *sarcastically*

specific + ally = *specifically*

dramatic + ally = *dramatically*

automatic + ally = *automatically*

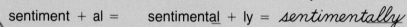
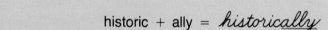

1. The seven words in the first column are all nouns. They become adjectives in

   the second column when the letters _____ are added. They become adverbs

   in the third column when the suffix _____ is added.

2. The last thirteen words in the second column can all be used as adjectives.

   What are the last two letters of these words? _____ What ending is added

   to form the adverbs in the last columns? _____

3. What are the last four letters of all of the words in the third column? _____

> Add **ly** to adjectives to form adverbs. Do not add **ly** directly to a noun.
> Add the ending **ally** to words that end with the letter **c** to form adverbs.
> Do not add **ly** directly to the letter **c**: **historical<u>ly</u>**, not **historicly.**

A Unscramble these syllables to make spelling words.

1. ly cal si mu _____
2. to ly au mat cal i _____
3. mo al e ly tion _____
4. dem ly ac i cal a _____
5. ti sen ly tal men _____
6. cal mis op ly ti ti _____
7. al di tion ly tra _____
8. ti ly cal dras _____
9. mat dra ly i cal _____
10. ly tal den ci ac _____

11. od ri pe ly i cal _____
12. cal let ly ath i _____
13. i cif cal spe ly _____
14. den in tal ly ci _____
15. ti ly fran cal _____
16. cal i tor ly his _____
17. ly sar cal cas ti _____
18. per tal tem ly a men _____
19. ly na al tion _____
20. man cal ro ly ti _____

Synonyms are words that have almost the same meaning.

B Write the spelling word that is a synonym for the underlined word.

1. John <u>unintentionally</u> brought the wrong book to class. _____

2. These sliding doors open <u>mechanically</u>. _____

3. The President visits our state <u>regularly</u>. _____

4. The camper looked <u>desperately</u> for water to douse the fire. _____

5. The actor behaved <u>moodily</u> when he didn't get his way. _____

6. This map shows <u>exactly</u> which route to take. _____

7. This town <u>customarily</u> has a parade on the Fourth of July. _____

8. Lara remarked <u>mockingly</u> that we all looked very busy. _____

9. The coach spoke <u>hopefully</u> about her team's chances of winning. _____

10. We thought that Roy presented his speech too <u>theatrically</u>. _____

11. The baseball scout was looking for <u>physically</u> talented players. _____

12. The drought will <u>severely</u> reduce our supplies of water. _____

Mnemonic Device: The "clee virus" causes words to shrivel away from lack of syllables:

        mu-si-cal-ly becomes musi-clee

Don't catch the clees!

C Use the noun, adjective, and adverb form of a spelling word to complete each set of phrases.

1. a traffic _____
   NOUN

   an _____ meeting
   ADJECTIVE

   broke the glass _____
   ADVERB

2. the _____ of love
   NOUN

   an _____ reunion
   ADJECTIVE

   an _____ delivered
   ADVERB
   speech

3. a family _____
   NOUN

   a _____ costume
   ADJECTIVE

   _____ celebrated the
   ADVERB
   holiday

4. an independent _____
   NOUN

   a _____ park
   ADJECTIVE

   a _____ televised show
   ADVERB

BUILD WORD POWER

Words spelled with **cal** are easily confused with words spelled with **cle**. Remember that **cal** is an adjective ending and **cle** is a noun ending. Use the clues to match each **cal** adjective with a **cle** noun. Write the phrase.

electrical	comical	clerical	article	uncle	vehicle
critical	typical	identical	tricycle	circle	spectacle
historical	practical	medical	chronicle	icicles	receptacle
optical	political	local	monocle	obstacle	clavicle

1. ordinary three-wheeler _____

2. record of past events _____

3. sensible relative _____

4. ambulance _____

5. visual barrier _____

6. uncomplimentary report _____

7. neighborhood show _____

8. ballot box _____

9. matching frozen objects _____

10. minister's collarbone _____

11. wired circuit _____

12. funny eyeglass _____

emotionally   incidentally   optimistically   musically   sarcastically
traditionally   specifically   periodically   athletically   temperamentally
nationally   sentimentally   academically   frantically   dramatically
historically   accidentally   romantically   drastically   automatically

New Words
Discover new words below!

REACH OUT FOR NEW WORDS

A Beginning with the first letter on each line, circle every other letter. Write the new word.

1. p a r l o i f m e t s o s y i n o z n _____

2. c e l t i u n a i m c _____

3. s b k o e l p a t h i s c _____

4. h l y e s a t c e m r o i n c d s _____

5. e f c a o g n j o b m l i q c r s _____

6. s a y o s l t b e r m r a i t k i w c _____

7. a b u c t d h f e z n u t v i k c _____

8. d x o r m j e o s y t g i a c _____

9. e l m a p b h y a s t u i k c _____

10. p l o h l s i a t r i n c h s _____

WRITING

B Use the **ly** form of one of the new words to complete each phrase. On your own paper, expand each phrase into a sentence.

1. _____ denied the reports

2. listened _____ to the product's exaggerated claims

3. sent the carpets to be _____ cleaned

4. laughed _____ at the ridiculous sight

5. _____ proven to be safe

6. a _____ wise statement by the governor

7. _____ portrayed the lives of Native Americans

8. went through the files _____

9. an _____ sound investment

10. animals raised _____

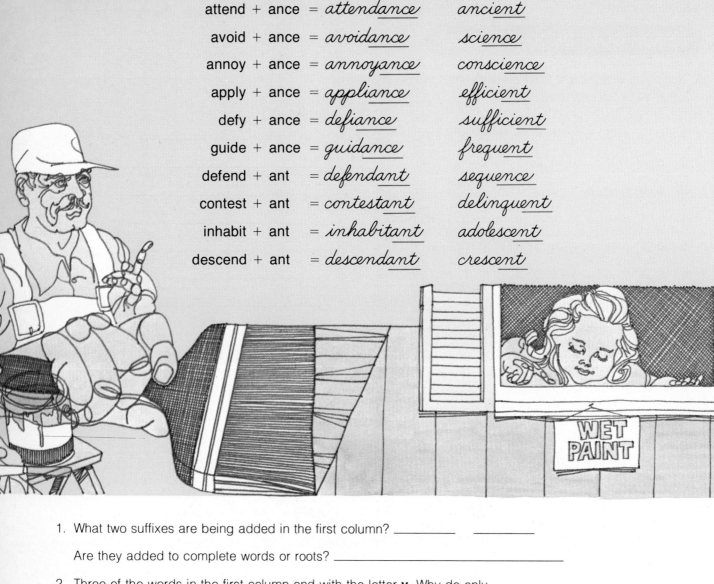

attend + ance = *attendance*   *anc**ient***

avoid + ance = *avoid**ance***   *sci**ence***

annoy + ance = *annoy**ance***   *consci**ence***

apply + ance = *appl**iance***   *effic**ient***

defy + ance = *def**iance***   *suffic**ient***

guide + ance = *guid**ance***   *freq**uent***

defend + ant = *defend**ant***   *seq**uence***

contest + ant = *contest**ant***   *delinq**uent***

inhabit + ant = *inhabit**ant***   *adole**scent***

descend + ant = *descend**ant***   *cre**scent***

1. What two suffixes are being added in the first column? _____ _____

   Are they added to complete words or roots? _____

2. Three of the words in the first column end with the letter **y**. Why do only

   two of the words change when a suffix beginning with a vowel is added?

   _____

3. What two suffixes are added to form the words in the last column? _____ _____

   Are they added to complete words? _____

4. How many of the words in the last column have the letters **ci** immediately

   before the **ent** or **ence**? _____ the letters **qu**? _____ the letters **sc**? _____

The **a** in **ance/ant** is difficult to distinguish from the **e** in **ence/ent**. The endings sound alike.
The suffixes **ance** and **ant** are commonly added to complete words.
The suffixes **ence** and **ent** are commonly used with roots. They are used after the letters **ci**,
   qu, and **sc**.
Mnemonic device: Many words that begin with the letter **a** use the suffix that begins with
   the letter **a**.

A Rewrite each sentence, finishing each incomplete word with the correct ending.

1. The defend_____ was released due to the lack of suffici_____ proof.

_____

2. This cave contains the fossils of an anci_____ inhabit_____.

_____

3. Sara's defi_____ of the rules caused us great annoy_____.

_____

4. We need some guid_____ to make more effici_____ use of our time.

_____

5. A kitchen appli_____ is a practical application of sci_____.

_____

6. This contest_____ was delinqu_____ in paying his entry fees.

_____

7. A cresc_____ is one stage in the moon's sequ_____ of change.

_____

8. Requirements of our drama class include frequ_____ attend_____ at plays.

_____

9. Ted's avoid_____ of his neighbor bothered his consci_____.

_____

B Write the spelling word that is related in some way to each group of words.

1. stove, refrigerator, vacuum cleaner _____

2. teen-ager, youth, juvenile _____

3. native, resident, citizen _____

4. biology, chemistry, physics _____

5. heir, grandson, great-granddaughter _____

6. first, second, third _____

7. competition, judge, winner _____

8. pest, bother, irritation _____

9. lawyer, judge, jury _____

10. modern, antique, futuristic _____

A **synonymy** is a special section at the end of some word entries in a dictionary. It contains a list of synonyms for the entry word. Short phrases or sentences may be included to show the slight differences between the word meanings.

C Look up **adolescent** and **sequence** in your spelling dictionary. Read the synonymy at the end of each entry. Write the synonyms after each word.

adolescent _____ _____

sequence _____ _____ _____

Now complete each sentence with the entry word or synonym that best fits the meaning.

1. Mrs. Field's daily exercises help her keep her _____ appearance.

2. The Orioles begin a _____ of home games tomorrow.

3. The _____ years are full of growth and discovery.

4. Who can complete this numerical _____?

5. I took my little brother to the _____ section of the public library.

6. Adding this chemical will start a _____ reaction.

BUILD WORD POWER

Synonyms have different shades of meaning. Complete each phrase by writing one of the two synonyms in each blank.

1. (disagreement/defiance)

   Not simply _____, but outright _____

2. (delinquent/late)

   Not merely _____, but seriously _____

3. (able/efficient)

   Not merely an _____ worker, but an _____ one

4. (aggravation/annoyance)

   Not a petty _____, but a serious _____

5. (avoidance/evasion)

   Not casual _____, but a planned _____

attendance defiance inhabitant conscience sequence
avoidance guidance descendant efficient delinquent
annoyance defendant ancient sufficient adolescent
appliance contestant science frequent crescent

New Words
Discover new words below!

REACH OUT FOR NEW WORDS

A Find eight new words using the International Morse Code.

A	B	C	D	E	F	G	H	I
·_	_···	_·_·	_··	·	··_·	__·	····	··

J	K	L	M	N	O	P	Q	R
·___	_·_	·_··	__	_·	___	·__·	__·_	·_·

S	T	U	V	W	X	Y	Z
···	_	··_	···_	·__	_··_	_·__	__··

1. ·_· / · / ·_·· / ·· / _ / _· / _·_· / · _____

2. _·· / · / ··_· / ·· / _·_· / ·· / · / _· / _ _____

3. ·_ / _· / ·_·· / ·· / ·_ / _· / _·_· / · _____

4. ·_· / ·_· / ___ / ··_· / ·· / _·_· / ·· / · / _· / _ _____

5. ___ / _··· / ··· / · / ·_· / ··· / ·_ / _· / _·_· /· _____

6. ··_· / ·_·· / ··_ / ___ / ·_· / · / ··· / _·_· / · / _· / _ _____

7. __· / ·_ / ·· / · / ··· / ·_ / _· / _·_· / · _____

8. ·· / ·_· / ·· / _·· / · / ··· / _·_· / · / _· / _ _____

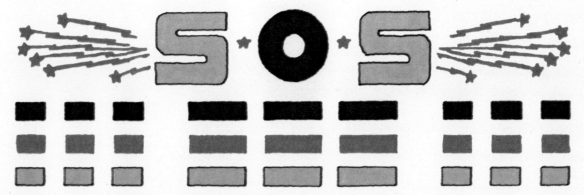

B Complete each sentence using one of the new words.

1. Randy has become a _____ carpenter.

2. The _____ lights in the ceiling began to flicker.

3. She complained loudly, but her _____ was minor.

4. The soap bubbles looked _____ in the sunlight.

5. Many businesses were closed in _____ of the holiday.

6. Which cereals are _____ in those vitamins?

7. A young monkey's _____ on its mother may last for several years.

8. The countries formed an _____ to strengthen their positions.

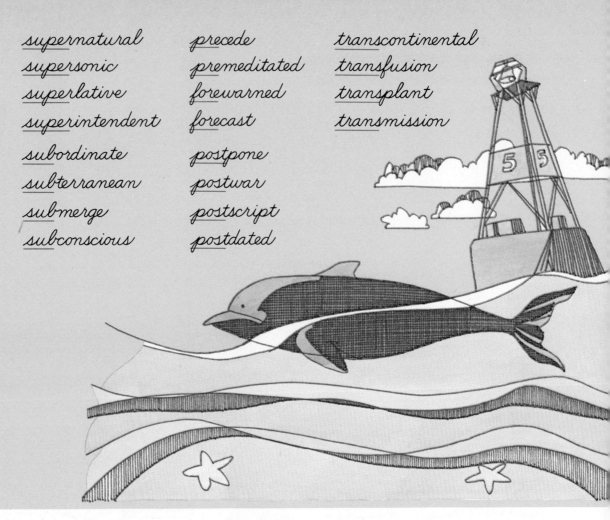

supernatural   precede   transcontinental
supersonic   premeditated   transfusion
superlative   forewarned   transplant
superintendent   forecast   transmission

subordinate   postpone
subterranean   postwar
submerge   postscript
subconscious   postdated

pre (before) + position = preposition

A **preposition** is placed *before* a word to show that word's relation to another word in the sentence: over, under, before, after, across.

1. The prefix **super** means "over," "above," or "beyond." What word in the first

   group refers to a happening that is above or beyond what seems natural?

   _____

2. The prefix **sub** means "under" or "below." The Latin root **terra** means "earth."

   What word means "below ground"? _____

3. Write the two prefixes that mean "before" or "ahead of." _____ _____

4. The prefix **post** means "after." Which word refers to a message written after

   the signature on a letter? _____

5. The prefix **trans** means "across" or "over." Which word means "across a

   continent"? _____

A prefix often carries the meaning of a preposition before a word.

PRACTICE THE WORDS

A Write the spelling word that matches each definition. Then circle the word in the definition that gives the meaning of the prefix.

1. below
   consciousness _____

2. note after
   a letter _____

3. to predict
   beforehand _____

4. person who
   oversees a job _____

5. to go before _____

6. a pouring or
   transferring of
   something across _____

7. under the earth _____

8. the sending of a
   message across _____

9. beyond the
   speed
   of sound _____

10. after a war _____

11. to put under
    water _____

12. planned or
    schemed
    beforehand _____

13. dated after the
    present _____

14. below another
    in rank _____

15. above all others
    in quality _____

16. beyond the laws
    of nature _____

17. to dig up and
    move over to
    another place _____

18. across a
    continent _____

19. to put off until
    later or after _____

20. warned
    beforehand _____

B Each word below means the same as one or more of the prefixes from your list. In alphabetical order beneath each word, write the spelling words that contain that prefix.

under	**before**	**above**
_____	_____	_____
_____	_____	_____
_____	_____	_____
_____	_____	_____

across	**after**
_____	_____
_____	_____
_____	_____
_____	

C Write the prefix from the spelling list that has the same meaning as the underlined word in each line of the prepositional poem. Then write your own prepositional poem. Choose a noun for the title, and write five lines about the title word.
Begin each line with a preposition.

Seagulls _____

<u>Over</u> the waves _____ _____

<u>Under</u> the clouds _____ _____

<u>Across</u> the bay _____ _____

<u>Before</u> the sunset _____ _____

<u>After</u> the storm _____ _____

BUILD WORD POWER

DICTIONARY

Common abbreviations are listed alphabetically in the dictionary as separate
entries. For example, the abbreviation for *postscript* (**P.S.**), is listed as
though it were a word that began with the letters **ps**. Abbreviations may be
punctuated or capitalized in different ways.

Use spelling words to complete the first part of this story. Then help the superintendent read her prepared itinerary by writing the complete word or words for
each underlined abbreviation.

The busy _____ boarded the _____

jet to begin her _____ trip from New York to California.

Although the weather _____ was poor, she did not want to

_____ her trip again. She read the itinerary that had been prepared by

one of her _____.

<u>Mon.</u>, <u>Jul.</u> 31   Depart <u>N.Y.</u>, <u>s.</u> to Washington <u>D.C.</u> Visit offices in <u>n.e.</u> <u>Va.</u>
<u>Wed.</u>, <u>Aug.</u> 2   Take flight 302 <u>w.</u> to Chicago, <u>Ill.</u> Stop at Michigan <u>Ave.</u> office for
                 briefing.
<u>Thurs.</u>, August 3   Continue to San Francisco, <u>CA.</u> Robert Crane of Images, <u>Inc.</u> will meet
                 you at the airport.

1. _____   6. _____   11. _____

2. _____   7. _____   12. _____

3. _____   8. _____   13. _____

4. _____   9. _____   14. _____

5. _____   10. _____   15. _____

supernatural   subordinate   precede   postpone   transcontinental   New Words
supersonic   subterranean   premeditated postwar   transfusion   Discover
superlative   submerge   forewarned   postscript   transplant   new words
superintendent subconscious   forecast   postdated   transmission   below!

REACH OUT FOR NEW WORDS

A Build a word pyramid by following the code. Use your spelling dictionary to find the four pyramid words that match the definitions.

TERR

The root **terr(a)** means "earth."

1. under the earth

   _____

2. small glass enclosure containing earth

   _____

3. famous sea in the middle of land

   _____

4. natural features of the land

   _____

TERR __ __ __
     1 3 5

TERR __ __ __
     1 6 8

TERR __ __ __ __ __
     6 12 9 10 14

TERR __ __ __ __ __
     1 10 6 13 7

S U B TERR A N E A N
11 13 2   1 8 5 1 8

__ __ __ __ TERR __ __ __ __ __
 7 5 4 6   1 8 5 1 8

A B C D E I M N O R S T U Y
1 2 3 4 5 6 7 8 9 10 11 12 13 14

B Build another word pyramid. Find the four pyramid words that match the definitions.

SON

The root **son** means "to sound."

1. poetry with a strict arrangement of sounds

   _____

2. device that uses sound to detect objects

   _____

3. repetition of the same vowel sound

   _____

4. clashing sounds

   _____

SON __ __
    1 9

SON __ __ __
    6 4 11

__ __ SON __ __ __ __
 1 10   1 6 2 4

__ __ __ SON __ __ __ __
 3 5 10   1 6 2 4

__ __ __ SON __ __ __
 2 7 6   1 6 11

S U P E R SON I C
10 12 8 4 9   5 2

A C D E I N O P R S T U
1 2 3 4 5 6 7 8 9 10 11 12

61

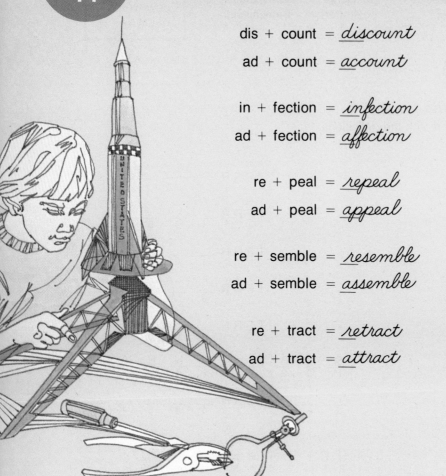

dis + count = *discount*   re + cent = *recent*

ad + count = *account*   ad + cent = *accent*

in + fection = *infection*   in + fluence = *influence*

ad + fection = *affection*   ad + fluence = *affluence*

re + peal = *repeal*   dis + proved = *disproved*

ad + peal = *appeal*   ad + proved = *approved*

re + semble = *resemble*   re + sistance = *resistance*

ad + semble = *assemble*   ad + sistance = *assistance*

re + tract = *retract*   in + tention = *intention*

ad + tract = *attract*   ad + tention = *attention*

1. Do the words in each pair have the same root? _____

   Do they have the same prefix? _____

2. Look at the first word in each pair. Does the spelling of the prefix change

   when it is added to the root? _____

3. What prefix is added to the second root in each pair? _____

   How is the prefix spelled when it is joined to a root that begins with:

   a **c**? _____ an **f**? _____ a **p**? _____ an **s**? _____ a **t**? _____

4. Is it easier to pronounce **adtract** or **attract**? _____

   Adfection or affection? _____

> When the last letter of a prefix changes to match the first letter of a root, the prefix is said to
> become assimilated.
>
>   ad   +   similated   =   assimilated
>   (to)   (same or similar)   (to make similar)
>
> The prefix **ad** is assimilated more than any other prefix. It also causes more double con-
> sonant spelling problems than any other prefix.
>
> **Mnemonic device**: Remember that one of the double consonants is really the **Mad
>   Ad** in disguise.

A Complete each sentence with two spelling words that have the same root.

1. Can you _____ the pieces of this puzzle to _____ a dog?

2. Everyone _____ of the scientist's research until his findings were _____ .

3. The council may _____ the new law if we _____ directly to the mayor.

4. This coupon entitles shoppers to a _____ when they open a charge _____ .

5. My _____ is to attract the _____ of the audience.

6. Nations with great _____ sometimes use their wealth to _____ other countries.

7. Her _____ visit to England may account for her slight _____ .

8. The mother showed much _____ when treating her baby's _____ .

9. I need your _____ in overcoming the _____ to my plan.

10. The candidate wanted to _____ his earlier statement to _____ more voters.

B Mrs. Mixit has done it again! She has mixed the wrong prefix with the right root.
Help her say what she really means by rewriting the nine underlined words correctly.

    I have been elected head of CHIRP, the Committee to Halt Injuries to Resident Pigeons. I intend to <u>retract</u> the public's <u>intention</u> to the important work of this organization. First, I plan to <u>resemble</u> all bird owners in the city. At this meeting, I will ask the owners for their <u>resistance</u> with my work. First, I will <u>repeal</u> to their <u>infection</u> for their own birds. I will give a true <u>discount</u> of all <u>accent</u> calamities that have befallen pigeons. I will then list safety measures that have been suggested and <u>disproved</u> by my committee. This should convince everyone that CHIRP's work is truly for the birds.

1. _____   4. _____   7. _____

2. _____   5. _____   8. _____

3. _____   6. _____   9. _____

C Read the meanings of the following roots. Then write the spelling words that contain these roots and match the definitions below. Checking the meaning of the prefix will help you decide if you have chosen the right word.

tract— to pull	**sist**— stand
semble— similar, together	**count**— to tell, count

1. to gather together _____

2. to pull toward oneself _____

3. a stand against something _____

4. an amount not counted _____

5. to pull back _____

6. to look similar to _____

7. a report that tells what happened _____

8. help that is "standing" by _____

BUILD WORD POWER

WRITING

Alliteration is the repetition of a beginning consonant sound:
Peter Piper picked a peck of pickled peppers . . .

All of the words on the spelling list begin with one of five letters: **a**, **r**, **d**, **i**, **c**.
Use as many spelling words as possible in five alliterative sentences. Circle the spelling words.

Detective Dawson (disproved) the department director's description of the daring (discount) deal.

1. _____

_____

2. _____

_____

3. _____

_____

4. _____

_____

5. _____

_____

discount	repeal	retract	influence	resistance
account	appeal	attract	affluence	assistance
infection	resemble	recent	disproved	intention
affection	assemble	accent	approved	attention

New Words

Discover new words below!

REACH OUT FOR NEW WORDS

A Build a word pyramid by following the code. Use your spelling dictionary to find the four pyramid words that match the definitions.

The root **tract** means "to pull or draw."

1. pulling attention away from

   _____

2. pulled or drawn back

   _____

3. vehicle for pulling

   _____

4. the act of pulling out

   _____

T R A C T

$\underset{1}{A}$ $\underset{11}{T}$ T R A C T

T R A C T $\underset{8}{}$ $\underset{9}{}$

$\underset{2}{}$ $\underset{8}{}$ $\underset{7}{}$ T R A C T

$\underset{9}{}$ $\underset{4}{}$ T R A C T $\underset{4}{}$ $\underset{3}{}$

$\underset{4}{}$ $\underset{12}{}$ T R A C T $\underset{6}{}$ $\underset{8}{}$ $\underset{7}{}$

$\underset{3}{}$ $\underset{6}{}$ $\underset{10}{}$ T R A C T $\underset{6}{}$ $\underset{7}{}$ $\underset{5}{}$

A	C	D	E	G	I	N	O	R	S	T	X
1	2	3	4	5	6	7	8	9	10	11	12

B Build another word pyramid. Find the four pyramid words that match the definitions.

The root **flu** means "to flow."

1. the condition of flowing smoothly and easily

   _____

2. a "flow" of power to affect others

   _____

3. to flow back and forth like a wave

   _____

4. a flow of riches

   _____

F L U

F L U $\underset{6}{}$ $\underset{3}{}$

F L U $\underset{4}{}$ $\underset{7}{}$ $\underset{2}{}$ $\underset{13}{}$

$\underset{1}{A}$ $\underset{5}{F}$ F L U $\underset{4}{E}$ $\underset{7}{N}$ $\underset{2}{C}$ $\underset{4}{E}$

F L U $\underset{2}{}$ $\underset{11}{}$ $\underset{12}{}$ $\underset{1}{}$ $\underset{11}{}$ $\underset{4}{}$

F L U $\underset{8}{}$ $\underset{9}{}$ $\underset{4}{}$ $\underset{10}{}$ $\underset{2}{}$ $\underset{4}{}$ $\underset{7}{}$ $\underset{11}{}$

$\underset{6}{}$ $\underset{7}{}$ F L U $\underset{4}{}$ $\underset{7}{}$ $\underset{2}{}$ $\underset{4}{}$

A	C	D	E	F	I	N	O	R	S	T	U	Y
1	2	3	4	5	6	7	8	9	10	11	12	13

cancel *gadget*
conceal *garage*
conceited *gorgeous*
cynical *gigantic*
circular *argument*
capacity *tragedy*
concentrate *gymnastics*

physician *religion*
delicious *contagious*
innocence *intelligence*

In this spelling list, the letters **c** and **g** have both a hard sound (<u>c</u>ake, <u>g</u>et) and a soft sound (fa<u>c</u>e, artifi<u>c</u>ial, pa<u>g</u>e).

1. When the **c** or **g** has a hard sound, it is followed by one of three vowels.

   Write the vowels. _____   _____   _____

2. When the **c** or **g** has a soft sound, it is followed by one of three letters.

   Write the letters. _____   _____   _____

3. Look at the last three words in each column.

   What suffixes follow soft **c**? _____   _____   _____

   What suffixes follow soft **g**? _____   _____   _____

When the letters **c** and **g** have a hard sound, they will be followed by **a**, **o**, or **u**.
When they have a soft sound, they will be followed by the letters **i**, **e**, or **y**.
Suffixes that follow the soft **c** or **g** will always begin with an **i** or an **e**:
   ian, ion, ious, ence

PRACTICE THE WORDS

A Complete each word by adding the missing vowels. Then write the word.

1. tr __ g __ dy _____
2. c __ p __ c __ ty _____
3. c __ n __ c __ l _____
4. c __ nc __ l _____
5. c __ nc __ ntr __ t __ _____
6. g __ r __ g __ _____
7. c __ rc __ l __ r _____
8. g __ g __ nt __ c _____
9. c __ nc __ __ t __ d _____
10. c __ nt __ g __ __ __ s _____

11. c __ nc __ __ __ l _____
12. r __ l __ g __ __ n _____
13. ph __ s __ c __ __ n _____
14. __ nt __ ll __ g __ nc __ _____
15. g __ dg __ t _____
16. __ nn __ c __ nc __ _____
17. g __ rg __ __ __ __ s _____
18. g __ mn __ st __ cs _____
19. d __ l __ c __ __ __ s _____
20. __ rg __ m __ nt _____

B Unscramble the following word groups to form complete sentences. Circle each spelling word.

1. small of is the capacity the garage.

   _____

2. weather forced gymnastics meet cancel bad to us the.

   _____

3. gorgeous gingerbread delicious those houses also are.

   _____

4. the mixer gigantic cement stirred motion a with circular the.

   _____

   _____

5. disease contagious could not he the doctor his conceal from.

   _____

   _____

6. helped lawyer's the argument the win him intelligence.

   _____

7. proud was the inventor of gadget the not conceited but.

   _____

PROOFREADING

C Read the descriptions of possible new daytime TV dramas. Cross out the nine misspelled words and write them correctly.

1. AS THE GIRL TURNS   A gorgous young gymnastics star tries to conseal her fear of circular jumps.

2. SEARCH FOR SORROW   An amnesia victim forces himself to consentrate on remembering the tragedy buried in his past.

3. THE BLINDING LIGHT   A conceted inventor proclaims his innocence after his gadjet causes a gigantic power failure.

4. MINERAL HOSPITAL   The cynicle story of disease spread by contageous pet rocks.

5. DAZE OF OUR LIVES   A physicion uses her intelligince to help bewildered individuals recover from head injuries.

1. _____   4. _____   7. _____

2. _____   5. _____   8. _____

3. _____   6. _____   9. _____

BUILD WORD POWER

The letter **c** at the end of words has a hard sound: giganti<u>c</u>, pani<u>c</u>. Adding endings that begin with **e**, **i**, or **y** would change the hard final **c** to a soft **c**.
To prevent this change of pronunciation, the letter **k** is added to some final **c** words before the endings **ed**, **ing**, or **y** are added:
panicked   panicking   panicky

Add the endings shown to these final c words.

1. colic + y   _____

2. picnic + ing   _____

3. mimic + ing   _____

4. frolic + ing   _____

5. shellac + ed   _____

6. politic + ing   _____

cancel · circular · delicious · gorgeous · gymnastics
conceal · capacity · innocence · gigantic · religion
conceited · concentrate · gadget · argument · contagious
cynical · physician · garage · tragedy · intelligence

New Words
Discover new words below!

REACH OUT FOR NEW WORDS

A Beginning with the letter **F**, count every three letters to find ten new **g** or **c** words. Cross out each letter as you use it. There will be one letter left over.

1. _____
2. _____
3. _____
4. _____
5. _____
6. _____
7. _____
8. _____
9. _____
10. _____

B Find the new word that would fit in the colored boxes. Then find the other words that would fit in the puzzle.

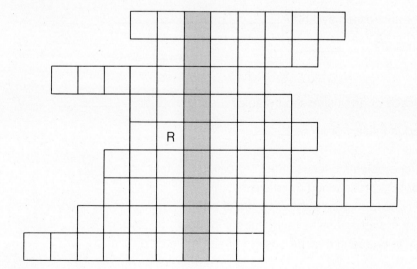

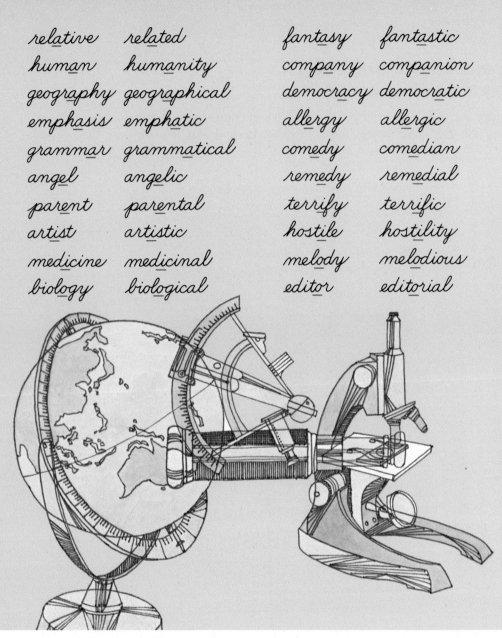

relative   related   fantasy   fantastic
human   humanity   company   companion
geography   geographical   democracy   democratic
emphasis   emphatic   allergy   allergic
grammar   grammatical   comedy   comedian
angel   angelic   remedy   remedial
parent   parental   terrify   terrific
artist   artistic   hostile   hostility
medicine   medicinal   melody   melodious
biology   biological   editor   editorial

1. Say the first word in each pair aloud.

   Is the underlined vowel in a stressed or unstressed syllable? _____

   Can the vowel be clearly heard or identified? _____

2. Say the second word in each pair aloud.

   Is the same underlined vowel in a stressed or an unstressed syllable? _____

   Can the vowel be more easily identified in these words? _____

Unstressed vowels cause spelling problems because they are difficult to hear and identify.
   A vowel in an accented syllable is pronounced more clearly.
      Is the **e** more clearly pronounced in **com'e dy** or **co me'di an**?
Many words have a form in which the accent shifts to a different syllable.
A vowel that is difficult to identify in one form may be easier to hear in the other form.

DICTIONARY

A Use your spelling dictionary to mark the accented syllable in each word shown below. Then write the related form in syllables and mark the accent.

1. gram mar _____
2. fan ta sy _____
3. bi ol o gy _____
4. ter ri fy _____
5. mel o dy _____
6. hu man _____
7. com pa ny _____
8. med i cine _____
9. rem e dy _____
10. de moc ra cy _____

11. par ent _____
12. com e dy _____
13. rel a tive _____
14. art ist _____
15. ed i tor _____
16. em pha sis _____
17. an gel _____
18. hos tile _____
19. al ler gy _____
20. ge og ra phy _____

B Use the clues to find spelling words that fit the puzzle.

Across

2. drug used to treat disease
6. pertaining to the earth's surface
7. person skilled in the fine arts
8. guests
10. person who revises written work
12. person who makes others laugh
13. concerning parents

Down

1. showing an abnormal sensitivity to a substance
3. of or for all people
4. showing special attention or stress
5. a highly imaginative image
9. rules for speaking or writing a language
11. study of living things

Antonyms are words that have opposite meanings.

C Find the spelling word that is the synonym (S) or antonym (A) of each word shown below. Be sure to use the correct form of the word.

1. scare (S) _____

2. tragedy (A) _____

3. cure (S) _____

4. anger (S) _____

5. forceful (S) _____

6. stranger (A) _____

7. amazing (S) _____

8. devilish (A) _____

9. tune (S) _____

10. child (A) _____

11. drug (S) _____

12. unconnected (A) _____

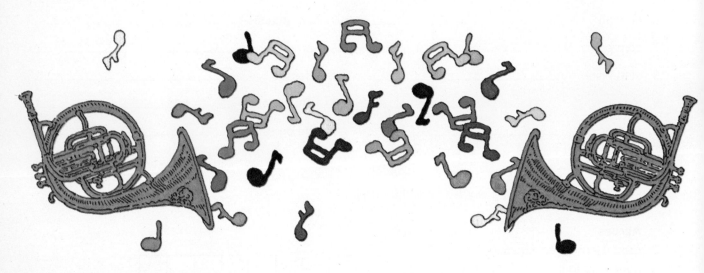

BUILD WORD POWER

WRITING

Choose two spelling words and write acrostic poems with each.

Grammar

Grappling with
Rules
And
Methods to
Make
Admirable sentences from
Rejected ones.

1. _____

2. _____

_____

_____

_____

_____

_____

_____

_____

_____

relative   grammar   medicine   democracy   terrify
human   angel   biology   allergy   hostile
geography   parent   fantasy   comedy   melody
emphasis   artist   company   remedy   editor

New Words
Discover new words below!

REACH OUT FOR NEW WORDS

A Find eight new spelling words by following this code. Each letter in a word is represented by a capital letter and a number.

	A	B	C	D	E	F	G	H
1	i	l	a	s	t	y	o	o
2	m	h	v	e	i	f	n	t
3	p	t	m	n	u	o	a	r
4	s	o	r	l	i	p	i	m
5	e	a	t	o	n	a	m	y
6	a	u	i	l	f	n	s	e
7	o	s	p	h	r	i	d	r
8	n	o	c	a	m	l	e	i

1. $\overline{E1}$ $\overline{G4}$ $\overline{A2}$ $\overline{A1}$ $\overline{G7}$

2. $\overline{D1}$ $\overline{A3}$ $\overline{A7}$ $\overline{F6}$ $\overline{C5}$ $\overline{C1}$ $\overline{D3}$ $\overline{H6}$ $\overline{G1}$ $\overline{B6}$ $\overline{A4}$

3. $\overline{C7}$ $\overline{B2}$ $\overline{A1}$ $\overline{D6}$ $\overline{B4}$ $\overline{B7}$ $\overline{A7}$ $\overline{F4}$ $\overline{D7}$ $\overline{F1}$

4. $\overline{G3}$ $\overline{E5}$ $\overline{A6}$ $\overline{H2}$ $\overline{D5}$ $\overline{E8}$ $\overline{H5}$

5. $\overline{G5}$ $\overline{B8}$ $\overline{F8}$ $\overline{D2}$ $\overline{C8}$ $\overline{E3}$ $\overline{F8}$ $\overline{A5}$

6. $\overline{E2}$ $\overline{H4}$ $\overline{F4}$ $\overline{H3}$ $\overline{D5}$ $\overline{C2}$ $\overline{H8}$ $\overline{B7}$ $\overline{H6}$

7. $\overline{E4}$ $\overline{A8}$ $\overline{F2}$ $\overline{F7}$ $\overline{G2}$ $\overline{C6}$ $\overline{C5}$ $\overline{G8}$

8. $\overline{F3}$ $\overline{E7}$ $\overline{B5}$ $\overline{B3}$ $\overline{H1}$ $\overline{H7}$ $\overline{H5}$

B Complete these sentences with forms of your new words. Use the suffixes that are in parentheses at the end of each sentence.

1. We did an _____ comparison of a fish and a frog in science class. (ical)

2. The speech was given with too much _____ to have been planned. (ity)

3. Mr. Jeffries has a very _____ outlook on life. (ical)

4. Our first activity in drama class was _____. (ation)

5. Ruben's _____ skills helped our team win the debate. (ical)

6. Karen's _____ made it difficult for her to speak up. (ity)

7. The _____ structure of this metal enables it to withstand great heat. (ular)

8. It is difficult to understand the concept of _____. (ity)

10 cavity   cavities
    delay   delays   delayed   delaying
    multiply   multiplies   multiplied   multiplying
    society   societies

11 accidental   accidentally   12 appliance
    athletic   athletically   guidance
    historic   historically   ancient
    specific   specifically   frequent
                                         adolescent

13 subconscious   14 resemble
    forecast   assistance   15 tragedy
    postpone   recent   conceited
    transcontinental   affection   physician
    supernatural   contagious

16 allergy   allergic
    medicine   medicinal
    relative   related
    comedy   comedian

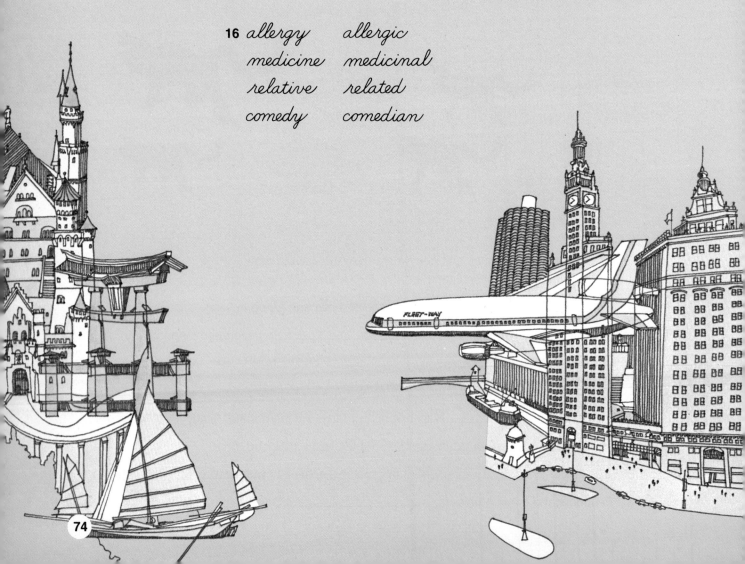

A Complete each analogy with a word from the spelling list.

1. **sonic** is to **supersonic** as **natural** is to _____

2. **cavities** is to **cavity** as **tragedies** is to _____

3. **access** is to **recess** as **accent** is to _____

4. **merge** is to **submerge** as **conscious** is to _____

5. **contract** is to **contracted** as **conceit** is to _____

6. **assist** is to **resist** as **assemble** is to _____

7. **apology** is to **apologies** as **society** is to _____

8. **warn** is to **forewarn** as **cast** is to _____

9. **intention** is to **attention** as **infection** is to _____

10. **created** is to **creative** as **related** is to _____

11. **angel** is to **angelic** as **allergy** is to _____

12. **company** is to **companion** as **comedy** is to _____

13. **religion** is to **religious** as **contagion** is to _____

14. **music** is to **musically** as **athletic** is to _____

15. **active** is to **activity** as **cave** is to _____

B Complete the sentences with spelling words.

1. This reproduction of the _____ city is _____ accurate.

2. The _____ events for _____ boys in this category will be _____ by five minutes.

3. The _____ saw that Lara had _____ taken too much of the strong _____.

4. The customer _____ asked for that particular kitchen _____.

5. After hearing the weather _____, we decided to _____ our long _____ plane trip until tomorrow.

6. Her _____ causes her to have _____ sneezing attacks, which have _____ now that spring is here.

7. We appreciated his wise _____ and able _____.

8. Psychics and other people interested in the _____ exchanged ideas at a _____ convention.

75

PROOFREADING

C Improve this paragraph. First, cross out the misspelled words and write them correctly. Then replace each underlined phrase with a spelling word. You may have to add endings.

   Highway accidence are <u>awful things</u> that could often be prevented. One thing we must realize is that safe driving is definitely related to the attitude of the person behind the wheel. For example, irritated drivers make frequant mistakes. Sometimes they become annoyed by minor <u>hold-ups that slow them down</u>, and they speed to make up for lost time. The usual risks are multiplyed by their impatience. Also, some adolescant drivers don't have the proper attitude. They may drive recklessly, believing that they don't need to be careful since most reactions are <u>something they don't deliberately intend or think about</u>. Such drivers need <u>some good advice and instruction</u> to show them how wrong they are. Soceity needs drivers who are in control of themselves and their cars.

Misspelled Words

1. _____ 4. _____

2. _____ 5. _____

3. _____

Word Substitutions

1. _____

2. _____

3. _____

4. _____

USING MORE REVIEW WORDS

A Follow the directions to make other words from spelling words.

1. gymnastics	-tics +ium	=	_____
2. physician	-ian +al	=	_____
3. resistance	-re -ance +tran +or	=	_____
4. attract	-at +or	=	_____
5. sequence	+con +s	=	_____
6. frequent	+in +ly	=	_____
7. descendant	-de +a -ant	=	_____
8. company	+ac +ist	=	_____
9. nation	+al +inter +ly	=	_____
10. accidental	-ac +in +co	=	_____
11. premeditated	-pre -ed +ion	=	_____
12. inhabitant	-in -ant +ual	=	_____
13. society	-ety +al +ize	=	_____
14. subordinate	-sub -ate +ary	=	_____
15. specific	-fic +ally +e	=	_____

B Three words in each row follow the same spelling pattern. Write the word that does not follow the pattern.

1. enjoyed   appliance   replies   copied   _____

2. delicious   innocence   physician   musical   _____

3. postwar   precede   disproved   supersonic   _____

4. contestant   accident   resistance   annoyance   _____

5. tragedy   apology   argument   gymnastics   _____

6. appeal   affection   attention   resemble   _____

7. recent   attract   discount   repeal   _____

8. counties   highways   essays   journeys   _____

9. guidance   medicinal   hostility   humanity   _____

10. angels   balconies   comedies   remedies   _____

C Complete each analogy with one word from the box. Each word is used once.

descendant	crescent	postpone	affection	transplant
medicine	science	assemble	delicious	optimistic
gymnastics	specific	appliance	innocence	sufficient

1. **answer** is to **respond** as **delay** is to _____

2. **grandfather** is to **daughter** as **ancestor** is to _____

3. **color** is to **yellow** as **shape** is to _____

4. **music** is to **jazz** as **general** is to _____

5. **planned** is to **premeditated** as **enough** is to _____

6. **ancient** is to **recent** as **hostility** is to _____

7. **chair** is to **furniture** as **toaster** is to _____

8. **ring** is to **jewelry** as **biology** is to _____

9. **display** is to **conceal** as **guilt** is to _____

10. **calm** is to **frantic** as **pessimistic** is to _____

11. **sound** is to **melodious** as **taste** is to _____

12. **copy** is to **duplicate** as **congregate** is to _____

13. **daisy** is to **flower** as **aspirin** is to _____

14. **person** is to **move** as **tree** is to _____

15. **language** is to **French** as **sports** is to _____

stalled	blocked	vehicle	brakes
engine	honked	traffic	lane
died	jinxed	driven	haul
embarrassed	episode	towed	crossed
intersection	police	trailer	bumper

Prewriting. Prewriting is the thinking, planning, and organizing you do before you begin to write. In this lesson, you will plan and write a **narrative composition**. You will write about an embarrassing moment you have had.

When you write about a personal experience, the material is within you. You must draw this material from your memory and make prewriting notes on paper. Do not worry about the order of these notes. You can organize them later. Just write down as many details as you can.

USE PREWRITING SKILLS

A Use spelling words to complete this list of prewriting notes.

usually ride my bike in the right-hand _____

bizarre mishap that stopped _____ for 30 minutes

bike has had so many problems, sometimes I think it's _____

_____ officer asked me to identify the unusual

_____ I was riding

tried to stay calm as dozens of horns _____ around me

every lane in the intersection was _____

_____ on my bike working perfectly earlier

I'll never try to _____ groceries on the back of my bike again

hit a car's _____, flew off my bike

car was _____ by an off-duty policeman

car was pulling a _____ behind it

_____ the street to find a phone

B Each paragraph of a composition should develop one **main idea**. Use your prewriting notes to decide what the main ideas of your composition will be. Then group your details under these main ideas.

Read the following set of prewriting notes and the main idea below. Write the notes that are related to that main idea. Leave out those that are unrelated.

The engine on our Model T Ford stalled.   I was so embarrassed I could have died.
My brother builds models of cars.   The parade continued around us.
The car had to be towed.   There were fireworks that night.

Main Idea: We had car trouble in the middle of a Fourth of July parade.

_____

_____

_____

_____

C A composition should include an introductory paragraph, several body paragraphs, and a conclusion. The body paragraphs must be organized in an order that makes sense. Narrative compositions are usually best organized in **chronological order**, or **time sequence**.

Read the following prewriting notes. Rewrite them in chronological order.

• Gordon had an appointment with the vet at ten o'clock.

• The episode began with our dog, Gordon.

• At the first busy intersection, Gordon leaped out of the car window.

• We coaxed him from the house to the car at about 9:30.

• Lying down under the front bumper, Gordon refused to move.

• It took two police officers and the animal warden to haul Gordon out.

_____

_____

_____

_____

_____

_____

NOW THINK Make prewriting notes about an embarrassing experience you have had. Once you have made your prewriting notes, plan the body of your composition. Follow these steps:

    1. Identify your main ideas.
    2. Group your details under these ideas.
    3. Organize your ideas in a logical order.

Writing. Good writers choose their words carefully. When you write, use strong specific verbs rather than weak, vague ones. Exact verbs will help your details come alive for the reader.

Example:

General verb: George, the garage mechanic, <u>took</u> our car to the station.
Specific verb: George, the garage mechanic, <u>towed</u> our car to the station.

Also, try to mention the person or thing that does an action before you mention the action itself. This produces a stronger effect. It is called "using the active voice."

Example:

Weak: The trailer <u>was driven</u> by Dan.   The lane <u>was blocked</u>.
Strong: Dan <u>drove</u> the trailer.   I <u>blocked</u> the lane.

USE WRITING SKILLS

Rewrite the following paragraph. Replace the underlined general verbs with stronger, more specific ones. Also, change one sentence so that it is in the active voice.

The very last thing on my mind as I <u>went</u> down that country road on my new ten-speed was my brakes. As I came over a hill, I <u>saw</u> some traffic ahead. The brakes were applied. Nothing happened. Rather than <u>go</u> into the bumper of a car, I <u>went</u> off the road. Unfortunately, a roadside fruit stand <u>was</u> in my way. I was so embarrassed by what happened next. I missed the customers, but not the crates. You might say I went bananas!

_____

_____

_____

_____

_____

_____

_____

W
TE Use your prewriting notes to write a first draft of your narrative composition. Write an introductory paragraph that catches the reader's attention. In the body, develop the events of your story. Write a conclusion that is a clear, interesting ending for your composition. Use fresh, exact verbs throughout your composition. Try to stay in the active voice.

Revising. Check your writing to make sure that your sentence beginnings vary. Not all sentences in a paragraph should begin the same way. For example, some writers begin almost every sentence with *the, I,* or *we.* That makes a composition dull and choppy. Remember that other parts besides the subject can begin a sentence.

Example: The stalled vehicle sat in the middle of the busy intersection.
In the middle of the busy intersection sat the stalled vehicle.

USE REVISING AND PROOFREADING SKILLS

A Rewrite the following paragraph on your own paper. Vary the beginnings of the sentences marked with a *.

*I entered the Winston bicycle race last month. I hoped it would be an important episode in my cycling history. *I was jinxed from the beginning, unfortunately. *The car stalled on the way to the track. The bike fell off the back bumper where I had secured it. *I found my lane blocked by another unlucky rider only fifteen seconds into the race. *I crossed the finish line first in spite of it all.

B Dialogue, or conversation, can add interest to your writing. Make sure you know how to punctuate it correctly.

Proofread the following piece of dialogue. Mark all mistakes in grammar, capitalization, punctuation, and spelling. Then rewrite it correctly on your own paper.

Remember
- In a divided quotation, words such as *he said* break up what a speaker is saying: "Come here," she said. "I want to talk to you." The first part of a divided quotation is followed by a comma. The comma is placed inside the quotation marks.
- Explanatory words in a divided quotation are followed by either a comma or a period. A comma is used if the second part does not begin a new sentence. A period is used if the second part of the quotation is a new sentence.
- The second part of a divided quotation begins with a small letter. Use a capital letter only if the second part is a proper noun, the pronoun **I**, or the beginning of a new sentence.

"I was so embarrassed at that intersektion today", Complained Mom, that I could have

died."

"The episod was not your fault," I reminded her. "did you feel jinxsed?"

"Every vehicle within a mile honked at me, she continued." "I couldn't hear myself think."

"You can't really blame them i said. after all, traffic was blocked for quite a while.

C Revise the following first draft. These directions will help you. Then rewrite the composition correctly on your own paper.

1. Replace the two underlined verbs with more specific ones.

2. Put the last sentence in the first paragraph in active voice.

3. Correct the capitalization errors in lines 1, 3, and 4.

4. Correct punctuation errors in lines 8, 9, and 11.

5. Correct the error in verb agreement in line 9.

6. Cross out the six misspelled words. Write them correctly on the lines below.

1   Ordinarily, I wouldn't mind being in a car when the enjine dyed. But last satur-

2 day was different. I happened to be dressed like a rabbit when our car staled. I

3 was wearing my costume for the play that our english class was <u>doing</u> at the pub-

4 lic library. i had been too embarrassed to ride my bike in the outfit. I was being

5 driven to the library by my mom.

6   Suddenly there I was standing at the main intersection of town. Every vehicel

7 passing by saw a giant rabbit <u>looking</u> under the hood of a car. My worst fears

8 were realized, when Mom told me I'd have to run, or hop, to the library by myself. I

9 took off while Mom waited until the car were toed. It was an unforgettable episode?

10 I remember well every street I crosst in that outfit. I can still hear all the cars that

11 honked at me. My only consolation, was that none of my friends recognized me.

_____   _____   _____

_____   _____   _____

NOW REVISE Revise your own first draft. Make sure your sentence beginnings vary. Did you use strong, active verbs? Proofread your composition for errors in grammar, capitalization, punctuation, and spelling. Make a clean, final copy.

Now you have written a narrative composition about an interesting, if embarrassing, situation. Share these in class. Notice how enjoyable it is to share personal experiences through writing.

A Writer's Journal

During a childhood illness, Helen Keller lost both her sight and her hearing. However, because of her strong desire to learn and through the help of others, she was able to overcome her handicaps. The paragraph to the left is from Keller's *The Seeing See Little*. Here she discusses an important lesson she has learned about people. Read the paragraph. Then discuss the questions with your class.

1. Why does the author feel that temporary blindness and deafness would be good for every human being?

2. What complaint about human beings does the author appear to have?

Perhaps the paragraph or discussion has already given you an idea to explore in your journal. If so, start writing. If not, you might want to choose one of these ideas to write about.

1. Choose a scene that is very familiar to you—for example, a classroom, the kitchen in your home, or the street where you live. Pretend that you are looking at it for the first time. Using all your senses, observe it closely. Then describe what you see, hear, and smell.

2. Close your eyes for thirty seconds, and listen closely to all the sounds around you. Try to describe everything you hear.

3. The author refers to the "joys of sound." Describe some sounds that are especially joyful to your ears. Then describe some sounds that make you feel sad.

4. Tell whether or not you agree that "darkness would make people more appreciative of sight." Explain why or why not.

> I have often thought it would be a blessing if each human being were stricken blind and deaf for a few days at some time during his or her early adult life. Darkness would make people more appreciative of sight; silence would teach them the joys of sound.
>
> —HELEN KELLER

Building a Personal Word List

How can your personal word list help you become a better speller? First, the list makes you aware of the words you need to learn to spell. Second, it helps you understand the kinds of spelling mistakes you make.

As you enter words on your personal word list, think about the kinds of spelling mistakes you made. You may begin to notice that you are repeating the same kinds of spelling errors. If you know the kinds of spelling errors you make, you may be able to keep them from recurring.

plan	planning	planned	
star	starring	starred	
slip	slipped	slippery	
jog	jogging	jogger	
grab	grabbing	grabbed	
stop	stopping	stopped	
swim	swimming	swimmer	
ship	shipping	shipped	shipment
sad	sadder	saddest	sadness
dim	dimmed	dimmer	dimly
upset	upsetting		
begin	beginning	beginner	
control	controlling	controlled	
regret	regretting	regrettable	
patrol	patrolling	patrolled	
rebel	rebelled	rebellion	
forgot	forgotten		
forget	forgetting		forgetful
equip	equipping	equipped	equipment
commit	committing	committee	commitment

A word that has **1** syllable, **1** vowel, and **1** final consonant is called a **1 + 1 + 1** word: set.
A word that has a single **v**owel in a final **a**ccented syllable with one final **c**onsonant is
called a **VAC** word: up set.'

The first ten words in the list are **1 + 1 + 1** words. The last ten are **VAC** words.

1. What happens to the final consonant of these words when a suffix beginning with

   a vowel is added? _____

2. What happens when a suffix beginning with a consonant is added?

   _____

3. In what **VAC** word are the letters **qu** treated as a single consonant? _____

Double the final consonant of a **1 + 1 + 1** word or a **VAC** word before a suffix that
begins with a vowel. Do not double before a suffix that begins with a consonant.

A Form spelling words by adding endings to the base words.

1. commit + ment _____
2. star + ed _____
3. equip + ing _____
4. forget + ful _____
5. jog + er _____
6. rebel + ion _____
7. patrol + ed _____
8. plan + ing _____
9. dim + ly _____
10. commit + ing _____
11. sad + ness _____
12. slip + ery _____

13. forgot + en _____
14. dim + er _____
15. grab + ed _____
16. control + ed _____
17. equip + ment _____
18. regret + able _____
19. begin + er _____
20. forget + ing _____
21. sad + est _____
22. stop + ing _____
23. commit + ee _____
24. swim + ing _____

B Answer each riddle with two spelling words that rhyme and fit the letters and spaces. Write the complete answer.

1. What was the waiter doing after he knocked over a stack of plates?

re __ __ __ __ __ ing the up __ __ __ __ ing

_____

2. What is the job of the police chief?

co __ __ __ __ __ __ __ ng the pa __ __ __ __ __ __ ng

_____

3. What did the truck deliver to the warehouse?

a sh __ __ __ __ nt of eq __ __ __ __ __ nt

_____

4. What do you call a fish who is less colorful than some others in his school?

a d __ __ __ __ r s __ __ __ __ __ r

_____

5. What did the clumsy sailor do when he went aboard?

sl __ __ __ __ d when he sh __ __ __ __ d

_____

DICTIONARY

An **idiom** is a phrase that has a meaning different from what the individual words usually mean. For instance, "to let the cat out of the bag" means "to let a secret be found out." The meanings of idiomatic phrases are usually found in the entry for the key word.

for·get (fər get', fôr-) *v.* **-got'**, **-got'ten** or **-got'**, **-get'ting** [OE. *forgietan*] **1.** to be unable to remember **2.** to fail to do without meaning to [to *forget* to lock the door] **3.** to overlook [let's *forget* our differences] —**forget it** don't trouble to think about it —**forget oneself** to behave in an improper or unseemly manner —**for·get'ta·ble** *adj.*

C Each of these sentences contains an idiom. The key word in each idiom is a spelling word. First find the spelling word and look it up in your spelling dictionary. Then write the idiom and the definition for it that is shown in the entry.

1. Nicole is always in the swim of things.

   _____

   _____

2. Philip let slip what the surprise was going to be.

   _____

   _____

3. My uncle says he'll buy a new car when his ship comes in.

   _____

   _____

4. The town pulled out all the stops to make the carnival a success.

   _____

   _____

BUILD WORD POWER

WRITING

Under each **1 + 1 + 1** word, write the word formed by adding a final silent **e**. Complete the sentence with a form of each of the two words. Remember the rules for adding suffixes to **1 + 1 + 1** and silent **e** words.

1. **star**   Susan _____ at the poster that said she was

   _____ _____ in the school play.

2. **dim**   I dropped the roll of _____ just as the lights were _____.

   _____

3. **plan**   We had _____ to change _____ in Kansas City.

   _____

On your own paper, write a sentence with each pair of words. Use as many endings as possible.

   scrap/scrape   hug/huge   hop/hope   scar/scare   tap/tape

86

planning	grabbed	saddest	controlled	forgotten
starred	stopping	dimmer	regrettable	forgetting
slippery	swimmer	upsetting	patrolled	equipment
jogging	shipment	beginning	rebellion	commitment

New Words
Discover new words below!

REACH OUT FOR NEW WORDS

A Each sentence in this story contains a **VAC** word or a **1 + 1 + 1** word. Find each word and write it.

One afternoon, the famous Dr. Creaky invited me to join a mountain-climbing trip to photograph some nesting eagles. Although I am terrified of heights, I decided to defer to the doctor's wishes.

As we climbed the mountainside, I said, "I just hope we don't stir up the eagles. They might think we've come to rob their eggs for food." I glanced worriedly at our bag of supplies.

"We're able to repel any attackers," said Dr. Creaky.

Just then I spied a huge eagle getting ready to propel himself toward our ropes. The ropes were stretched tight as a drum, and the bird's sharp beak could easily slice them!

Dr. Creaky accepted the situation with a quip: "I don't think I want to 'hang around' here any longer today."

1. _____   4. _____   7. _____

2. _____   5. _____   8. _____

3. _____   6. _____   9. _____

B Make a word that matches each clue or definition by adding a suffix from the box to one of the new words.

| ed er s ing age ery |

1. pushed away _____

2. seen in a band _____

3. stumbles _____

4 giving in to _____

5. something you take on vacation _____

6. found on some planes _____

7. joked _____

8. theft _____

9. mixed _____

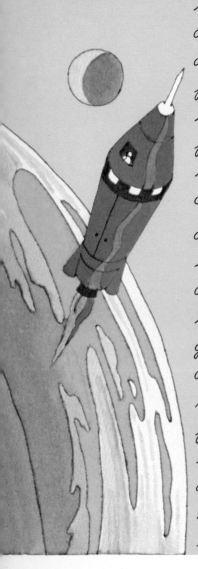

transmit	transmitting	transmitted	
omit	omitting	omitted	
admit	admitting	admitted	
permit	permitting	permitted	
transfer	transferring	transferred	
prefer	preferring	preferred	preference
refer	referring	referred	reference
confer	conferring	conferred	conference
differ	differing	differed	difference
suffer	suffering	suffered	
offer	offering	offered	
happen	happening	happened	
gallop	galloping	galloped	
orbit	orbiting	orbited	
visit	visiting	visited	
pilot	piloting	piloted	
enter	entering	entered	
alter	altering	altered	
murmur	murmuring	murmured	
labor	laboring	labored	

1. All of the words in the first column end with a single consonant that follows a single vowel. What

   syllable is accented in the first eight words? _____ in the last twelve

   words? _____ Which words are **VAC** words? _____

2. What happens to the final consonant when **ed** and **ing** are added to the **VAC** words?

   _____

3. Three of the **VAC** words also use the **ence** suffix. What syllable is stressed or accented

   in these words? _____ Why isn't the final consonant doubled?

   _____

A **VAC** word must have a final accented syllable. Some **VAC** words have a form in
which the accent shifts to a different syllable when the suffix is added. For these
forms, do *not* double the final consonant of the base word when you add the suffix:
con·fer′ con′fer·ence

A Each spelling word is divided into two syllables. Say each word aloud and listen for the accented or stressed syllable. Mark the accented syllable. Then write the **ed** and **ing** forms of the word.

	ed	ing
1. con fer		
2. en ter		
3. suf fer		
4. trans mit		
5. hap pen		
6. la bor		
7. ad mit		
8. dif fer		
9. re fer		
10. mur mur		
11. al ter		
12. gal lop		
13. vis it		
14. or bit		
15. pre fer		

B Mrs. Mixit is still combining the wrong prefix with the right root. Help her say what she really means by writing the eight underlined words correctly.

Let your public library work for you! Become aware of all the services that are suffered by your library, and learn how to find the information you need. If you need an encyclopedia, go to the preference room. When you need a book that your library doesn't own, see if you can have a copy conferred from another library. If mystery stories are your favorite, express your reference to the librarian. He or she may be able to suggest some new titles. If you have left out the author's name on a book report, use the card catalog to find the name you have admitted. When you need a place to work on a project with someone, see if your library has a special difference room. Here talking would be omitted. Finally, notice how your public library suffers from your school library. Learn to be at home in both.

1. _____   4. _____   7. _____

2. _____   5. _____   8. _____

3. _____   6. _____

DICTIONARY

C Complete each pair of sentences with one spelling word. You may add endings.
Then look up the word in your spelling dictionary. Write the abbreviation for the
part of speech that fits the use of the word in each sentence. If there is more
than one definition, write the number of the correct definition next to the abbreviation.

1. The _____ landed the airplane safely. _____

   The sailor had to _____ the boat through stormy waters. _____

2. The store owner does not _____ food in the shop. _____

   Bill's brother applied for a driving _____. _____

3. The worker was tired after eight hours of hard _____. _____

   The overloaded truck _____ up the steep hill. _____

4. Maria plans to _____ to a different school. _____

   The bus driver took the _____ from the passenger. _____

5. The campers could hear the soft _____ of the creek. _____

   Disappointed members of the audience began _____ to each other. _____

BUILD WORD POWER

Answer each question. Then complete the last statement.

1. Write the seven spelling words in which **fer** is the last syllable of the base word.

   _____ _____ _____ _____

   _____ _____ _____

2. Which of these words have a double consonant in the base form?

   _____ _____ _____

3. Which of the seven **fer** words are not **VAC** words?

   _____ _____ _____

The **fer** words that have a _____ in the

base form do not double the _____ when

a suffix is added.

90

transmitting	transferring	difference	galloping	entered
omitted	preference	suffered	orbiting	altered
admitted	referred	offered	visiting	murmuring
permitted	conference	happened	piloted	labored

REACH OUT FOR NEW WORDS

A Unscramble these letters to make words that match the definitions.
The underlined letters are in the correct position.

1. eimt—to give off _____

2. ucocr—to happen, take place _____

3. tbgoi—prejudiced person _____

4. eucrr—to happen again _____

5. tusbim—present or offer to others _____

6. tilaqurn—calm, peaceful _____

7. wspihor—take part in a religious service _____

8. groparm—to schedule, set up _____

B On the blanks after the numbers below, write your eight new words in the
order you found them. Use each word plus the suffix shown after the
blank to complete the first five sentences.

1. _____ + **ed**   The factory chimneys _____ clouds of dark smoke.

2. _____ + **ence**   The eclipse was the most talked–about _____ of the year.

3. _____ + **ed**   His _____ remarks showed his ignorance of others.

4. _____ + **ing**   Ralph has a _____ dream in which he stars in a play.

5. _____ + **ed**   Cora _____ her report two days late.

For the last three words, look up each word in your dictionary. Write the spelling
or spellings you find for each new form. Then answer the questions.

6. _____ + **ity** = _____

Are the letters **qu** treated as a single consonant in **VAC** words? _____

Is the base form of this word a **VAC** word? _____

Does the accented syllable change when **ity** is added? _____

Is the final consonant of the base word doubled when **ity** is added? _____

7. _____ + **ing** = _____   _____

Some dictionaries list more than one spelling for a word form. The form that is listed first

is the preferred form. What is the preferred spelling of this **ing** word? _____

8. _____ + **ing** = _____   _____

What is the preferred spelling of this **ing** word? _____

adapt + able = *adaptable*　　vis + ible = *visible*

avail + able = *available*　　aud + ible = *audible*

attain + able = *attainable*　　leg + ible = *legible*

agree + able = *agreeable*　　ed + ible = *edible*

regret + able = *regrettable*　　poss + ible = *possible*

forget + able = *forgettable*　　cred + ible = *credible*

control + able = *controllable*　　tang + ible = *tangible*

adore + able = *adorable*

advise + able = *advisable*

excite + able = *excitable*

notice + able = *noticeable*

change + able = *changeable*

manage + able = *manageable*

1. Is the suffix **able** added to complete words or to roots? _____

2. How do the three **VAC** words change when **able** is added?

_____

3. Six of the base words end with a silent **e**. What happens to the final **e** in

   the first *three* words when **able** is added? _____

4. Now look at the last three silent **e** words. Is the **e** dropped in these words

   when **able** is added? _____ What letter would follow the **c** and **g** in these

   words if the **e** were not kept? _____ Would the **c** and **g** have a hard sound

   (c̲able, g̲able) or a soft sound (lac̲e, pag̲e) if they were followed by **a**? _____

5. Is the suffix **ible** added to complete words or to roots? _____

> The suffix **able** is commonly added to complete words to form adjectives meaning "able
> to be." When **able** is added to words that end in **ce** or **ge**, the **e** must be kept to
> protect the soft sound of **c** or **g**.
> The suffix **ible** is more commonly added to roots than to complete words.
> The **i** in **ible** gives the letter **g** a soft sound: legible, tangible.
> **Mnemonic device:** Many words that begin with **a** use the suffix that begins with **a**.

A Unscramble the letters and write the spelling words. First find and circle the **able** or **ible** endings. They are not scrambled.

1. sibleiv _____
2. cixeablet _____
3. ableroda _____
4. ptaaabled _____
5. ssibleop _____
6. vlableaia _____
7. gnatible _____
8. tablegreert _____
9. sadvablei _____
10. ibledua _____

11. ganaableme _____
12. eableearg _____
13. icenotable _____
14. deible _____
15. lableltornoc _____
16. hagablecen _____
17. dreiblec _____
18. tatableain _____
19. torfeablegt _____
20. iblegle _____

B Answer each question with a sentence that uses the **ible** form of a spelling word. The underlined words will give you a clue to the word you should use.

1. Was the handwriting in the old letter still able to be read?

_____

2. Does Paul's story about his adventure seem believable to you?

_____

3. Could the plant cells be seen without a microscope?

_____

4. Is the leftover food still fit to be eaten?

_____

5. Can the actor's voice be heard throughout the theater?

_____

6. Did the explorers discover physical evidence of the lost city?

_____

7. Is an earthquake capable of happening in your state?

_____

PROOFREADING

C Proofread the following magazine article. Cross out the nine misspelled words. Then write the words correctly.

Everyone loves an adoreable puppy, but not everyone knows how to choose or raise one. Check out your puppy carefully. Make sure it is healthy and has an agreeable personality. It is adviseable that your puppy be about eight weeks old before you bring it home. Once it's home, it is possable to avoid many common problems by remembering certain tips. A puppy is easily excittible, so treat it gently. Make sure it gets a proper diet. Do not simply feed it anything you think is edible. You should also get the special vitamins that are availible for puppies. Brush your pet daily to remove the noticeable specks that can get caught in its hair. Your pet's behavior must be very managable at all times. Allowing your pet to be uncontrollable would certainly be a regretable mistake. Keep your voice low but audable when training your dog. Be patient but firm. If you treat your pet properly, you will soon have tangable proof that a dog can be a best friend.

1. _____   4. _____   7. _____

2. _____   5. _____   8. _____

3. _____   6. _____   9. _____

BUILD WORD POWER

A negative prefix gives a word the opposite meaning of its base word. Write the words formed by adding negative prefixes. Then underline the first letter of the prefix and the first letter of the suffix.

visible   (in) = _____   adaptable   (un) = _____

audible   (in) = _____   available   (un) = _____

legible   (il) = _____   attainable   (un) = _____

edible   (in) = _____   forgettable (un) = _____

possible (im) = _____   agreeable   (dis) = _____

credible (in) = _____   changeable (un) = _____

tangible (in) = _____   noticeable   (un) = _____

Look at the negative words in the first column and complete this statement:

Many words formed by adding the _____ suffix also use a negative prefix

that begins with the letter _____.

adaptable   regrettable   advisable   manageable   edible
available   forgettable   excitable   visible   possible
attainable   controllable   noticeable   audible   credible
agreeable   adorable   changeable   legible   tangible

New Words
Discover
new words
below!

REACH OUT FOR NEW WORDS

A Unscramble each group of syllables to make a new **able** or **ible** word.

1. ble bat de a _____

2. a cur ble _____

3. vis ble i di in _____

4. pos dis a ble _____

5. ci vin ble in _____

6. ta tec ble de _____

7. ble cep sus ti _____

8. plor a de ble _____

9. si ble mis per _____

10. tin guish a dis ble _____

B Write the new word that might be used in relation to the following things.

1. paper plates, plastic bottles _____

2. radioactivity _____

3. the United States, best friends _____

4. driving with a license _____

5. an important issue, a questionable policy _____

6. superheroes, championship teams _____

7. sweet from sour _____

8. telling lies, spreading rumors _____

9. measles, sprained ankle _____

10. someone likely to become sick _____

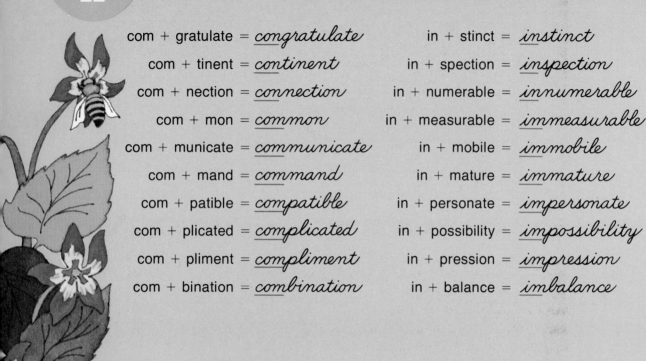

com + gratulate = *congratulate*

com + tinent = *continent*

com + nection = *connection*

com + mon = *common*

com + municate = *communicate*

com + mand = *command*

com + patible = *compatible*

com + plicated = *complicated*

com + pliment = *compliment*

com + bination = *combination*

in + stinct = *instinct*

in + spection = *inspection*

in + numerable = *innumerable*

in + measurable = *immeasurable*

in + mobile = *immobile*

in + mature = *immature*

in + personate = *impersonate*

in + possibility = *impossibility*

in + pression = *impression*

in + balance = *imbalance*

A prefix may be spelled in several different ways.

1. Look at the first three words in each column.
   Are the prefixes **com** and **in** spelled with an **n** or
   an **m** when they are added to form these words? _____
   Why do the words **connection** and **innumerable** have double consonants?

   _____

   _____

2. Look at the remaining words in each column.
   How is the prefix **com** spelled when it is
   added to roots that begin with **m**, **p**, or **b**? _____
   How is the prefix **in** spelled when it is added
   to words or roots that begin with **m**, **p**, or **b**? _____

The prefixes **com** and **in** follow the same spelling pattern. Both are spelled with an **n** before most letters of the alphabet. Both are spelled with an **m** before roots or words that begin with the letters **m**, **p**, or **b**. They are spelled this way to make more compatible combinations that are easier to pronounce.
Say **inmobile** and **immobile**.   Say **comtinent** and **continent**.

Mnemonic device: Remember co**mm**on co**mp**atible co**mb**inations.

Double consonants often result from joining prefixes and roots.
Remember that one consonant belongs to the prefix, and one belongs to the root.

A Find and circle 15 spelling words hidden in three directions in the puzzle. →↑↓
Write each word after you have circled it in the puzzle.

T	R	C	O	M	B	I	N	A	T	I	O	N
E	C	O	N	G	R	A	T	U	L	A	T	E
T	O	M	E	I	G	N	N	D	E	N	I	I
A	N	M	C	M	U	O	E	F	H	O	M	N
N	T	U	N	M	D	I	M	G	R	I	M	S
O	I	N	A	O	N	T	I	O	V	S	A	T
S	N	I	L	B	A	C	L	A	M	S	T	I
R	E	C	A	I	M	E	P	B	L	E	U	N
E	N	A	B	L	M	P	M	C	E	R	R	C
P	T	T	M	E	O	S	O	L	N	P	E	T
M	O	E	I	B	C	N	C	O	M	M	O	N
I	M	P	O	S	S	I	B	I	L	I	T	Y

1. _____
2. _____
3. _____
4. _____
5. _____
6. _____
7. _____
8. _____
9. _____
10. _____
11. _____
12. _____
13. _____
14. _____
15. _____

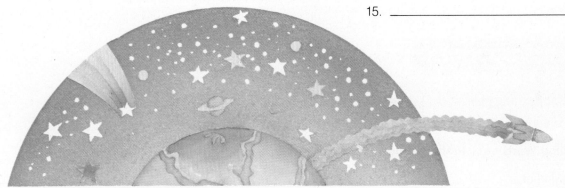

B Find the misspelled word in each group. Write the word correctly.

1. common
   conection
   compliment
   combination

   _____

2. impersonate
   immeasurable
   immature
   imobile

   _____

3. instinct
   innumerable
   inpression
   inspection

   _____

4. continent
   congratulate
   conpatible
   connection

   _____

5. immature
   immobile
   immeasurable
   immbalance

   _____

6. communicate
   comand
   common
   connection

   _____

C Write the spelling word that is related to the two words on each line. One of the two words is a synonym for the spelling word. The other word is an antonym of the same spelling word. Mark the synonym with the letter **S**. Mark the antonym with the letter **A**.

1. simple _____   complex _____   _____

2. countless _____   few _____   _____

3. ordinary _____   extraordinary _____   _____

4. adult _____   childish _____   _____

5. order _____   obey _____   _____

6. separation _____   link _____   _____

7. movable _____   stationary _____   _____

8. agreeable _____   hostile _____   _____

9. limited _____   boundless _____   _____

10. flattery _____   insult _____   _____

BUILD WORD POWER

Add and subtract letters to make new forms of spelling words. Remember the final silent **e** when adding or subtracting suffixes.

Spelling Word	Prefix Change	Suffix Change		New Word Form
compliment	+un	+ary	=	_____
immeasurable	-im	-able, +ment	=	_____
immature	-im	+ity	=	_____
instinct		+ive, +ly	=	_____
common	+un	+ly	=	_____
impersonate	-im	-ate, +al, +ity	=	_____
immobile	-im	+ity	=	_____
congratulate	-con	-ulate, +itude	=	_____
complicated	-com, +du	-ed, +ion	=	_____
innumerable	-in	-able, +ator	=	_____
communicate	-com, +im	-cate, +ity	=	_____

congratulate   communicate   compliment   innumerable   impersonate
continent   command   combination   immeasurable   impossibility
connection   compatible   instinct   immobile   impression
common   complicated   inspection   immature   imbalance

New Words
Discover
new words
below!

REACH OUT FOR NEW WORDS

A Build a word pyramid by following the code. Use your spelling
dictionary to find the four pyramid words that match the definitions.

S P E C

The root **spec** means "to look at, see."

S P E C $\underset{1}{\_}$ ... $\underset{10}{\_}$

1. extraordinary to look at

_____

$\underset{8}{\_}\underset{9}{\_}\underset{7}{\_}$ S P E C $\underset{10}{\_}$

2. what is seen to be ahead

_____

S P E C $\underset{10}{\_}\underset{1}{\_}\underset{10}{\_}\underset{7}{\_}\underset{9}{\_}$

3. a looking back on things past

_____

$\underset{4}{I}\underset{6}{N}$ S P E C $\underset{10}{T}\underset{4}{I}\underset{7}{O}\underset{6}{N}$

$\underset{9}{\_}\underset{3}{\_}\underset{10}{\_}\underset{9}{\_}\underset{7}{\_}$ S P E C $\underset{10}{\_}$

4. one view of something

_____

S P E C $\underset{10}{\_}\underset{1}{\_}\underset{2}{\_}\underset{11}{\_}\underset{5}{\_}\underset{1}{\_}\underset{9}{\_}$

A	C	E	I	L	N	O	P	R	T	U
1	2	3	4	5	6	7	8	9	10	11

B Build another word pyramid. Find the four pyramid
words that match the definitions.

P R E S S

The root **press** means "to press."

P R E S S $\underset{12}{\_}\underset{11}{\_}\underset{5}{\_}$

1. pressed together

_____

$\underset{11}{\_}\underset{5}{\_}$ P R E S S $\underset{5}{\_}\underset{4}{\_}$

2. an effect "pressed" on the mind

_____

$\underset{4}{\_}\underset{5}{\_}$ P R E S S $\underset{6}{\_}\underset{10}{\_}\underset{9}{\_}$

3. a low or "pressed down" place

_____

$\underset{3}{\_}\underset{10}{\_}\underset{8}{\_}$ P R E S S $\underset{5}{\_}\underset{4}{\_}$

4. restrained or kept "pressed down"

_____

$\underset{6}{I}\underset{8}{M}$ P R E S S $\underset{6}{I}\underset{10}{O}\underset{9}{N}$

$\underset{6}{\_}\underset{8}{\_}$ P R E S S $\underset{6}{\_}\underset{10}{\_}\underset{9}{\_}\underset{1}{\_}\underset{2}{\_}\underset{7}{\_}\underset{5}{\_}$

A	B	C	D	E	I	L	M	N	O	R	U
1	2	3	4	5	6	7	8	9	10	11	12

ad + preciate = *appreciate*

ad + petite = *appetite*

ad + paratus = *apparatus*

ad + parently = *apparently*

ad + propriate = *appropriate*

ad + proximately = *approximately*

ob + ponent = *opponent*

ob + portunity = *opportunity*

sub + ported = *supported*

sub + posed = *supposed*

com + respond = *correspond*

com + rection = *correction*

in + rigation = *irrigation*

in + regular = *irregular*

in + ritate = *irritate*

in + legal = *illegal*

in + lustration = *illustration*

com + lapse = *collapse*

com + lege = *college*

com + lection = *collection*

1. With what letter do all of the roots in the first column begin? _____
   When joined to a root that begins with the letter **p** . . .

   the prefix **ad** is spelled _____,

   the prefix **ob** is spelled _____,

   the prefix **sub** is spelled _____.

2. Look at the words in the second column.
   When joined to a root that begins with the letter **r** . . .

   the prefix **com** is spelled _____,

   the prefix **in** is spelled _____.

   When joined to a root that begins with the letter **l** . . .

   the prefix **in** is spelled _____,

   the prefix **com** is spelled _____.

Assimilated prefixes often result in double consonants that cause spelling problems.
The spelling of the prefixes **ad**, **ob**, and **sub** changes when they are joined to roots
    or base words that begin with the letter **p**:
       ad becomes **ap**   **ob** becomes **op**   **sub** becomes **sup**
The spelling of the prefixes **com** and **in** changes when they are joined to roots or
    base words beginning with the letter **r**:
       com becomes **cor**   **in** becomes **ir**
The spelling of the prefixes **com** and **in** changes when joined to the letter **l**:
       com becomes **col**   **in** becomes **il**

A Unscramble the syllables to make spelling words. Cross out the extra syllable or syllables in each group.

1. ri in tate ir _____

2. posed des sup er _____

3. de col es lapse _____

4. i mate prox da ap ly _____

5. lec on tion col _____

6. pre ate ci non ap _____

7. tra in lus il tion _____

8. tite pe ap ly con _____

9. spond dis re cor _____

10. ty ob ni por op tu _____

11. un ly ap ent par _____

12. lege tor oc col _____

13. ed sup ly port _____

14. le ni gal il _____

15. u reg sa lar ir _____

16. ob nent po op _____

17. ri tion ir ga or _____

18. tus ra pa ad ap _____

19. pro ate up pri ap _____

20. de rec cor tion _____

Sometimes a word must be broken at the end of a line of writing. Divide the word between syllables. Use a hyphen to show that the word is continued on the next line.

DICTIONARY

B Write each spelling word as though it had to be divided between the two lines of the sentence. Use your dictionary to see how the word is broken into syllables. Put a hyphen after the break. Some words can be divided in more than one way.

1. **illustration**
   Who drew the _____

   _____ in the magazine?

2. **irritate**
   Did the smoke _____

   _____ your eyes?

3. **irregular**
   The music has an _____

   _____ beat.

4. **supposed**
   It is not _____

   _____ to rain.

5. **collection**
   Maria has a _____

   _____ of shells.

6. **supported**
   The building is _____

   _____ by steel beams.

7. **illegal**
   Parking is _____

   _____ on this street.

8. **college**
   Mr. Kent has a _____

   _____ degree.

9. **appetite**
   The boy's _____

   _____ was hearty.

C Find the spelling words that fit in the shapes. Then write each word.

1. _____

2. _____

3. _____

4. _____

5. _____

6. _____

7. _____

8. _____

9. _____

10. _____

BUILD WORD POWER

WRITING

Rewrite each phrase by substituting a spelling word similar in meaning for each underlined word. On your own paper, expand each rewritten phrase into a sentence.

1. communicate with the university _____

2. annoy your rival _____

3. a set of equipment _____

4. like the drawing _____

5. suitable chance _____

6. visibly unlawful _____

7. occasional hunger _____

8. upheld the improvement _____

9. ought to provide water _____

appreciate   appropriate   supported   irrigation   illustration
appetite   approximately   supposed   irregular   collapse
apparatus   opponent   correspond   irritate   college
apparently   opportunity   correction   illegal   collection

New Words
Discover new words below!

REACH OUT FOR NEW WORDS

A Build a word pyramid by following the code. Use your spelling dictionary to find the four pyramid words that match the definitions.

The root **leg** means "law."

1. being within the law

_____

2. lawful inheritance

_____

3. to make or pass a law

_____

4. lawful representative

_____

L E G

L E G $\frac{}{1}$ $\frac{}{2}$ $\frac{}{14}$

$\frac{I}{6}$ $\frac{L}{7}$ L E G $\frac{A}{1}$ $\frac{L}{7}$

$\frac{}{3}$ $\frac{}{4}$ L E G $\frac{}{1}$ $\frac{}{12}$ $\frac{}{4}$

L E G $\frac{}{6}$ $\frac{}{12}$ $\frac{}{6}$ $\frac{}{8}$ $\frac{}{1}$ $\frac{}{12}$ $\frac{}{4}$

$\frac{}{9}$ $\frac{}{10}$ $\frac{}{6}$ $\frac{}{13}$ $\frac{}{6}$ L E G $\frac{}{4}$

L E G $\frac{}{6}$ $\frac{}{11}$ $\frac{}{7}$ $\frac{}{1}$ $\frac{}{12}$ $\frac{}{4}$

A	C	D	E	G	I	L	M	P	R	S	T	V	Y
1	2	3	4	5	6	7	8	9	10	11	12	13	14

B Build another word pyramid. Find the four pyramid words that match the definitions.

The root **port** means "to carry."

1. carried into a country

_____

2. means of carrying

_____

3. one who carries back news

_____

4. able to be carried

_____

P O R T

$\frac{}{11}$ $\frac{}{4}$ P O R T $\frac{}{4}$ $\frac{}{11}$

$\frac{}{4}$ $\frac{}{15}$ P O R T $\frac{}{4}$ $\frac{}{3}$

$\frac{}{5}$ $\frac{}{7}$ P O R T $\frac{}{4}$ $\frac{}{3}$

$\frac{S}{12}$ $\frac{U}{14}$ $\frac{P}{10}$ P O R T $\frac{E}{4}$ $\frac{D}{3}$

P O R T $\frac{}{1}$ $\frac{}{2}$ $\frac{}{6}$ $\frac{}{4}$

$\frac{}{13}$ $\frac{}{11}$ $\frac{}{1}$ $\frac{}{8}$ $\frac{}{12}$ P O R T $\frac{}{1}$ $\frac{}{13}$ $\frac{}{5}$ $\frac{}{9}$ $\frac{}{8}$

A	B	D	E	I	L	M	N	O	P	R	S	T	U	X
1	2	3	4	5	6	7	8	9	10	11	12	13	14	15

antique   quite   aquarium
boutique   quiet   squirrel
technique quickly   equality
           quarterly equator
mosquito   quarrel   banquet
etiquette quotation ventriloquist
bouquet   quotient
           quilted

1. Look at the underlined letters in each word. What letter always follows the letter **q**? _____

2. Say the first three words aloud. What two letters make the single sound of the letter **k**? _____ What silent letter follows these letters? _____

3. In the next three words, what two letters make the sound of the letter **k**? _____

4. In the remaining words, what two letters make the sound of **kw**? _____

The letter **q** is always followed by the letter **u** in the English language.
When **qu** is pronounced like **k**, it can appear in the middle of a word or at the end of a word: mosquito, antique. The spelling is always **que** at the end of a word.
When **qu** is pronounced like **kw**, it can appear in the middle of a word or at the beginning of a word: equator, quarrel.

A First find the one spelling word that will fit in the colored boxes. Then find eight more words to fit in the boxes going across.

B The words in each group are related in some way. Find the spelling word that fits in each group.

1. chipmunk, gopher, beaver   _____

2. fight, argument, dispute   _____

3. zoo, stable, kennel   _____

4. fly, gnat, bee   _____

5. divisor, dividend, remainder   _____

6. shop, store, salon   _____

7. feast, party, dinner   _____

8. courtesy, manners, politeness   _____

9. bunch, corsage, arrangement   _____

10. still, silent, calm   _____

11. monthly, yearly, semi-annually   _____

12. method, system, style   _____

105

C Rewrite each phrase, using an **'s** to show the possessive form of the underlined word.

1. the wings of the <u>mosquito</u> _____

2. the boutique of the <u>owner</u> _____

3. the voice of the <u>ventriloquist</u> _____

4. the nest of the <u>squirrel</u> _____

5. the quarrel of the <u>children</u> _____

6. the source of the <u>quotation</u> _____

7. the colors of the <u>bouquet</u> _____

8. the technique of the <u>artist</u> _____

9. the value of the <u>antique</u> _____

10. the banquet of the <u>association</u> _____

BUILD WORD POWER

WRITING

Write acrostic poems with some of your spelling words.

Squirrel

Swinging _____   _____

Quickly _____   _____

Up _____   _____

Into the tree, _____   _____

Racing _____   _____

Rapidly with _____   _____

Ease from _____   _____

Limb to limb. _____   _____

106

antique etiquette quickly quotient equality
boutique bouquet quarterly quilted equator
technique quite quarrel aquarium banquet
mosquito quiet quotation squirrel ventriloquist

New Words
Discover new words below!

REACH OUT FOR NEW WORDS

A Write the letter **P** on the first line. Then count every three letters to find nine new **q** words. Cross out each letter as you use it.

P I E H S Q Y E U S S A I Q D Q U R U A

1. _____
2. _____
3. _____
4. _____
5. _____
6. _____
7. _____
8. _____
9. _____

B Write the new word that goes with each definition and fits in each set of boxes.

1. done or growing in water   _____

2. compressed coal dust   _____

3. bodily structure   _____

4. group of five   _____

5. non-transparent   _____

6. crush   _____

7. greenish blue   _____

8. multiply by four   _____

9. attractive, like a picture   _____

107

justice   challenge
juice   language
jumbo   damage
juvenile   mileage
jacket   marriage
journal   judge
pajamas   pledge
conjunction   bridge
rejoice   badge
injury   dodge

1. Look at the words in the first column. Does the letter **j** ever appear at the

   end of a word? _____ The letter **j** is followed by one of three vowels in

   these words. Write the vowels. _____   _____   _____

   If the letter before these vowels were a **g**, would the **g** have a hard sound

   (g̲um, g̲ame, g̲o) or a soft sound (g̲inger)? _____

2. Look at the first five words in the second column. What silent vowel follows

   the letter **g**? _____ How many syllables are in each of these words? _____

   Where in each word do the letters **ge** appear? _____

3. In the last five words, what consonant comes before the **ge** in each word? _____

   How many syllables are in each word? _____

   Is the vowel in each word long or short? _____

> The letters **j** and **g** often sound alike.
> The letter **j** is used at the beginning and in the middle of words, not at the end.
>   Unlike the letter **g**, it has a *soft* sound before the vowels **a**, **o**, **u**.
> The letters **ge** spell the soft sound of **j** at the ends of words.
> The letters **dge** are used only in a one-syllable word with a short vowel.

PRACTICE THE WORDS

A Find the missing vowels. Write the complete word.

1. d__dg__ _____
2. d__m__g__ _____
3. br__dg__ _____
4. __nj__r__ _____
5. j__mb__ _____
6. b__dg__ _____
7. j__ck__t _____
8. j__ __c__ _____
9. j__dg__ _____
10. pl__dg__ _____

11. p__j__m__s _____
12. m__rr__ __g__ _____
13. ch__ll__ng__ _____
14. c__nj__nct__ __n _____
15. l__ng__ __g__ _____
16. j__ __rn__l _____
17. j__v__n__l__ _____
18. r__j__ __c__ _____
19. m__l__ __g__ _____
20. j__st__c__ _____

B Unscramble these groups of words to make complete sentences. Be sure to use correct capitalization and punctuation. Circle the spelling words.

1. wore each jacket badge delegate a his on.

   _____

2. a language learning foreign challenge is a.

   _____

3. engineers bridge the damage to the repaired.

   _____

4. a marriage judge the performed ceremony.

   _____

5. to dodge to injury the tried pitcher ball the avoid an.

   _____

6. in journal his kept record a the mileage of travelers the of one.

   _____

An **Americanism** is a word, or one meaning of a word, that first appeared in the English language in America. A dictionary may use a special symbol such as a star to point out which words and meanings are Americanisms.

C Read the entries in the spelling dictionary for **jumbo**, **jacket**, **challenge**, and **pledge**. Then use one word in each sentence below. After the sentence, write the definition of the Americanism that applies to the sentence.

1. Robin's brother is a _____ in a college fraternity. _____

   _____

2. Put the phonograph record back in its _____ . _____

   _____

3. Have you ever flown in a _____ jet? _____

4. The loser of the election plans to _____ the vote counts. _____

   _____

BUILD WORD POWER

One underlined word in each phrase is part of a spelling word. The other under-lined word is a clue to its meaning. Write the spelling word. Then write the plural form of the word. Use your dictionary to check the spelling of some of the plural forms.

1. the right <u>age</u> for a <u>wedding</u>   _____   _____

2. no <u>award</u> for being <u>bad</u>   _____   _____

3. <u>dare</u> to give your <u>all</u>   _____   _____

4. <u>ruined</u> by <u>age</u>   _____   _____

5. <u>across</u> the <u>ridge</u>   _____   _____

6. <u>ice</u> in your <u>drink</u>   _____   _____

7. <u>jam</u> on your <u>nightshirt</u>   _____   _____

8. hid the <u>diary</u> in the <u>urn</u>   _____   _____

9. <u>joined</u> with the prefix <u>con</u>   _____   _____

10. ran a good <u>distance</u> for his <u>age</u>   _____   _____

11. <u>promised</u> to <u>edge</u> the lawn   _____   _____

12. Cleopatra's <u>youth</u> on the <u>Nile</u>   _____   _____

110

justice   jacket   rejoice   damage   pledge

juice   journal   injury   mileage   bridge

jumbo   pajamas   challenge   marriage   badge

juvenile   conjunction   language   judge   dodge

New Words
Discover new words below!

REACH OUT FOR NEW WORDS

A Nine new **j** or **g** words are hidden in three directions in this puzzle. →↓↘
Each word will match one set of blanks and letters. Write the words.

```
J  J  E  O  P  A  R  D  Y  Z
O  U  R  V  M  I  S  G  J  P
E  B  D  E  A  L  H  U  A  J
S  I  L  I  N  D  U  L  G  E
B  L  X  I  C  E  C  T  U  A
I  E  W  E  G  I  H  O  A  L
L  E  O  C  A  E  A  K  R  O
J  A  R  G  O  N  F  L  N  U
Q  R  A  N  V  E  D  A  Y  S
M  E  J  A  U  N  D  I  C  E
```

1. __ a __ __ o __   _____

2. j __ b __ __ __ __   _____

3. __ b __ __ g __   _____

4. __ eo __ __ __ __ y   _____

5. __ __ d __ __ __ __ l   _____

6. __ ea __ __ __ __   _____

7. __ __ __ __ lg __   _____

8. j __ __ __ d __ __ __   _____

9. __ __ g __ __ r   _____

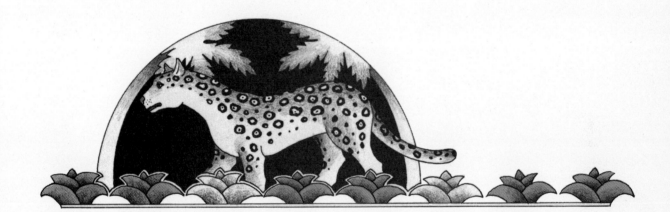

B Complete these sentences with the new words.

1. The _____ sensed that its life was in _____ when it heard the hunters.

2. The highest _____ power in the United States is the Supreme Court.

3. Her doctor's medical _____ confused her, but Cheryl could see she had

   _____ by the yellowish color of her skin.

4. The store celebrated its twenty-fifth year with an anniversary _____.

5. The child's parents tried not to _____ him even though he was _____

   of the new baby.

6. Because the film crew was so considerate, the town tried to _____

   them in any way they could.

19 begin   beginning   beginner
control   controlling   controlled
equip   equipping   equipped   equipment
forget   forgetting   forgetful

20 offer   offering   offered
differ   differing   differed   difference
happen   happening   happened
refer   referring   referred   reference

21 advisable
agreeable
noticeable
changeable
visible

22 impossibility
communicate
immature
connection

23 appetite
opponent
supposed
correspond
illegal

24 mosquito
antique
quarrel
equator

25 justice
judge
marriage
language

A Complete each analogy with a word from the spelling list.

1. **commit** is to **commitment** as **equip** is to _____

2. **bouquets** is to **bouquet** as **mosquitos** is to _____

3. **prefer** is to **refer** as **preference** is to _____

4. **carry** is to **carriage** as **marry** is to _____

5. **legible** is to **illegible** as **legal** is to _____

6. **complication** is to **complicate** as **communication** is to _____

7. **differ** is to **differed** as **offer** is to _____

8. **replaced** is to **replaceable** as **noticed** is to _____

9. **believe** is to **believable** as **advise** is to _____

10. **premature** is to **mature** as **prejudge** is to _____

11. **forgot** is to **forgetting** as **began** is to _____

12. **incredible** is to **credible** as **injustice** is to _____

13. **managed** is to **manageable** as **changed** is to _____

14. **inaudible** is to **invisible** as **audible** is to _____

15. **regrettable** is to **regretting** as **controllable** is to _____

B Complete these sentences with spelling words.

1. There was only a slight weight _____ between Sean and

   his _____ in the wrestling match.

2. There is a definite _____ between the size of your _____

   and the size of your waist.

3. This _____ desk is _____ to be 150 years old.

4. A foolish _____ sounds the same in any _____.

5. Although they _____ in their beliefs, they were both _____

   and willing to compromise.

6. I keep _____ to _____ with my pen pal, who lives in

   a country near the _____.

7. His _____ attitude made reaching an agreement

   an _____.

8. I think it is _____ for Lee to report what _____ to the police.

PROOFREADING

C Improve these paragraphs. First, cross out the misspelled words and write them correctly. Then replace each underlined phrase with a spelling word.

Last summer, my Uncle Jed offerred to take me flying in his small plane. As I sat down beside him in the cabin, I thought the controll panel of the plane looked much more complicated than the dashboard of a car. The plane had so much more <u>stuff</u> to be studied and checked before we could take off. I hoped Uncle Jed wasn't forgeting anything important! He tested the radio to make sure we could <u>talk back and forth</u> with the airport tower. Then he checked the wind direction. He explained that the winds, which are <u>likely to shift around a lot</u>, make a difference in the direction of our take-off.

Once we were off the ground, the motion of the plane was barely noticable. I was surprised that the houses and roads were so <u>easy to see</u> from the air. Before we landed, I controlled the plane by myself for a few seconds. Uncle Jed said I wasn't bad for a beginner, and he promised to take me flying again next summer.

Misspelled Words

1. _____
2. _____
3. _____
4. _____

Word Substitutions

1. _____
2. _____
3. _____
4. _____

USING MORE REVIEW WORDS

A Follow the directions to make other words from spelling words.

1. immature	-im +ity	=	_____
2. advisable	-able +or	=	_____
3. bridge	+a +ment	=	_____
4. immobile	-im +ity	=	_____
5. agreeable	-able +ment +dis	=	_____
6. quotation	-ation +ed +mis	=	_____
7. changeable	-able +ing +un	=	_____
8. immeasurable	-able +ment -im	=	_____
9. congratulate	-ulate +itude -con	=	_____
10. justice	-ice +ment +ad	=	_____
11 apparently	-ly -ap +trans	=	_____
12. impersonate	-im -ate +al +ity	=	_____
13. supposed	-sup +op -ed +ition	=	_____
14. innumerable	-ble -in +tor	=	_____
15. approximately	-ap -ate -ly +ity	=	_____

114

B Three words in each row follow the same spelling pattern. Write the one word that does not fit the pattern.

1. offer   differ   refer   enter   _____

2. inspection   impression   irregular   illustration   _____

3. badge   damage   bridge   dodge   _____

4. noticeable   changeable   excitable   manageable   _____

5. quotient   equality   quotation   etiquette   _____

6. appreciate   admitted   appropriate   approximately   _____

7. quite   plan   grab   stop   _____

8. credible   edible   agreeable   possible   _____

9. collapse   command   correction   correspond   _____

10. technique   bouquet   antique   quiet   _____

C Complete each analogy with one word from the box. Each word is used once.

challenge	squirrel	piloted	bridge	apparatus	galloping
language	mosquito	bouquet	orbit	continent	aquarium
appetite		judge		visible	

1. **fish** is to **trout** as **insect** is to _____

2. **sound** is to **audible** as **sight** is to _____

3. **France** is to **French** as **country** is to _____

4. **fabric** is to **silk** as **animal** is to _____

5. **kangaroo** is to **horse** as **hopping** is to _____

6. **train** is to **route** as **spaceship** is to _____

7. **drink** is to **thirst** as **food** is to _____

8. **Spain** is to **Europe** as **country** is to _____

9. **birds** is to **flock** as **flowers** is to _____

10. **cage** is to **zoo** as **tank** is to _____

11. **promise** is to **pledge** as **dare** is to _____

12. **car** is to **drove** as **plane** is to _____

13. **under** is to **tunnel** as **over** is to _____

14. **hospital** is to **doctor** as **courtroom** is to _____

15. **tennis** is to **rackets** as **gymnastics** is to _____

climate	snaked	liner	constellation
humid	diamonds	sunset	monuments
dampness	tugboat	avenue	skyscrapers
piers	swirling	golden	smokestacks
steel	ocean	muggy	heaven

Prewriting. Prewriting is the thinking, planning, and organizing you do before you begin to write. In this lesson, you will plan and write a **descriptive composition**. You will describe a city scene.

The details you think of when making prewriting notes are important. They will help your reader to form a mental picture of what you are describing.

USE PREWRITING SKILLS

A Answer these questions with spelling words. The words will help you think of details for a city scene.

1. What two words are names for types of boats you might see in a city harbor?

_____   _____

2. What is another name for a city street? _____

3. What three nouns are names of structures you might see in a city?

_____   _____   _____

4. What word is a name for walkways that reach into the water? _____

5. What three nouns are names for things in the sky?

_____   _____   _____

6. Write four words that can be used to talk about the weather. _____

_____   _____   _____

7. What word is the name of a material used to build a skyscraper? _____

8. What adjective could describe a sunset? _____

9. What two verbs could be used to tell how a river moves?

_____   _____

10. What could you compare bright, twinkling city lights to? _____

B The feeling that a piece of writing creates is called the **mood**. Before you begin to write, you must decide what mood you want your description to have. You might choose a feeling of excitement, fear, peace, or sadness. Choose your words and details carefully to give this feeling. Also, try to use words that appeal to the senses.

Write the detail from each pair that you would choose to create a peaceful feeling in your description.

1. a tugboat resting at the pier
the harsh whistle of a tugboat

_____

2. swirling ocean waters
calm ocean waves

_____

3. golden sunset glowing in the west
fiery red sunset streaking the western sky

_____

4. smokestacks puffing billows of dark smoke
rows of smokestacks, silent and still

_____

5. quiet, tree-lined avenue
traffic clogging the busy avenue

_____

6. a constellation of diamonds twinkling in the heavens
lightning snaking its way across the sky

_____

C The details in a set of prewriting notes can usually be grouped around two or three main ideas. Look at this list of main ideas and details. On your own paper, write each detail under the main idea that it supports.

First Main Idea: The weather was hot.
Second Main Idea: We could see the harbor from our boat.
Third Main Idea: We could see the city skyline in the distance.

Supporting Details
stately ocean liner docked at a nearby pier
humid, muggy air was stifling
rows of steel and glass skyscrapers
felt the dampness of a tropical climate
factory smokestacks belching black clouds
sturdy tugboat churning through the swirling waters

NOW THINK Make prewriting notes for your own description of a city scene. Picture the scene in your mind. Decide what mood you want to create. List your main ideas. Write supporting details for each idea. Word your details carefully to appeal to the reader's senses.

Writing. Writers create pictures with words. They do this by using vivid details that appeal to the reader's senses. They often use comparisons to help the reader see in a new way how things are similar.

A comparison that is introduced by the words *like* or *as* is called a **simile**.

Examples: The skyscrapers towered over us *like mountains*.
The ocean water was *as smooth as glass*.

USE WRITING SKILLS

Use your imagination to add one or more words to each simile. Then expand each simile into a complete sentence.

1. _____ sparkled like diamonds.

_____

_____

2. ocean liner as big as a _____

_____

_____

3. as humid and muggy as a _____

_____

_____

4. skyscrapers as tall as _____

_____

_____

5. sunset glowing like a _____

_____

_____

6. _____ swirling like a _____

_____

_____

7. traffic snaked through the city like a _____

_____

_____

NOW WRITE   Now look at your prewriting notes. Use them to write a description of a city scene. Write a paragraph for each main idea. Use sensory details to develop each paragraph. Include some similes to create a vivid picture.

Revising. When you revise your writing, check to see if you have chosen the best words to express your ideas. In a descriptive composition, use precise words to create a more vivid picture. Choose vocabulary to strengthen the mood and appeal to the senses.

USE REVISING AND PROOFREADING SKILLS

A The following sentences contain some words that do not express the writer's ideas precisely enough. Rewrite the sentences. Substitute more descriptive words or phrases for the underlined words.

1. The building is made of steel.

_____

2. We went down the tree-lined avenue.

_____

3. Dark smoke poured from the smokestacks.

_____

4. The boat bounced in the deep ocean water.

_____

5. I gazed at the constellation in the air above me.

_____

B Proofread the following sentences. Mark all mistakes in grammar, capitalization, punctuation, and spelling. Then rewrite the sentences on your own paper.

Remember
- Use the **er** form of an adjective to compare two things. Use the **est** form to compare more than two.
- Capitalize the names of particular trains, ships, airplanes, and automobiles.
- The antecedent of a pronoun is the noun or pronoun which it replaces or to which it refers. Use a singular pronoun for a singular antecedent. Use a plural pronoun for a plural antecedent.

   Example: The sunset (singular) filled the horizon with its (singular) golden streaks.

1. The concorde jet soared into the sunsett.

2. The luxury linar titanic sank on their first voyage.

3. Yesterday was the muggier of the three days.

4. The orient express snaked through the mountains and forests.

5. The climat is mild in Washington, D.C. than in New York city.

C Revise the following first draft of a descriptive composition. These directions will help you. Then rewrite the composition correctly on your own paper.

1. In line 8, change a detail that does not fit the feeling, or mood, of the composition.

2. Use a more precise verb in place of each underlined verb.

3. Correct a grammar error in line 9.

4. Correct capitalization errors in lines 2 and 4.

5. Correct punctuation errors in lines 4 and 6.

6. Cross out the six misspelled words. Write them correctly on the lines below.

1   The night was really too humed and muggy for a walk. However, the thought of

2   fresh air drew me outside. The close dampeness of the august night blanketed me.

3   Hoping a breeze might find its way from the ocaen, I stopped for a moment on

4   the bridge? Ahead of me the harbor lay asleep. The darkened liner plymouth <u>was</u>

5   in the water with its faithful tugboat bobbing beside it. Along the shore, weather-

6   beaten peirs reached into the water They beckoned silently like long fingers.

7   To my right was the sleepy city. Dark, deserted skyskrapers stretched to the heav-

8   ens. The noisy buildings lined the shore. I watched as night-crawling taxis snaked

9   down the avenue between them. Each set of headlights seemed brightest than the

10   one before. The strings of street lights <u>were</u> like one giant, fallen constelation. The

11   sudden wail of a lonely foghorn startled me; it called me home.

_____   _____   _____

_____   _____   _____

NOW REVISE   Now read your own composition. Do the sentences in each paragraph tell about the main idea? Do the details all contribute to the mood? Have you used precise words? Remember to proofread for mistakes in grammar, capitalization, punctuation, and spelling. Then write your final copy.

Now you have written a descriptive composition. Share your work with other students in your class. Compare the different moods and images in the compositions.

Read this poem. Think about what it means. Then discuss the questions with your class.

1. What kind of dreams are the subject of the poem?

2. What does the poet mean when he says, "Hold fast to dreams"?

3. What two comparisons does the poet make to describe life without dreams? How do these comparisons make you feel?

Now use the poem as a starting point for your next journal entry. Here are some ideas you might want to use.

1. Imagine that one of your hopes or wishes comes true. Describe what happens.

2. Allow yourself to dream about the future. Decide how you might complete this sentence: "In twenty years, I will be. . ." Then describe your life twenty years from now.

3. Add another stanza to the poem. Use "Hold fast to dreams" as your first line. Include your own comparison to describe a life without dreams.

Building a Personal Word List

Now that you have collected words you misspelled and have written them on your personal word list, you know the words you need to practice. How can you go about learning these words? You might try one of these ways.

1. Carefully examine the words on your list. Are any of them similar in spelling to words you already know how to spell? Knowing how to spell **judge** may help you spell **pledge,** for example.

2. Search for patterns. Do any of the words on your personal list have familiar spelling patterns? In **visible, legible,** and **possible,** for example, the suffix **ible** was added to a root. Practice spelling these words as a group.

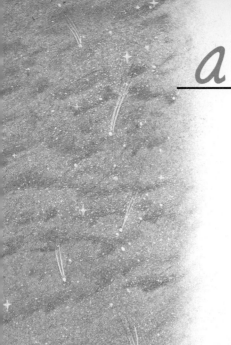

DREAMS

Hold fast to dreams
For if dreams die
Life is a broken-winged bird
That cannot fly.

Hold fast to dreams
For when dreams go
Life is a barren field
Frozen with snow.

—LANGSTON HUGHES

stere	*stereo*	*stereophonic*
typos, typi	*typical*	*stereotype*
psycho	*psychic*	*psychology*
logi, logy	*logical*	*technology*
techni	*technical*	*architect*
arch	*archives*	*archeology*
patri	*paternal*	*patriarch*
genes	*genesis*	*genealogy*
hydro	*hydrant*	*hydrophobia*
phobia	*phobia*	*acrophobia*

Combining forms are word elements that, unlike prefixes and suffixes, may be used in different positions when they are combined with other word elements.

1. The Greek combining forms in the first column become English nouns or adjectives when suffixes are added to form the words in the second column. Does the spelling of some combining forms change when endings are added? _____

2. The words in the last column have been formed by joining two Greek combining forms. Can the same Greek form sometimes be used at the beginning of one word and at the end of another? _____

Suffixes can be added to some Greek combining forms to make English nouns and adjectives.
   The noun suffix **ant** forms the noun **hydrant**: hydro+ant.
   The adjective suffix **ic** forms the adjective **psychic**: psycho+ic.
The spelling of the Greek combining form may change slightly when it is joined to other word parts.
Greek combining forms may be joined like the two parts of a compound word:
   fireproof/proofread   patriarch/archeology.
Knowing the meaning of the separate parts will help you to understand the different words made by combining the parts.

PRACTICE THE WORDS

A First look at the meaning of each of these Greek word parts. Then use the meanings of the Greek parts to find spelling words that match the definitions below.

phobia—fear	**psycho**—mind	**logi**, **logy**—reason; study of
genes—origin	**hydro**—water	**patri**—father
stere—strong	**techni**—skilled	**arch**—first
phon—sound	**typos**, **typi**—type, example	**acro**—highest

1. fatherly _____

2. dealing with a skill _____

3. street pipe for water _____

4. reasonable _____

5. "first father," or leader _____

6. strong type _____

7. fear _____

8. strong sounding _____

9. "first documents" or records _____

10. "first" skilled builder _____

11. fear of water _____

12. study of origins _____

13. study of skill _____

14. study of first people _____

15. strong-sounding record player _____

16. study of the mind _____

17. fear of heights _____

18. a usual type _____

19. concerning the mind _____

20. origin _____

B Write the word from each pair of spelling words that best completes the sentence.

1. Joyce will not swim because she suffers from (hydrophobia, acrophobia). _____

2. Ralph's family has traced its (archeology, genealogy) back to the sixteenth century. _____

3. A home computer is one product of modern (technology, psychology). _____

4. The discovery of fire marked the (genesis, genealogy) of a new way of life. _____

5. Consider all aspects of a problem carefully to arrive at a (logical, technical) solution. _____

6. Students of (archeology, archives) may work at actual "digs" while learning about that science. _____

7. Thomas Jefferson was the (patriarch, architect) who designed and built Monticello. _____

8. The term for any extreme fear is (phobia, acrophobia). _____

C Cross out the misspelled words that appear in Helpful Hannah's newspaper column. Write the words correctly.

DEAR HELPFUL HANNAH: My school project has been to trace the genology of my family. I have made a thorough, logical search of family records and the city arkives. I have discovered some disturbing facts about the paternel side of my otherwise typikal family. The family patriark suffered from both hydrophobia and accrophobia. His son, an architect, developed a terrible fear of fire hyderants. Is there a chance that I could develop a strange fobia?

FRIGHTENED IN PHOENIX

DEAR FRIGHTENED: I have not studied much psycology, but I do know that the teknical term for "fear of a phobia" is phobophobia. Therefore, in answer to your question, all you have to fear is fear itself!

HELPFUL HANNAH

1. _____
2. _____
3. _____
4. _____
5. _____
6. _____
7. _____
8. _____
9. _____
10. _____

BUILD WORD POWER

Combine **phobia** with each form to make a word meaning "fear of _____." The spelling of both forms remains the same when they are combined.

1. **photo** means "light" fear of light = _____

2. **pyro** means "fire" fear of fire = _____

3. **biblio** means "book" fear of books = _____

4. **zoo** means "animal" fear of animals = _____

5. **helio** means "sun" fear of the sun = _____

6. **claustro** means "closed space" fear of closed spaces = _____

Now complete each phrase with one of the new words.

Wouldn't it be strange if . . .

a librarian had _____

a lion tamer had _____

an elevator operator had _____

a firefighter had _____

a lifeguard at the beach had _____

a television performer had _____

stereo	psychic	technical	paternal	hydrant	**New Words**
stereophonic	psychology	architect	patriarch	hydrophobia	Discover
typical	logical	archives	genesis	phobia	new words
stereotype	technology	archeology	genealogy	acrophobia	below!

REACH OUT FOR NEW WORDS

A Each letter in this code stands for the letter that comes immediately before it in the alphabet. Find ten new words using the code.

1. bouispqpmphz   _____

2. qijmbouispqz   _____

3. npobsdiz   _____

4. npopmphvf   _____

5. ijfsbsdiz   _____

6. bobsdiz   _____

7. qspmphvf   _____

8. qijmptpqiz   _____

9. izesphfo   _____

10. hfofujdt   _____

B Write the new word that has the same meaning as the underlined phrase in each sentence. The meanings of the Greek word parts you have not yet studied are given in the box. Underline each of the Greek parts within the word.

anthropo—human	**pro**—before	**an**—without
logos—word, speech	**monos**—alone, one	**heros**—sacred
philo—to love	**archos**—leader	**soph**—wisdom

1. Thomas read the <u>speech before the play</u> from *Romeo and Juliet*.   _____

2. The revolution had left the country in a state of <u>being without a leader</u>.   _____

3. Margaret Mead is known for her work in <u>the study of mankind</u>.   _____

4. The lightest of elements is <u>a gas once thought to have its origin in water</u>.   _____

5. Carol delivered a <u>speech for one person</u> for her audition.   _____

6. Socrates taught his followers <u>the love of wisdom</u>.   _____

7. We are studying <u>the science of origins and heredity</u> in biology.   _____

8. He contributes to many charities out of his feelings of <u>love for mankind</u>.   _____

9. This country has a <u>one-leader government</u>.   _____

10. Selection of tribal leaders followed a strict <u>sacred order of leadership</u>.   _____

125

quad	*quarter*	*quadrangle*
ped	*pedestrian*	*quadruped*
cent	*century*	*centipede*
grad	*gradual*	*centigrade*
annus	*annual*	*anniversary*
uni	*united*	*universal*
anima	*animated*	*unanimous*
magni	*magnify*	*magnanimous*
fac	*factory*	*manufacture*
manu	*manual*	*manuscript*

1. The Latin combining forms in the first column become complete words

    when suffixes or word endings are added to form the words in the second column. Does

    the spelling of some combining forms change when endings are added? _____

2. The words in the last column have been formed by joining two Latin

    combining forms. Can a combining form be a first syllable? _____

    Can it be a last syllable? _____ Can it be a middle syllable? _____

> Suffixes can be added to Latin combining forms to make complete words. The spelling
> may change slightly when other word parts are added, but the meaning will remain
> the same.
> Two Latin combining forms may be joined like the two parts of a compound word. Unlike
> prefixes and suffixes, a combining form can be used in any position in a word.

PRACTICE THE WORDS

A First look at the meaning of these Latin word parts. Then write the spelling word that can replace the underlined words in the phrases.

fac—do	**magni**—large, great	**annus**—year	**quad**—four
manu—hand	**anima**—spirit	**cent**—one hundred	**vers**—turn
grad—degree	**uni**—one	**ped**—foot	**scrip**—to write

1. submitted his <u>handwritten paper</u> _____

2. a generous or <u>great-spirited</u> person _____

3. a <u>fourth</u> of the pie _____

4. a bridge for <u>a person on foot</u> _____

5. the <u>yearly</u> report _____

6. a <u>hundred degree</u> thermometer _____

7. saw a <u>four-footed</u> animal _____

8. celebrate the <u>turn of a year</u> _____

9. <u>one</u> in their opinions _____

10. caught a <u>creature with one hundred feet</u> _____

11. <u>do or make the parts by hand</u> _____

12. a <u>hand-operated</u> switch _____

13. once in a <u>hundred years</u> _____

14. <u>make larger</u> with the microscope _____

15. a change that is <u>by degrees</u> _____

16. <u>spirited</u> conversation _____

B Complete each analogy with a spelling word.

1. **often** is to **frequent** as **yearly** is to _____

2. **rider** is to **walker** as **passenger** is to _____

3. **three** is to **triangle** as **four** is to _____

4. **quiet** is to **active** as **separated** is to _____

5. **one hundred** is to **twenty-five** as **dollar** is to _____

6. **two** is to **biped** as **four** is to _____

7. **far** is to **distant** as **worldwide** is to _____

8. **ten** is to **decade** as **one hundred** is to _____

9. **greedy** is to **miserly** as **generous** is to _____

10. **decrease** is to **reduce** as **increase** is to _____

C Complete this story using spelling words. Capitalize where necessary.

In the attic of his house, Josh found an old, yellowed __1__ that had been written by his great-grandfather. It was a collection of __2__ reports that covered over a __3__ of a __4__ of his life. The papers told about the great-grandfather's arrival in the __5__ States, and his __6__ adjustment to life in a new country. Josh read about the __7__ friend who had given his great-grandfather a place to live and food to eat. He read about the strenuous __8__ labor his great-grandfather did in a __9__ for a few dollars a week. Other papers told about how Josh's great-grandfather had met his wife, and of their family and every __10__ they celebrated together. Josh showed the papers to his own family, and they made a __11__ decision to read the papers every year to remind them of their rich family history.

1. _____   5. _____   9. _____

2. _____   6. _____   10. _____

3. _____   7. _____   11. _____

4. _____   8. _____

BUILD WORD POWER

The meaning of each combining form below is a number. Substitute those numbers for the combining forms in the mathematical equations. Write the answer for each problem, using a combining form instead of a number.

uni = 1	quad = 4	cent = 100	quin = 5	tri = 3	bi = 2	deca = 10

1. quad + uni + tri − quin = _____   4. tri × bi + quin − uni = _____

2. deca − quad + bi − quin = _____   5. quin × tri − deca × bi = _____

3. uni + quin ÷ tri + bi = _____   6. cent ÷ deca − quad − bi = _____

Complete each sentence with a word that contains a Latin combining form from above. The underlined words are clues to the combining form. Use your dictionary to check the correct spelling of the words.

1. Mr. and Mrs. <u>Quin</u>n are the parents of _____.

2. I will <u>try</u> to draw a _____ and a square.

3. <u>By</u> nightfall, both tires on the _____ were flat.

4. Building this <u>deck</u> without help will take me a _____.

quarter   century   annual   animated   factory
quadrangle   centipede   anniversary   unanimous   manufacture
pedestrian   gradual   united   magnify   manual
quadruped   centigrade   universal   magnanimous   manuscript

New Words
Discover
new words
below!

REACH OUT FOR NEW WORDS

A Find nine new words by following the code. Each letter in a word is represented
by a capital letter and a number.

	A	B	C	D	E	F	G	H
1	n	i	n	a	m	i	u	o
2	i	g	i	m	a	t	p	e
3	a	e	s	f	e	c	i	m
4	b	l	t	e	c	a	d	n
5	e	a	o	i	t	m	e	l
6	n	m	a	t	i	p	a	t
7	i	e	r	a	i	e	b	u
8	x	u	e	d	o	t	n	r

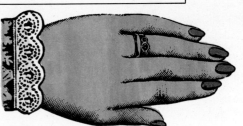

1. ___ E1 A3 G8 C2 F3 G1 H8 H2

2. ___ B6 D1 H4 G3 F6 B8 H5 E2 D6 B3

3. ___ G2 D4 G4 B7 C3 E5 G6 B4

4. ___ G5 A8 F6 B3 D8 E6 C4 D5 H1 A1

5. ___ D2 C6 B2 C1 G3 F8 H7 G4 A5

6. ___ A2 C1 D7 G8 A7 F5 A3 H6 F7

7. ___ D3 B5 E4 C3 E7 H3 E7 H5 C8

8. ___ A4 E3 A1 B7 D3 F4 F3 H6 C5 C7

9. ___ G7 B3 H4 D4 D8 F1 E4 F2 E6 H1 A6

WRITING

B Using the meaning of each Latin combining form, match each new word with a
definition. On your own paper, write a sentence with each word.

1. **bene** means "well, good"
   a blessing, or good things that are spoken _____

   someone who does good for another _____

2. **manu** means "hand"
   care of the hands and fingernails _____

   handle skillfully _____

3. **ped** means "foot"
   a long trip or march, sometimes on foot _____

   the foot or base of a statue or pillar _____

4. **anima** means "spirit, life, or motion"
   lack of life or movement _____

5. **magni** means "great" or "large"
   greatness of size _____

6. **simile** means "the same"
   an exact reproduction, or made the same _____

129

marvel + ous = *marvelous*   real + ize = *realize*

industry + ous = *industrious*   critic + ize = *criticize*

adventure + ous = *adventurous*   apology + ize = *apologize*

courage + ous = *courageous*   memory + ize = *memorize*

outrage + ous = *outrageous*   sympathy + ize = *sympathize*

virus   *despise*

circus   *televise*

census   *exercise*

genius   *advertise*

surplus   *compromise*

All of the words in the first column end with the same sound.

1. What suffix is added to make the first five words? _____

   Is the suffix added to complete words or to roots? _____

   When it is added to **adventure**, what happens to the final silent **e**? _____

   Why is the final silent **e** kept in **courageous** and **outrageous?**

   _____

2. What are the last two letters of the next five words in the first column? _____

   All of the words in the second column end with the same sound.

3. What suffix is added to make the first five words? _____

   Is the suffix added to complete words or to roots? _____

4. What are the last three letters of the next five words? _____

> The suffix **ous** is added to words to form adjectives meaning "full of" or "having
> certain characteristics."
>   **adventurous** = full of adventure
> The **us** spelling is not a suffix. It is a noun ending.
> The suffix **ize** is added to words to form verbs meaning "to make or become."
>   **apologize** = to make an apology
> The **ise** ending is not a suffix.

A Decide whether **ize** or **ise** should be added to each word or letter group. Write the complete word. Then write the **ing** form.

1. desp _____ _____

2. apology _____ _____

3. comprom _____ _____

4. real _____ _____

5. sympathy _____ _____

6. memory _____ _____

7. telev _____ _____

8. advert _____ _____

9. critic _____ _____

10. exerc _____ _____

B Use the clues to find spelling words that fit in the puzzle. Use the past tense of some words.

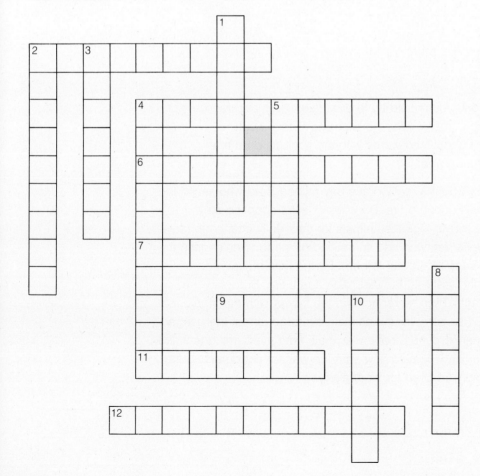

Across

2. wonderful
4. settled differences
6. hard-working
7. brave
9. say you're sorry
11. to hate
12. daring

Down

1. amount left over
2. committed to memory
3. to know
4. found fault
5. shocking
8. official count
10. brilliant person

C Each group of words below contains a noun, an adjective, and a verb. Write a sentence that uses all three words. Add endings to the words if necessary.

1. circus, marvelous, televise

_____

_____

2. virus, courageous, sympathize

_____

_____

3. adventurous, genius, memorize

_____

_____

4. realize, outrageous, census

_____

_____

5. industrious, advertise, surplus

_____

_____

BUILD WORD POWER

When you revise your written work, you should try to eliminate slang, overused expressions, and vague language. Improve the word choice in this rough draft by replacing each group of underlined words with the spelling word that could be used in the rewritten paragraph.

> *Fire!* was a super show about a really brave boy named Brad who saved the lives of many circus animals during a fire. Bunches of extra supplies were stored in the tent where a trainer took the animals for their daily chance to move around and work out. The trainer, who had some kind of a bug, didn't notice the smell of smoke when the supplies began to burn. By the time he figured out why the animals were acting restless, the tent had caught fire. Brad saw the flames and spread the alarm. Then he ran to help the trainer with the frightened animals. Because Brad felt so sorry for the animals, he forgot about the danger. Together, he and the trainer rescued all of the animals from the burning tent. No one cut down the poor trainer, who said how sorry he was for not detecting the smell of the smoke and thanked Brad for his bravery.

1. _____   4. _____   7. _____

2. _____   5. _____   8. _____

3. _____   6. _____   9. _____

marvelous   outrageous   genius   apologize   televise
industrious   virus   surplus   memorize   exercise
adventurous   circus   realize   sympathize   advertise
courageous   census   criticize   despise   compromise

New Words
Discover new words below!

REACH OUT FOR NEW WORDS

A Beginning with the first letter on each line, circle every other letter. Write each new word.

1. e l n o t a e s r f p j r l i n s x e   _____

2. s n i v n l u o s   _____

3. f t r p a o n q c u h y i e s r e   _____

4. d c e o v a i m s z e   _____

5. m l o b m a e g n a t r o p u e s   _____

6. p y e w r a s b o g n u a f l p i e z a e   _____

7. b h u g r a g o l w a t r c i x z e e   _____

8. l u o m c n a i l o i s z o e   _____

9. s y u e p w e t r b v u i q s p e   _____

10. c a o d m i p f r j i u s k e   _____

B Use the new words to complete these sentences.

1. Lee often gets a _____ headache when the weather is bad.

2. The first moon landing was a _____ occasion.

3. Our committee chose Dan to _____ the project.

4. The pain seemed to _____ in her right shoulder.

5. My sister decided to _____ her luggage before she went to college.

6. That hamburger chain will try to _____ its restaurants all over the city.

7. Every _____ Tom has undertaken has been successful.

8. Ashley wants to _____ her own dance routine.

9. After several attempts had been made to _____ the house, my parents bought an alarm.

10. What are the elements that _____ a good story?

ex + pect = *expect*

ex + pired = *expired*

ex + pert = *expert*

ex + perience = *experience*

ex + pensive = *expensive*

ex + tremely = *extremely*

ex + tension = *extension*

ex + tinguish = *extinguish*

ex + terior = *exterior*

ex + tinct = *extinct*

ex + cuse = *excuse*

ex + clamation = *exclamation*

ex + cursion = *excursion*

ex + fort = *effort*

ex + fective = *effective*

ex + ficiency = *efficiency*

ex + lection = *election*

ex + levate = *elevate*

ex + scape = *escape*

ex + vaporate = *evaporate*

1. In how many words is the prefix **ex** added to a root that begins with the
   letter **p**? _____ With the letter **t**? _____ With the letter **c**? _____
   Does the spelling of the prefix change when it is joined to these roots? _____

2. Is the letter **x** ever followed by the letters **s** or **z**? _____

3. In how many words does the spelling of the prefix change to match the
   first letter of a root? _____ What is that letter? _____

4. How does the spelling of the prefix change in the last four words?

   _____

Unlike the "Mad **ad**," the prefix **ex** seldom loses its identity. It causes few doubling
problems because the letter **x** is never doubled and seldom changes to match the
first letter of the root.

    ex remains **ex** before roots that begin with **p**, **t**, or **c**.

    ex changes to **ef** when joined to the roots that begin with the letter **f**.

    ex changes to **e** before most other consonants.

Spelling problems are caused by the **s** sound of the letter **x**. Do not add the letter **s**
between the prefix and the root.

A Alphabetize the spelling words that come between each pair of guide words.

expand	explain	effect	eleven

_____   _____

_____   _____

_____   _____

_____   _____

_____   _____

escalate	excuser	extend	extremist

_____   _____

_____   _____

_____   _____

_____   _____

WRITING

A **cliché** is an expression or idea that has become stale from too much use. "As light as a feather" and "sweet as honey" are clichés.

B The use of too many clichés and idioms can weaken your writing. Improve this paragraph by replacing each underlined phrase with the spelling word that could be used in a rewritten version. You may have to add endings.

I recently read an article about a scientist, a know-it-all in his field, who made a fascinating discovery. While traveling on some remote islands, he discovered a huge lizard that scholars thought had been dead as a doornail for years. The scientist was extremely excited. Although he wished that he could bring the animal back with him, he knew that it would cost an arm and a leg. He settled for taking a picture of the creature and recording data about it. Then he flew the coop before the lizard could get too interested in him!

1. _____   3. _____

2. _____   4. _____

Now write the spelling words that could replace these phrases.

1. worldly wisdom _____   3. be "on the alert" for _____

2. kicked the bucket _____   4. disappear into thin air _____

135

C Look up **escape**, **expect**, and **expensive** in the spelling dictionary and read the synonomies. Write the synonyms for each word.

escape   _____   _____

expect   _____   _____

expensive   _____

Decide which entry word or synonym best fits each sentence. Write the word.

1. A warm dinner will _____ you when you return.

2. Did the prisoner _____ from the jail?

3. The museum displayed the _____ jewels.

4. We _____ six guests for dinner.

5. The performer tried to _____ reporters by wearing a disguise.

6. Hank could not afford the _____ jacket.

7. Try to _____ walking in the rain puddles.

8. I _____ that your wish comes true.

BUILD WORD POWER

No common English words begin with the letters **exs**. When the prefix **ex** is joined to certain roots that begin with the letter **s**, the **s** is dropped from the spelling.

     Write the words formed by adding the prefix **in** to the roots **spect**, **spire**, **sist**, and **stinct**. Then write the words formed by adding the prefix **ex** to the same roots.

1. in + spect = _____   ex + spect = _____

2. in + spire = _____   ex + spire = _____

3. in + sist   = _____   ex + sist   = _____

4. in + stinct = _____   ex + stinct = _____

Are the words formed with the **ex** prefix spelled with the letters **exs**? _____

Can you still hear the sound of **s** when you say the **ex** words? _____

What letter makes the sound of **s** in the **ex** words? _____

expect	expensive	exterior	excursion	election
expired	extremely	extinct	effort	elevate
expert	extension	excuse	effective	escape
experience	extinguish	exclamation	efficiency	evaporate

New Words
Discover new words below!

REACH OUT FOR NEW WORDS

A Build a word pyramid by following the code. Use your spelling dictionary to find the four pyramid words that match the definitions.

The root **ten(d)** means "to stretch."

1. swollen or stretched out

_____

2. mental or nervous strain

_____

3. an increase or "stretching" in degree or amount

_____

4. stretching the mind toward

_____

TEN

TEN ⎽ ⎽ ⎽ ⎽
    8 5 7 6

E X TEN S I O N
4 11   8 5 7 6

⎽ ⎽ ⎽ TEN ⎽ ⎽ ⎽
3 5 8   3 4 3

TEN ⎽ ⎽ ⎽ ⎽ ⎽
    3 4 6 2 12

⎽ ⎽ TEN ⎽ ⎽ ⎽ ⎽
5 6   8 5 10 4

⎽ ⎽ TEN ⎽ ⎽ ⎽ ⎽
1 9   9 5 10 4

A	C	D	E	I	N	O	S	T	V	X	Y
1	2	3	4	5	6	7	8	9	10	11	12

B Build another word pyramid. Find the four pyramid words that match the definitions.

The root **lec** means "to gather or choose."

1. gather together

_____

2. ability to think, understand, or choose between ideas

_____

3. a chosen way of speaking

_____

4. act of choosing from

_____

LEC

⎽ ⎽ ⎽ LEC ⎽
3 7 1   12

⎽ ⎽ ⎽ LEC ⎽
2 10 8   12

E LEC T I O N
4   12 7 10 9

⎽ ⎽ ⎽ ⎽ ⎽ LEC ⎽
7 9 12 4 8   12

⎽ ⎽ LEC ⎽ ⎽ ⎽ ⎽
11 4   12 7 10 9

⎽ ⎽ ⎽ LEC ⎽ ⎽ ⎽ ⎽
9 4 6   12 5 13 8

A	C	D	E	F	G	I	L	N	O	S	T	U
1	2	3	4	5	6	7	8	9	10	11	12	13

mis + spelled = *misspelled*   ad + sume = *assume*

re + spelled = *respelled*   re + sume = *resume*

dis + solved = *dissolved*   sub + ceed = *succeed*

re + solved = *resolved*   ex + ceed = *exceed*

com + mission = *commission*   ad + cess = *access*

ad + mission = *admission*   pro + cess = *process*

ad + tend = *attend*   com + lapse = *collapse*

pre + tend = *pretend*   re + lapse = *relapse*

ob + fense = *offense*   com + ruption = *corruption*

de + fense = *defense*   ex + ruption = *eruption*

1. Look at the two words in each pair. Do they have the same root? _____

   Do they have the same prefix? _____ Do both words contain a double

   consonant when the prefix and root are joined? _____

2. Write the three words in which a double consonant results without any

   change in the spelling of the prefix.

   _____   _____   _____

3. How many words have double consonants caused by an assimilated prefix

   that has been changed to match the first letter of the base word or root? _____

> Some double consonants occur because the last letter of the prefix is the same
>   as the first letter of the base word or root: mi**ss**pelled.
> Most double consonants occur because the prefix is assimilated. The last letter of the
>   prefix changes to match the first letter of the base word or root: a**d** + tend = a**tt**end.
> **Mnemonic device:** Associating the words in each pair will help you to remember that
>   one of the double consonants belongs to the prefix, and one belongs to the root
>   or base word.

A Complete each sentence with two spelling words that contain the same root.

1. Only two scientists have _____ to the secret _____.

2. The football coach praised both the _____ and the _____.

3. Will this year's fund-raising drive _____ in its attempt to _____ last year's result?

4. The student _____ each word that she had _____ on the pretest.

5. The newspaper's accusations of _____ resulted in an

   _____ of angry denials from several officials.

6. Mark tried to _____ that he was thrilled to _____ the boring meeting.

7. I _____ that the show will _____ after the special news report.

8. As the decorations _____ in the rain, Sue _____ never to have an outdoor party again.

9. The college established a _____ to study its _____ policies.

10. A _____ of his illness caused the patient to _____ in exhaustion.

B Mrs. Mixit is still combining the wrong prefix with the right root. Help her say what she really means by writing the underlined words correctly.

Recently I was asked to <u>pretend</u> a meeting of a <u>remission</u> on TV programming. Barely five minutes into a most useless discussion, I was <u>dissolved</u> to set them straight.

"I <u>resume</u>," I said, "that you are not going to waste our time on too many issues like this. If you are to <u>exceed</u> in reaching your goals, you cannot continue to <u>attend</u> that more serious problems don't exist! Now, I do not mean to <u>succeed</u> my status as an observer, and I don't mean to set up an automatic <u>offense</u> for musicians. However, I really cannot see the harm in violins on television. It certainly won't cause the <u>relapse</u> of the television industry or threaten the democratic <u>recess</u>."

"That's *violence*, Mrs. Mixit," said one of the commissioners. "We're discussing *violence* on television."

"Now that's worthwhile," I said, and let the commissioners <u>presume</u> the meeting.

1. _____   5. _____   9. _____

2. _____   6. _____   10. _____

3. _____   7. _____   11. _____

4. _____   8. _____

C The words **assume**, **process**, and **commission** each have several definitions in
the dictionary. Read the entry for each word. Then complete each sentence
with one of the words. Finally, write the abbreviation for the part of speech of
the word as it is used in the sentence. If there is more than one definition for
that part of speech, write the number of the definition that matches the
sentence.

1. The real estate agent received a _____ for each house that she

   sold. _____

2. Superman had to _____ the appearance of a mild-mannered reporter. _____

3. The king plans to _____ an artist to paint his portrait. _____

4. Mother has to _____ the vegetables before she freezes them. _____

5. Straightening teeth can be a long and expensive _____. _____

6. The rebel soldiers tried to _____ control of their government. _____

7. The mayor formed a _____ to study the transportation problem. _____

8. The judges _____ you know the rules of the competition. _____

BUILD WORD POWER

The Latin root **cede** means "go" or move. It is spelled in three different ways.

1. The root **cede** changes to **cess** in many noun and adjective forms. Write
   the words formed by adding prefixes to **cede** and **cess**.

   ad   + cede = _____   ad   + cess   = _____

   re   + cede = _____   re   + cess + ion = _____

   se   + cede = _____   se   + cess + ion = _____

   con + cede = _____   con + cess + ion = _____

2. The root is spelled **ceed** in only three words.

   ex   + ceed = _____   ex   + cess + ive = _____

   suc + ceed = _____   suc + cess + ful = _____

   pro + ceed = _____   pro + cess + ion = _____

   Mnemonic device: Use your **ESP** to remember the three words with **ceed** spellings:
   (**e**xceed, **s**ucceed, **p**roceed).

---

3. The root is spelled **sede** in only one word: **supersede**. Write the word. Then
   write a mnemonic device to help you remember the unusual spelling of **supersede**.

   _____

   _____

misspelled	commission	offense	succeed	collapse
respelled	admission	defense	exceed	relapse
dissolved	attend	assume	access	corruption
resolved	pretend	resume	process	eruption

New Words

Discover new words below!

REACH OUT FOR NEW WORDS

A Build a word pyramid by following the code. Use your spelling dictionary to find the four pyramid words that match the definitions.

The root **rupt** means "to break."

1. broken or split open

_____

2. broken away from standards; wicked

_____

3. a bursting or breaking out of

_____

4. broken into or between

_____

RUPT

$\frac{}{1}\frac{}{6}\frac{}{7}$ RUPT

$\frac{E}{3}$ RUPT $\frac{I}{4}\frac{O}{6}\frac{N}{5}$

$\frac{}{2}\frac{}{4}\frac{}{8}$ RUPT $\frac{}{3}\frac{}{2}$

RUPT $\frac{}{10}\frac{}{7}\frac{}{3}\frac{}{2}$

$\frac{}{4}\frac{}{5}\frac{}{9}\frac{}{3}\frac{}{7}$ RUPT $\frac{}{3}\frac{}{2}$

$\frac{}{2}\frac{}{4}\frac{}{8}$ RUPT $\frac{}{4}\frac{}{11}\frac{}{3}$

C D E I N O R S T U V
1 2 3 4 5 6 7 8 9 10 11

B Build another word pyramid. Find the four pyramid words that match the definitions.

MISS

The root **miss** means "to send."

1. act of sending a message

_____

2. sent away

_____

3. permission to be sent in

_____

4. object sent through the air

_____

MISS $\frac{}{4}\frac{}{5}\frac{}{3}$

$\frac{}{2}\frac{}{4}\frac{}{10}$ MISS $\frac{}{3}\frac{}{2}$

$\frac{A}{1}\frac{D}{2}$ MISS $\frac{I}{4}\frac{O}{8}\frac{N}{7}$

$\frac{}{11}\frac{}{9}\frac{}{1}\frac{}{7}\frac{}{10}$ MISS $\frac{}{4}\frac{}{8}\frac{}{7}$

$\frac{}{4}\frac{}{7}\frac{}{11}\frac{}{3}\frac{}{9}$ MISS $\frac{}{4}\frac{}{8}\frac{}{7}$

MISS $\frac{}{4}\frac{}{8}\frac{}{7}\frac{}{1}\frac{}{9}\frac{}{12}$

A D E I L M N O R S T Y
1 2 3 4 5 6 7 8 9 10 11 12

1 *amateur*   2 *bureau*   3 *beret*

chauffeur   *plateau*   *ballet*

grandeur   *trousseau*   *buffet*

pasteurize   *chateau*   *gourmet*

4 *tongue*   5 *corsage*

league   *mirage*

fatigue   *espionage*

vague   *sabotage*

Many words taken from the French language have repeated letter patterns. Say each group of words out loud as you answer these questions.

1. What three-letter combination is repeated in the first group of words? _____

2. In the second group of words, what three letters make the long **o** sound? _____

3. Is the final **t** pronounced in the third group of words? _____

4. In the fourth group of words, does the letter **g** have a hard or a soft sound? _____

   What silent letters follow the **g**? _____

5. In the last group of words, does the letter **g** have a hard or a soft sound? _____

   What vowel follows the letter **g**? _____

6. Think of the pattern for hard and soft **g** in English words. When **g** is

   followed by **e**, **i**, or **y**, it usually has a _____ sound. When **g** is followed

   by **a**, **o**, or **u**, it usually has a _____ sound. Is the pattern for hard and soft

   g the same in English and French words? _____

Spelling follows certain patterns in every language. Some French letter patterns appear in words commonly used in the English language: **eur**, **eau**, final silent **t**, final silent **ue**.

In both English and French, a soft **g** is usually followed by **e**, **i**, or **y**. The hard **g** is usually followed by **a**, **o**, or **u**.

A Complete each sentence with a spelling word.

1. The dancers performed a classic _____, *Swan Lake*.

2. Does the dairy farm _____ its own milk?

3. Jeffrey reads books about spies because he likes tales of _____.

4. A high, flat stretch of land is called a _____.

5. Do the initials F.B.I. stand for the Federal _____ of Investigation?

6. "Hold your _____" is an idiom that means "do not speak."

7. The agents planned to _____ the railroads of the enemy's country.

8. Only _____ players can enter this special tournament.

9. The _____ image of a lake in the desert was only a _____.

10. Tourists are always impressed by the _____ of the French Alps.

11. Barry brought his date a _____ of roses.

12. The delicious _____ was prepared by a _____ chef.

13. The French family lived in a _____ that was over 300 years old.

14. Did you notice that the _____ driving that car wore a _____?

15. Doctors say that the exhausted athlete is suffering from _____.

16. The bride wore an outfit from her _____.

PROOFREADING

B Cross out the misspelled words in this story. Write them correctly.

George's face was lined with fatigeu as he drove the stranger up to the plateau. The stranger wore a berat but spoke in an unfamiliar language. Finally they arrived at an old chateaux. Its grander was disappearing with age. George watched from the car as the stranger walked to the door. The owners, Mr. and Mrs. Smith, appeared at the entrance. George recognized her as a famous ballet dancer, and he had a vaigue memory of seeing Mr. Smith before, too. The couple quickly invited George's passenger in to dinner. George crept over to the dining room window and listened. He overheard a fiendish plot to sabitage all the French bread factories in the country! George leaped through the window and announced that they were under arrest. He explained that he was only an amature chaufer. Actually he worked for the Bureau of Security. He handcuffed them to each other, and then sat down and finished their gourmay meal.

1. _____   4. _____   7. _____

2. _____   5. _____   8. _____

3. _____   6. _____   9. _____

Homographs are words that are spelled alike but have different meanings and origins. In many dictionaries, homographs are marked with small numerals after the entry word.

spell¹ (spel) *n.* [OE., a saying] **1.** a word or words supposed to have some magic power **2.** power or control that seems magical

spell² (spel) *v.* **spelled** or **spelt, spell'ing** [< OFr. *espeller*, to explain < Frank. *spellōn*] **1.** to say, write, or signal in order the letters of (a word, etc.) **2.** to mean [red *spells* danger]

spell³ (spel) *v.* **spelled, spell'ing** [OE. *spelian*] to work in place of (another) while he rests —*n.* **1.** a turn of working in place of another **2.** any period of work, duty, etc. [a two-year *spell* as reporter] **3.** a period [a *spell* of gloom]

C The spelling words **buffet** and **league** both have homographs. Look up and read the two entries for each word in your spelling dictionary. Write the word along with the numeral that tells which entry fits the sentence.

1. The guests served themselves from the <u>buffet</u> table. _____

2. A storm at sea caused high waves to <u>buffet</u> the small boat. _____

3. The voters formed a <u>league</u> to protect their interests. _____

4. The giant in the fairy tale could cover seven <u>leagues</u> with one step. _____

BUILD WORD POWER

In your spelling dictionary, read the unusual etymology and the definition for each of these words: **sabotage, pasteurize, Braille, boycott, cashmere**. First write each word beside the phrase that relates to its origin. Then write the common definition of the word.

1. a 19th century French chemist—_____

_____

2. a wooden shoe from Holland—_____

_____

3. a 19th century French teacher—_____

_____

4. region in southeast Asia near Tibet—_____

_____

5. a 19th century Irish land agent—_____

_____

amateur	bureau	beret	tongue	corsage
chauffeur	plateau	ballet	league	mirage
grandeur	trousseau	buffet	fatigue	espionage
pasteurize	chateau	gourmet	vague	sabotage

New Words
Discover
new words
below!

REACH OUT FOR NEW WORDS

A Find ten new words from the French language. Begin with **league** and find your way out of the maze. Write each word.

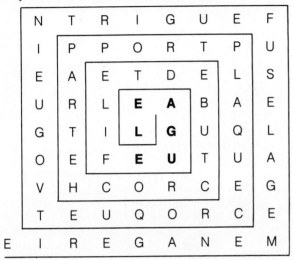

league

1. _____   6. _____

2. _____   7. _____

3. _____   8. _____

4. _____   9. _____

5. _____   10. _____

WRITING

B Write an answer for each question, using one of the new words. Use complete sentences.

1. Did the winning player receive an award?

_____

2. Is that style of clothing popular this year?

_____

3. What game requires mallets, wooden balls, and wickets?

_____

4. Does Lisa like to knit? _____

5. What part of the plane was damaged? _____

6. Why does Marty like mystery books? _____

7. Does this zoo have a good collection of animals?

_____

8. When is that new dancer's first performance?

_____

9. What cut of meat is served with the meal?

_____

10. Does Mr. Swidler communicate well with his class?

_____

ought *slight*
although *delightful*
throughout *sightseeing*
thoroughly *frightened*
thoroughbred *copyright*
doughnut *height*
fought *weighed*
brought *eightieth*
bought *freight*
thoughtless *neighborhood*

1. In the first ten words, what four-letter combination is repeated? _____

2. In the next five words, what four-letter combination is repeated? _____

3. In the last five words, what four-letter combination is repeated? _____

4. What two letters are silent in each of these combinations? _____

The letters **gh** are silent in a few familiar letter combinations:
ou**gh**   i**gh**t   ei**gh**

A Write the spelling words that contain the following words:

ought   rough   eight

_____   _____   _____

_____   _____   _____

_____   _____   _____

_____   _____

_____

light   right

_____   _____

_____   _____

You may want to use the small words as mnemonic devices to help you remember the spelling of the large words.

B Complete these analogies. The first two words will be either synonyms or antonyms. Write the spelling word that will make the same relationship between the next two words.

1. **happy** is to **glad** as **scared** is to _____

2. **commanded** is to **obeyed** as **sold** is to _____

3. **talked** is to **discussed** as **quarreled** is to _____

4. **generous** is to **stingy** as **considerate** is to _____

5. **may** is to **might** as **should** is to _____

6. **up** is to **down** as **width** is to _____

7. **big** is to **large** as **slender** is to _____

8. **hot** is to **cold** as **unpleasant** is to _____

9. **throwing** is to **tossing** as **touring** is to _____

10. **ship** is to **boat** as **cargo** is to _____

11. **illegally** is to **lawfully** as **incompletely** is to _____

12. **under** is to **below** as **during** is to _____

13. **maybe** is to **perhaps** as **though** is to _____

14. **finished** is to **concluded** as **measured** is to _____

C Find the two words in each sentence that can be combined to form a spelling word. Then write the spelling word.

1. My neighbor damaged the hood of her car. _____

2. Did you copy the right telephone number? _____

3. John has given less thought to the project than you have. _____

4. The cat ran through the door and out the window. _____

5. This cookie dough doesn't have a single nut in it. _____

6. Seeing a full theater was a welcome sight to the actors. _____

7. The German shepherd was bred to do a thorough job as a Seeing Eye dog. _____

BUILD WORD POWER

DICTIONARY

The underlined phrase in each sentence is an idiom that can be found in your spelling dictionary. First complete each sentence with a spelling word. Then write the dictionary definition of each idiomatic phrase.

1. After having _____ for years, they decided to bury the hatchet.

   _____

2. He was so _____, he almost jumped out of his skin.

   _____

3. Jerry got a kick out of riding the _____ horse.

   _____

4. We rolled out the red carpet for Mrs. Grant's _____ birthday.

   _____

5. Once in a blue moon a _____ train uses that crossing.

   _____

6. Paula was almost at the end of her rope when her friends _____ help to her.

   _____

7. Tom's _____ actions rubbed me the wrong way.

   _____

8. _____ we tried to be quiet, one of our neighbors raised the roof over the noise.

   _____

ought · thoroughbred · bought · sightseeing · weighed
although · doughnut · thoughtless · frightened · eightieth
throughout · fought · slight · copyright · freight
thoroughly · brought · delightful · height · neighborhood

New Words
Discover
new words
below!

REACH OUT FOR NEW WORDS

A Eight new silent **gh** words are hidden in three directions in this puzzle. → ↓ ↘
Find the words and write them.

A	D	M	L	A	U	D	E	L	S	Q
F	C	A	U	G	H	T	E	R	T	U
V	T	U	U	O	B	A	N	A	R	Y
F	A	G	N	G	L	O	T	N	A	N
R	U	N	A	H	H	N	U	U	I	A
E	G	T	N	J	T	O	G	G	U	
U	H	Z	O	X	L	F	E	P	H	G
G	T	I	P	L	E	A	N	R	T	H
H	D	I	S	T	R	A	U	G	H	T
B	F	O	P	L	I	G	H	T	O	Y

1. _____
2. _____
3. _____
4. _____
5. _____
6. _____
7. _____
8. _____

B Use spelling words to complete this old melodrama.

     Mrs. Trueheart wrung her hands, terribly __1__. The little bakery that she owned with her lovely __2__ Madeline was about to be taken from them by that evil villain, Blackbird. The mortgage was due, and someone had stolen all of their money. Madeline knew that only Gary Goodguy could help rescue them from their awful __3__. She told him their sorrowful story, and together they went __4__ to the local dance hall, __5__ Nellie's. There they found Blackbird. The villain laughed at Madeline's request for a little more time, but Gary noticed a small leaf stuck in Blackbird's collar. He whispered something to Madeline, and together they went to Blackbird's house. Sure enough, they found the stolen money in the __6__ of a large old oak.
    "Looks like we've __7__ Mr. Blackbird at his own game," said Gary.
    "Yes," said Madeline, "but was he never __8__ that crime doesn't pay?"

1. _____
2. _____
3. _____
4. _____

5. _____
6. _____
7. _____
8. _____

149

28
stereotype
stereophonic
archeology
technology

29
unanimous
centigrade
anniversary
manufacture

30
courageous
virus
memorize
realize
exercise

31
excuse
effort
escape
experience
extremely

32
misspelled
dissolved
process
succeed

33
amateur
chauffeur
bureau
league

34
thoroughly
weighed
frightened
neighborhood

USING REVIEW WORDS

A Complete each analogy with a word from the spelling list.

1 **circuses** is to **circus** as **viruses** is to _____

2. **complete** is to **completely** as **extreme** is to _____

3. **proved** is to **disproved** as **solved** is to _____

4. **critic** is to **criticize** as **real** is to _____

5. **industriously** is to **industrious** as **unanimously** is to _____

6. **outrage** is to **outrageous** as **courage** is to _____

7. **rough** is to **roughly** as **thorough** is to _____

8. **exploding** is to **explode** as **escaping** is to _____

9. **matched** is to **mismatched** as **spelled** is to _____

10. **apology** is to **apologize** as **memory** is to _____

11. **tongues** is to **tongue** as **leagues** is to _____

12. **fatigued** is to **fatigue** as **chauffeured** is to _____

13. **unexplored** is to **explore** as **unexcused** is to _____

14. **beginners** is to **beginner** as **amateurs** is to _____

15. **excess** is to **exceed** as **success** is to _____

B Complete the sentences with spelling words.

1. Daily _____ requires determination and physical _____.

2. Modern _____ has enabled companies to _____ complex

   equipment at an _____ reasonable cost.

3. A government _____ sent me information about the _____ of printing money.

4. Students of _____ are required to get actual _____

   in the field.

5. The huge _____ cake must have _____ 20 pounds.

6. The _____ child had wandered away from his own _____.

7. Clara Barton was a _____ woman who fought the _____ that

   women did not belong in nursing.

8. There was _____ agreement among the critics that _____

   sound helped movie musicals _____ as entertainment.

PROOFREADING

C Improve this paragraph. First, cross out the misspelled words and write them correctly. Then replace each underlined phrase with a spelling word.

The unanymous opinion of professional writers is that good writing requires <u>very, very</u> hard work. The idea that a writer is a person who produces perfect sentences and paragraphs without <u>trying hard</u> is a false sterotype. Amateur writers should realize that there is no easy <u>way to get away</u> from the difficult stages of the proccess between rough draft and finished composition. Revision is more than correcting <u>mistakes in the spelling of</u> words. Expereinced writers know that it takes as much perspiration as inspiration to succeed.

Misspelled Words	**Word Substitutions**
1. _____	1. _____
2. _____	2. _____
3. _____	3. _____
4. _____	4. _____

USING MORE REVIEW WORDS

A Follow the directions to make other words from spelling words.

1. league	+s +col	=	_____
2. defense	+in +ible	=	_____
3. extinguish	-ex +dis +ed	=	_____
4. neighborhood	-hood +ly +un	=	_____
5. courageous	-ous +ing +dis	=	_____
6. election	-ion +ed +re	=	_____
7. effort	+able -ef +com	=	_____
8. exclude	-ex +con +ing	=	_____
9. assume	-as +con +ing	=	_____
10. extinct	-ex +dis +ive	=	_____
11. adventurous	ad ous +ed	=	_____
12. memorize	+com -ize +ate	=	_____
13. anniversary	-anni +re -ary +ible	=	_____
14. century	-ury +ennial +bi	=	_____
15. effective	-ef +af -ive +ion +ate	=	_____

B Three of the words in each row follow the same spelling pattern. Write the word that does not follow the same pattern.

1. architect   patriarch   psychic   stereophonic   _____

2. marvelous   surplus   census   genius   _____

3. expect   expensive   extension   effective   _____

4. vague   corsage   fatigue   tongue   _____

5. apologize   criticize   despise   sympathize   _____

6. exclamation   elevate   election   evaporate   _____

7. manuscript   centigrade   quadruped   magnify   _____

8. access   process   attend   assume   _____

9. beret   ballet   weighed   gourmet   _____

10. genesis   centipede   hydrant   phobia   _____

C Complete each analogy with a word from the box. Each word is used once.

courageous	paternal	chateau	exterior	amateur
copyright	quadruped	genesis	archives	ballet
pedestrian	tongue	expense	beret	vague

1. **fruit** is to **apple** as **hat** is to _____

2. **man** is to **dog** as **biped** is to _____

3. **food** is to **doughnut** as **dance** is to _____

4. **car** is to **limousine** as **house** is to _____

5. **touch** is to **finger** as **taste** is to _____

6. **hate** is to **despise** as **cost** is to _____

7. **busy** is to **industrious** as **origin** is to _____

8. **mother** is to **father** as **maternal** is to _____

9. **vehicle** is to **driver** as **foot** is to _____

10. **internal** is to **external** as **interior** is to _____

11. **expert** is to **professional** as **novice** is to _____

12. **lively** is to **animated** as **unclear** is to _____

13. **afraid** is to **cowardly** as **brave** is to _____

14. **invention** is to **patent** as **book** is to _____

15. **books** is to **library** as **documents** is to _____

discipline	calories	straighten	pulse
muscles	floor	aerobics	ached
trampoline	sauna	sweating	track
demonstrate	cushions	calisthenics	hate
crazy	mattress	whirlpool	cramp

Prewriting. Prewriting is the thinking, planning, and organizing you do before you begin to write. In this lesson, you will plan and write an **explanatory composition that persuades**. You will state an opinion about exercise. Then you will try to persuade the reader to share that opinion.

USE PREWRITING SKILLS

A Begin your planning by jotting down thoughts and ideas about your subject. These ideas will help you decide what opinion you want to express.

Use spelling words to complete these statements. They express positive ideas about exercise.

1. Daily exercise can improve your _____ rate.

2. Exercise can strengthen your back and help _____ poor posture.

3. Two popular types of exercise programs are _____

and _____ .

4. You can easily exercise at home on your living room _____ . If the surface is too

hard, you can use a couple of _____ or an old _____ .

5. Nothing is more fun than bouncing up and down on a _____ in the gym.

6. After exercising, some people relax in a heated _____ or _____ .

Use more spelling words to complete the remaining statements. They express negative ideas about exercise.

1. Exercise always gives me sore _____ .

2. My muscles _____ for three days the last time I exercised.

3. Running causes me to get a _____ in my leg.

4. After a workout, my clothes are always dripping wet from _____ .

5. Anybody who runs around a _____ twenty times must be _____ .

6. I _____ aerobics!

B In a persuasive composition, you must present convincing reasons for your opinion. These reasons should persuade your audience to share your opinion. Before you can choose the best reasons, you must find out who your audience is. For example, if your audience will be senior citizens, you might choose one set of reasons. If your audience will be teen-agers, you might plan a different set of reasons.

Read this list of reasons. They support the opinion that any exercise program is beneficial. Write the three reasons that would be most appropriate to an audience of teen-agers.

Aerobics helps reduce the circulation problems caused by age.
The mental discipline of daily exercise can improve study habits.
Aerobics can straighten the poor posture that troubles office workers.
Calisthenics builds the muscles you'll need for team sports such as soccer.
Jazzercise lets you enjoy rock music while you burn off calories.

_____

_____

_____

_____

_____

_____

C Plan to support your reasons with thoughtfully chosen details. These details could include facts and figures, incidents, and examples.

Read the list of details below. On your own paper, write the three details that support the following reason.

One reason to exercise regularly is to prevent back problems.

DETAILS
A firm mattress provides proper back support.
Over 80% of Americans suffer from backaches.
The whirlpool relaxes sore muscles.
Studies demonstrate that weak stomach muscles cause back problems.
Just twenty floor sit-ups a day can strengthen your back.

NOW THINK

Make prewriting notes for an explanatory composition that persuades. Follow these steps:

1. Decide how you feel about your subject. State your opinion.
2. Identify your audience. Plan reasons that will convince that audience. You may have to do some research to find convincing arguments.
3. Choose details to support your reasons. These details may be facts and figures, examples, or incidents.
4. Organize your reasons and details in a logical order. One effective order is from the least important to the most important reason. This order leaves the strongest reason fresh in your readers' minds.

Writing. When you are writing to persuade, it is important to know the difference between fact and opinion. Facts are those statements that can be proven. Opinions are statements that can't be proven. Often, opinions use judgmental words such as *good, bad, the best,* and *the most.*

Example: Fact: Calisthenics is a form of gymnastic exercise.
Opinion: Calisthenics is the best form of exercise.

Begin a persuasive composition by stating an opinion. Then support that opinion with facts.

USE WRITING SKILLS

A Read the following facts. Rewrite each as an opinion. Include the underlined words in your opinion.

1. Aerobics is one form of exercise.

_____

2. An air mattress can be used as a cushion.

_____

3. Some instructors demonstrate their exercise methods on videos.

_____

4. Sweating in the sauna opens and cleans the pores of the skin.

_____

B Now change these opinions to facts. Include the underlined words in your rewritten facts.

1. Floor exercises are the hardest to do.

_____

2. The best health clubs have whirlpools and saunas.

_____

3. Isometrics is the hardest method of exercise.

_____

4. Track isn't as much fun as calisthenics.

_____

NOW WRITE Use your prewriting notes to write a first draft of your persuasive composition. Begin with an introductory paragraph that states your opinion. Use the body paragraphs to present reasons that support your opinion. Present each reason in a topic sentence. Support each reason with details such as facts and figures, examples, or incidents. Conclude with a summary of the main points and a restatement of the opinion. You may want to request that some action be taken. Make your conclusion as strong as the rest of your composition.

Revising. When you revise a persuasive composition, make sure that all of your details are related to your main idea. Also make sure that you include some facts to support the reasons you give.

USE REVISING AND PROOFREADING SKILLS

A Rewrite the following paragraph. Omit one unrelated detail. Also include these facts in your rewritten paragraph:

A full workout is only twenty minutes long.

An aerobics routine quickens the pulse, which makes the heart work harder.

Aerobics is the perfect form of exercise. Thousands of Americans who were bored by calisthenics are now crazy about aerobics. The routines are usually done to peppy music, which can make even floor exercise fun. Aerobics also doesn't take a lot of time. One important benefit of this method is that it strengthens the heart. Aerobics also helps firm the muscles. Most people hate sit-ups.

_____

_____

_____

_____

_____

_____

_____

_____

B Proofread the following sentences. Mark the mistakes in grammar, capitalization, punctuation, and spelling. Rewrite the sentences correctly on your own paper.

Remember
* The verb must agree with the subject in number.
* Use commas to set off words or groups of words that interrupt the train of thought.
  Example: Too much exercise, however, can be dangerous.
* Capitalize the pronoun **I**.

1. My pusle race whenever i run around the track.

2. It takes discipline after all to perfect a trampoline routine?

3. Some floor exercises i suppose require a matress.

157

C Revise the following paragraph from the first draft of a composition. The directions below will help you. Then write the corrected paragraph on your own paper.

1. Cross out one reason that is an opinion, not a fact.

2. Cross out one reason not suitable to a teen-age audience.

3. Correct punctuation errors in lines 2 and 7.

4. Correct capitalization errors in lines 3 and 5.

5. Correct mistakes in verb agreement in lines 1 and 8.

6. Cross out the six misspelled words. Write them correctly on the lines below.

1 The benefits of a daily exercise program is medically documented. Most stu-

2 dents however still haet to exercise. They lack the discipline to structure it into their

3 daily lives. Therefore, every School should offer a morning exercise program in ad-

4 dition to regular gym classes. Mild exercise has improved the circulation of many

5 elderly people. classes in airobics and calisthanics would bring students together

6 for a healthy half-hour. Jazzercise classes would be more fun. Such a program

7 would also have additional benefits In addition to strong mussels, daily exercize

8 improve concentration. Students might begin the day with a quickened pulss, but

9 their minds would be ready for work.

_____ _____ _____

_____ _____ _____

NOW REVISE Read your own persuasive composition. Does your introductory paragraph state an opinion? Do your reasons apply to the audience you are addressing? Did you support your reasons with facts? Now proofread for mistakes in grammar, capitalization, punctuation, and spelling. Make a clean, final copy.

Plan to read your composition aloud in class. See if you have succeeded in persuading your audience.

HANDBOOK

I The Structure of Words

Syllables
Base Words
Roots
Prefixes
Suffixes
Words Formed from Other Words
Abbreviations

II The Function of Words

Nouns
Pronouns
Verbs
Adjectives
Adverbs
Prepositions
Conjunctions
Interjections

III The Sound of Words

Vowels
Consonants
Silent Letters
Stressed and Unstressed Syllables

I The Structure of Words means the way words are put together.

Syllables

Words are made up of parts called syllables. The dictionary shows how words are divided into syllables.

but·ter = two syllables   dress = one syllable

Base Words

Base words are words before any changes have been made.

Base word   wrap
Base word with endings added   wrap<u>s</u>   wrapp<u>ed</u>   wrapp<u>ing</u>
Base word with prefix added   <u>un</u>wrap

Roots

Roots are word parts that cannot stand alone. They grow into words when they are joined to prefixes or suffixes.

pend   (root meaning "to hang")
<u>de</u>pend   (root + prefix)
pend<u>ant</u>   (root + suffix)
<u>de</u>pend<u>ant</u>   (root + prefix *and* suffix)

Prefixes

A prefix is a group of letters added to the beginning of a word or root to change the meaning. For example, **pre** is a prefix meaning "before." Therefore, the word **prefix** literally means "to fix before."

The word **informed** means "having information or news."

1.   He was an <u>informed</u> speaker.
    (He knew what he was talking about.)
2.   He was a <u>misinformed</u> speaker.
    (He had wrong or incorrect information.)
3.   He was an <u>uninformed</u> speaker.
    (He had no information.)

Suffixes

A suffix is an ending added to a word or root to change the way it is used in a sentence. The meaning of the root or base word does not change.

inform   to give knowledge or news (verb)
informer   one who gives news (noun)
information   news (noun)
informative   providing news (adjective)

The base word **inform** keeps its basic meaning in all these forms. Its *use* changes from verb to noun to adjective.

Words Formed from Other Words

Contractions A contraction is made from two words. When two words are put together, an apostrophe takes the place of one or more letters.

we are = we **a**re = we're   he will = he **wi**ll = he'll

Compound Words A compound word is made from two smaller words. The spellings do not change when the words are put together.

class + room = classroom   after + noon = afternoon

Some compound words are joined with a hyphen.

three + fourths = three-fourths   cross + country = cross-country

Blends If you put two words together and drop some of the letters without adding punctuation, the resulting word is called a blend.

motor + hotel = motel   breakfast + lunch = brunch

Clipped Words Long words are often shortened in the English language to make them more convenient to use.

gymnasium → gym   omnibus → bus

Abbreviations

An abbreviation is a shortened form of a word.
Abbreviations may use the first few letters of a word followed by a period.

Days:	Tuesday-Tues.	Wednesday-Wed.
Months:	December-Dec.	September-Sept.
Titles:	Reverend-Rev.	Captain-Capt.
Addresses:	Avenue-Ave.	Street-St.
Businesses:	Company-Co.	Incorporated-Inc.

Measurements:	inch-in.	dozen-doz.
Parts of Speech:	noun-n.	adverb-adv.

Abbreviations may use the first and last letter of a word followed by a period.

Mister-Mr.   Road-Rd.   foot-ft.

Doctor-Dr.   yard-yd.   hour-hr.

Abbreviations may use all capital letters without periods.

Maryland-MD   New York-NY   California-CA

(A complete list of state abbreviations can be found on page 168.)

Abbreviations may use all capital letters with periods.

Doctor of Medicine-M.D.   Registered Nurse-R.N.

A few common abbreviations do not follow any of these patterns.

ounce-oz.   pound-lb.   manager-mgr.

Ms. may be used for either married or unmarried women instead of Miss or Mrs.

Acronyms Single words made from the first letters or the first few letters of a group of words are called acronyms.

radio **d**etecting **a**nd **r**anging = radar

self-**c**ontained **u**nderwater **b**reathing **a**pparatus = scuba

The Function of Words means the way words are used.

Nouns

A noun is a word that names something.

Common noun suffixes include:

ment	arrangement, government, measurement
tion, ion, sion, ation	introduction, opinion, depression, formation
ness	goodness, correctness, happiness
ity, ty, y	fatality, loyalty, difficulty
ence, ance	independence, importance
er, ar, or	banker, beggar, collector
ian, ist	librarian, chemist

Singular and Plural Nouns A noun that names one thing is called a singular noun: pencil. A noun that names more than one thing is a plural noun: pencils.

The plural of most nouns is formed by adding **s**.

building + s = buildings   dream + s = dreams

Most nouns that end in **o** also add **s**. Some add **es**. Check the spelling of final **o** plurals in your dictionary.

pianos   studios   tomatoes   echoes

The plural of nouns ending in **s**, **sh**, **ch**, **x**, and **z** is formed by adding **es**.

rash + es = rashes   box + es = boxes

The plural of some nouns is formed by a change of spelling.

tooth − teeth   child − children   crisis − crises   half − halves

The plural and singular forms are the same for some nouns.

deer   quail   trousers   scissors

Possessive Nouns The possessive form of a noun shows that something belongs to someone. Make the possessive form of a singular noun by adding **'s**.

That car belongs to my father.   That is my father's car.

When a plural noun ends in **s**, add only an apostrophe to make the possessive form.

Those uniforms belong to the players.

Those are the players' uniforms.

When a plural noun does *not* end in **s**, add **'s** to make the possessive form.

Is that the classroom of the children?

Is that the children's classroom?

Pronouns

A pronoun is a word used in place of a noun.

The students wrote as they listened.   She is bringing the dessert.

A possessive pronoun takes the place of a noun in the possessive form.

My father's car = his car

The Clark's house = their house

Ashley's book = her book

A possessive pronoun is *not* spelled with an apostrophe.

Verbs

A verb is a word that shows an action or state of being.

He runs on the beach.   He is on the beach.

The endings **ed** and **ing** may be added to verbs to show the tense of the verb or the time of the action.

I walk on the beach in the summertime. (present tense)

We walked a mile to the beach. (past tense)

We are walking to the beach. (present participle)

Common verb suffixes include:

ify	fortify, glorify, justify
ize, ise	advertise, compromise, visualize, idolize
ate	dictate, operate, investigate
ish	publish, punish, astonish
en	weaken, lighten

Adjectives

An adjective is a word that modifies a noun or pronoun by limiting it or describing it in some way.

We walked along the sandy shore. (Sandy describes the shore.)

This is my favorite. (Favorite describes this.)

Common adjective suffixes include:

ly	publicly, weekly (also an adverb suffix)

ous, ious	mountainous, serious
ful	painful, rightful, powerful
ive	attractive, inventive, active
al, ial	mechanical, official, colonial
able, ible	profitable, responsible
ate	delicate, private
ar, iar	similar, familiar
ery, ary, ory	slippery, temporary, accessory

Adverbs

An adverb is a word that tells *where, when, how,* or *how much.*

The sailor acted <u>bravely</u> during the storm.

(<u>Bravely</u> tells how the sailor acted.)

Two common adverb suffixes are **ly** and **ily**:

quick<u>ly</u>   sleep<u>ily</u>

Prepositions

A preposition is a word that relates its object to some other word in the sentence.

We walked <u>along</u> the shore.

(<u>Along</u> tells where we walked in relation to the shore.)

The box is <u>under</u> the stairway.

(<u>Under</u> tells where the box is in relation to the stairway.)

Conjunctions

A conjunction is a word that connects words, phrases, or clauses.

Vines <u>and</u> flowers covered the wall.

Traffic moved slowly <u>but</u> steadily.

We could buy tickets now <u>or</u> purchase them at the door.

Interjections

An interjection is a word or word group that has no grammatical relation to the rest of the sentence. It usually shows surprise or some other strong emotion.

Help!   Oh!   Terrific!   Hold it!

III The Sound of Words means the way you say words when you speak. Sometimes the sound will help you to spell a word.

Vowels

Five letters of the alphabet are called vowels. The vowels are **a**, **e**, **i**, **o**, and **u**. The letter **y** may also be used as a vowel: gym.

Each vowel may have a long sound (g<u>a</u>te) or a short sound (b<u>a</u>t).
Other pronunciations of each vowel are shown on page 172.

Indistinct Vowels Vowels that are difficult to hear or identify are called indistinct vowels.

begg_r   (The missing vowel could be **e** or **a**.)
ben_fit   (The missing vowel could be **i**, **e**, **u**, or **a**.)

Consonants

The consonants are all the letters of the alphabet except **a**, **e**, **i**, **o**, and **u**.

Silent Letters

Silent letters make no sound. You can see them in a word, but you cannot hear them. Silent letters may appear at the beginning, in the middle, or at the end of words.

<u>k</u>nee	strai<u>gh</u>t	autum<u>n</u>	ans<u>w</u>er	<u>gh</u>ost	<u>p</u>sychic
<u>w</u>rist	dou<u>b</u>t	amaz<u>e</u>	<u>w</u>hole	rhyme	cup<u>b</u>oard
<u>g</u>nat	stal<u>k</u>	thum<u>b</u>	recei<u>p</u>t	forei<u>g</u>n	<u>p</u>neumonia

Stressed and Unstressed Syllables

Stress is the amount of emphasis placed on a syllable when you pronounce a word. The accent mark in a dictionary shows you which syllable receives the most stress.

man'   The one syllable is stressed.
be•gin'   The second syllable is stressed.

Unstressed syllables cause spelling problems because they are hard to hear and likely to be pronounced carelessly.

gram'mar (the last syllable is often slurred)

vic'to•ry (often pronounced <u>vic-try</u>)

The more stress there is on a syllable, the more clearly it is heard and the easier it is to spell. Sometimes the unstressed syllable is stressed in a related form of the same word.

gram'mar   gram•ma'ti•cal

vic'to•ry   vic•tor'i•ous

The indistinct vowels **a** and **o** are no longer indistinct when they are in accented syllables.

PREFIXES, SUFFIXES, AND STATE ABBREVIATIONS

Prefixes

ad to or toward
ante before
com with; together
de to take away
dis not; opposite of
ex out of; from
fore before
in in, into *or* not
mis badly; wrongly
non not, lack of
per through
post after
pre before
pro before *or* forward
re again; back
sub beneath, under, lower
super over; above
syn with, together
un not

Suffixes

able that can be (adj.)
age condition of (n.)
al, ial like or suitable to (adj.)
ance act of; state of (n.)
ant one who (n. or adj.)
ar like (adj.)
ary person or thing that (n. or adj.)
ate to cause to be (v.)
ation the act or condition of (n.)
ence quality or state of (n.)
ent one who (n. or adj.)
er person or thing that (n.)
ery place for, occupation of; quality of (n.)
ful having; full of (adj.)
fy to make or become (v.)
ian of or having to do with (n. or adj.)

ible that can be (adj.)
ics body of facts (n.)
ion act of; state of (n.)
ity quality; condition, or state of being (n.)
ive of or having to do with (adj.)
ize to make or become (v.)
less without (adj.)
ly in a certain way (adv.)
ment product; process, or state (n.)
ness state of being; action; behavior (n.)
or person or thing that (n.)
ory having to do with (n. or adj.)
ous full of; having much (adj.)
ure act of (n.)
y full of; having (n. or adj.)

Abbreviations of State Names

The United States Postal Service has published a list of approved abbreviations for states to be used on the envelopes.

Alabama **AL**
Alaska **AK**
Arizona **AZ**
Arkansas **AR**
American Samoa **AS**
California **CA**
Canal Zone **CZ**
Colorado **CO**
Connecticut **CT**
Delaware **DE**
District of Columbia **DC**
Florida **FL**
Georgia **GA**
Guam **GU**
Hawaii **HI**

Idaho **ID**
Illinois **IL**
Indiana **IN**
Iowa **IA**
Kansas **KS**
Kentucky **KY**
Louisiana **LA**
Maine **ME**
Maryland **MD**
Massachusetts **MA**
Michigan **MI**
Minnesota **MN**
Mississippi **MS**
Missouri **MO**
Montana **MT**

Nebraska **NE**
Nevada **NV**
New Hampshire **NH**
New Jersey **NJ**
New Mexico **NM**
New York **NY**
North Carolina **NC**
North Dakota **ND**
Ohio **OH**
Oklahoma **OK**
Oregon **OR**
Pennsylvania **PA**
Puerto Rico **PR**
Rhode Island **RI**
South Carolina **SC**

South Dakota **SD**
Tennessee **TN**
Trust Territories **TT**
Texas **TX**
Utah **UT**
Vermont **VT**
Virginia **VA**
Virgin Islands **VI**
Washington **WA**
West Virginia **WV**
Wisconsin **WI**
Wyoming **WY**

How To Find a Word

A dictionary is organized like a telephone book. It lists information in alphabetical order with guide words at the top of each page.

Guide Words

The guide words help you find the right page quickly. They tell you at a glance what section of the alphabet is included on each page. The guide word on the left tells you the first word on that page. The guide word on the right tells you the last word on that page. If the word you are looking for comes alphabetically between those two words, you are on the right page.

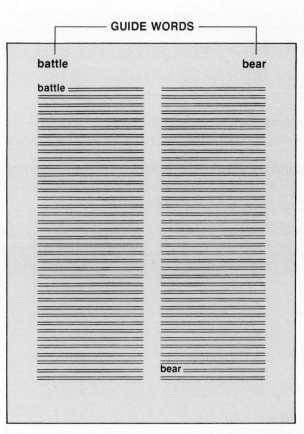

Alphabetical Order

Alphabetical order means words placed in the order of the letters in the alphabet. When two words begin with the same letter, you must look at the second letter of each word to determine alphabetical order. When several of the letters are the same, you will have to look at the third or fourth letter to determine the alphabetical order.

<u>a</u>bout toa<u>d</u>
<u>b</u>ear toa<u>s</u>t
<u>c</u>lass

Words Listed

The words listed in a dictionary are called entry words. A word is usually listed in its base form. Other forms of the word, such as the **ed** and **ing** forms of verbs or the plurals of nouns, may be listed within the same entry.

Word Forms	Base Form	Entry Word
hurrying	hurry	hurry
hurried		

Homographs are words that are spelled alike but have different meanings and origins. In this dictionary, homographs are marked with small numerals just after the boldface spelling of the entry word: **spell**[1]

Prefixes and suffixes have separate entries in a dictionary. Some words made with prefixes have separate entries. The meanings of other words with prefixes can be found by combining the meaning of the prefix with the meaning of the base word.

Some words made with suffixes may have separate entries. Other words may be found within the entry of the base word.

An Americanism, or a usage that first appeared in the English language in America, is marked by an open star before the word or meaning: ☆ **jumbo.**

Idiomatic phrases, or phrases that have a meaning different from the literal one, are defined at the end of the entry for the key word of that phrase: Ted is feeling *under the weather.*

What the Dictionary Tells About a Word

A dictionary tells you much more than the spelling and meaning of a word. The information it contains about each word is called the entry. The parts of an entry are labeled and explained below.

The *ENTRY WORD* is printed in heavy black type. It is divided into syllables.

A *SYNONYMY* contains a list of synonyms for the entry word. It may be shown in a special note at the end of an entry.

An *ETYMOLOGY*, or word history, may be shown in a special note within an entry.

The *PART OF SPEECH* is shown as an abbreviation after the pronunciation. Some words may have more than one part of speech.

OTHER FORMS of the entry word are included in the same entry. These words may be shown in a shortened form.

The *RESPELLING* tells you how to pronounce the word. The *Pronunciation Key* explains the respelling.

A *STRESS MARK* is placed after a syllable that gets an accent. Words may have both a primary (heavy) stress and a secondary (light) stress.

A sample *SENTENCE* or *PHRASE* can help you understand the meaning of the entry word.

The *DEFINITION* is the meaning of the word. If a word has more than one meaning, each meaning is given a number.

ex·pense (ik spens′) *n.* [< Anglo-Fr. < LL. *expensa (pecunia)*, paid out (money)] **1.** financial cost; fee **2.** any cost or sacrifice

ex·pen·sive (ik spen′siv) *adj.* requiring much expense; high-priced —**ex·pen′sive·ly** *adv.* —**ex·pen′sive·ness** *n.*
SYN.—**expensive** implies a price that is greater than the article is worth or more than the customer is willing to pay [an *expensive* dress]; **costly** refers to something that costs much and usually implies richness, magnificence, rareness, etc.

ex·pe·ri·ence (ik spir′ē əns) *n.* [< L. < prp. of *experiri*, to try] **1.** anything or everything observed or lived through [an *experience* he'll never forget] **2.** activity that includes training, practice, and work —*v.* **-en·ced, -enc·ing** to have experience; undergo

ex·pert (ek′spərt; *also, for adj.*, ik spʉrt′) *adj.* [< OFr. < L. pp. of *experiri*, to try] *n.* a person who is very skillful and informed in some field —**ex′pert·ly** *adv.* —**ex′pert·ness** *n.*

ex·pire (ik spīr′) *v.* **-pired′, -pir′ing** [< L. *exspirare* < *ex-*, out + *spirare*, to breath] **1.** to breathe out air **2.** to come to an end; terminate

ex·port (ik spôrt) *v.* [< L. < *ex-*, out + *portare*, to carry] to carry or send (goods, etc.) to other countries, esp. for sale —**ex·port′a·ble** *adj.* —**ex·port′er** *n.*

ex·ten·sion (ik sten′shən) *n.* **1.** a part that forms an addition [building an *extension* onto the library] **2.** an extra period of time allowed for some purpose

ex·te·ri·or (ik stir′ē ər) *adj.* [L., compar. of *exter(us)*, on the outside] on the outside; outer —*n.* an outside or outside surface

ex·tinct (ik stinkt′) *adj.* [< L. pp. of *extinguere* < *ex-*, out + *stinguere*, to extinguish] no longer living; having died out [an *extinct* species]

171

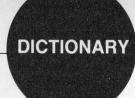

DICTIONARY

Pronunciation Key

SYMBOL	KEY WORDS	SYMBOL	KEY WORDS	SYMBOL	KEY WORDS
a	ask, fat	u	up, cut	n	not, ton
ā	ape, date	ur	fur, fern	p	put, tap
ä	car, lot			r	red, dear
		ə	a in ago	s	sell, pass
e	elf, ten		e in agent	t	top, hat
er	berry, care		e in father	v	vat, have
ē	even, meet		i in unity	w	will, always
			o in collect	y	yet, yard
i	is, hit		u in focus	z	zebra, haze
ir	mirror, here				
ī	ice, fire			ch	chin, arch
		b	bed, dub	ŋ	ring, singer
ō	open, go	d	did, had	sh	she, dash
ô	law, horn	f	fall, off	th	thin, truth
oi	oil, point	g	get, dog	*th*	then, father
oo	look, pull	h	he, ahead	zh	s in pleasure
o͞o	ooze, tool	j	joy, jump		
yoo	unite, cure	k	kill, bake	'	as in (ā'b'l)
yo͞o	cute, few	l	let, ball		
ou	out, crowd	m	met, trim		

A heavy stress mark ′ is placed after a syllable that gets a strong accent, as in **con·sid·er** (kən sid′ər).

A light stress mark ′ is placed after a syllable that also gets an accent, but of a weaker kind, as in **dic·tion·ar·y** (dik′shən er′ē).

The following abbreviations are the more common ones used in your dictionary. The parts of speech are usually shown in dark italic type. The language abbreviations are found within the etymologies.

n.	noun	**Afr.**	African	**Gr.**	Greek	**M.**	Middle, Medieval
v.	verb	**Am.**	American	**Heb.**	Hebrew	**Mod.**	Modern
pron.	pronoun	**Ar.**	Arabic	**Ind.**	Indian	**O.**	Old
adj.	adjective	**E.**	English	**Ir.**	Irish		
adv.	adverb	**Fr.**	French	**It.**	Italian		
prep.	preposition	**G.**	German	**L.**	Latin		
conj.	conjunction			**Sp.**	Spanish		
interj.	interjection			**Swed.**	Swedish		

A

ac·a·dem·ic (ak′ə dem′ik) *adj.* of colleges, universities, etc.; scholastic —**ac′a·dem′i·cal·ly** *adv.*

ac·cede (ak sēd′) *v.* -ced′ed, -ced′ing [< L. *accedere* < *ad-*, to + *cedere*, to yield] to give assent; agree (to)

ac·cent (ak′sent) *n.* [Fr. < L. < *ad-*, to + *cantus*, pp. of *canere*, to sing] 1. the emphasis given to a word or syllable when speaking it 2. a distinguishing regional or national way of pronouncing

ac·cess (ak′ses) *n.* [< OFr. < L. pp. of *accedere*, < *ad-*, to + *cedere*, to yield] a being able or allowed to enter or use [he has *access* to the information]

ac·ci·dent (ak′sə dənt) *n.* [< OFr. < L. prp. of *accidere*, happen < *ad-*, to + *cadere*, to fall] a happening that is not expected, foreseen, or intended

ac·ci·den·tal (ak′sə den′t'l) *adj.* happening by chance —**ac′ci·den′tal·ly** *adv.*

ac·count (ə kount′) *n.* 1. an arrangement by which a customer may pay for purchases within a specified future period 2. an explanation, report, or description [he gave an *account* of his travels]

ache (āk) *v.* ached, ach′ ing [OE. *acan*] to have or give dull, steady pain

ac·ro·pho·bi·a (ak′rə fō′bē ə) *n.* [<Gr. *akros*, at the end or top + *phobos*, fear] an abnormal fear of being in high places

ac·ti·vate (ak′tə vāt′) *v.* -vat′ed, -vat′ing to make active —**ac′ti·va′tion** *n.* —**ac′ti·va′tor** *n.*

ac·tive (ak′tiv) *adj.* [< OFr. < L. *activus* < base *act-*, a doing] 1. acting, working, moving 2. lively, busy, quick —**ac′tive·ly** *adv.* —**ac′tive·ness** *n.*

ac·tiv·i·ty (ak tiv′ə tē) *n., pl.* -ties the state of being active

ad- *a prefix meaning* motion toward, addition to, nearness to [*admit, adjoin, adrenal*]

a·dapt·a·ble (ə dap′tə b'l) *adj.* able to adjust oneself to changes —**a·dapt′a·bil′i·ty** *n.*

ad·join (ə join′) *v.* [< OFr. < L. *adjungere* < *ad-*, to + *jungere*, join] to be next to, be in contact —**ad·join′ing** *adj.*

ad·min·is·ter (ad min′ə stər, ad-) *v.* [< OFr. < L. *administrare* < *ad-*, to + *ministrare* to serve] 1. to manage or direct 2. to give out, dispense or apply (punishment, medicine, etc.) 3. to furnish help or be of service

ad·mis·sion (ad mish′ən, ad-) *n.* an admitting or being admitted —**ad·mis′sive** *adj.*

ad·mit (ad mit′, ad-) *v.* -mit′ted, -mit′ting [< L. *admittere* < *ad-*, to + *mittere*, to send] 1. to permit to enter or use 2. to acknowledge or confess

ad·o·les·cent (ad′ 'l es′ 'nt) *adj.* [Fr. < L. prp. of *adolescere*, to mature] of or characteristic of adolescence; youthful, exuberant, etc. —*n.* a boy or girl from puberty to adulthood; person in his or her teens **SYN.**—**adolescent** applies to one in the period between puberty and maturity and especially suggests the awkwardness, emotionalism, etc. of this period; **juvenile** applies to that which has to do with, is suited to, or intended for young persons; **youthful** applies to one who is or appears to be in the period between childhood and maturity

a	fat	ir	here	ou	out	zh	leisure
ā	ape	ī	bite, fire	u	up	ŋ	ring
ä	car, lot	ō	go	ur	fur		a *in* ago
e	ten	ô	law, horn	ch	chin		e *in* agent
er	care	oi	oil	sh	she	ə = i *in* unity
ē	even	oo	look	th	thin		o *in* collect
i	hit	ōō	tool	th	then		u *in* focus

a·dor·a·ble (ə dôr′ ə b'l) *adj.* [Colloq.] delightful; charming —**a·dor′a·bil′i·ty** *n.* —**a·dor′a·bly** *adv.*

ad·vance (əd vans′) *v.* -**vanced′**, -**vanc′ing** [< OFr. *avancer*, to forward < L. *ab*-, from + *ante*, before] to bring or move forward —**in advance** ahead of time

ad·vance·ment (əd vans′mənt) *n.* **1.** promotion, as to a higher rank **2.** progress or improvement

ad·ven·tur·ous (əd ven′chər əs) *adj.* fond of adventure; daring —**ad·ven′tur·ous·ness** *n.*

ad·ver·tise (ad′vər tīz′) *v.* -**tised′**, -**tis′ing** [< OFr. *advertir*, to call attention to] to call attention to (a product, service, etc.), so as to promote sales —**ad′ver·tis′er** *n.*

ad·vis·a·ble (əd vī′zə b'l) *adj.* being good advice; wise; sensible [it is *advisable* to leave early] —**ad·vis′a·bil′i·ty** *n.* —**ad·vis′a·bly** *adv.*

aer·o·bics (er′ ō′ biks *or* ar′ ō′ biks) *n.* a system of physical exercises that increases the body's consumption of oxygen and improves the functioning of the circulatory system

af·fec·tion (ə fek′shən) *n.* fond or tender feeling; warm liking

af·flu·ence (af′loo wəns) *n.* [< L. < *affluere* < *ad*-, to + *fluere*, to flow] much riches; wealth; great plenty

a·gree·a·ble (ə grē′ə b'l) *adj.* pleasing or pleasant —**a·gree′a·bil′i·ty** *n.* —**a·gree′a·bly** *adv.*

-al (əl, 'l) *a suffix meaning* of, like, or suitable for [*comical, hysterical*]

☆ **al·ler·gic** (ə lʉr′jik) *adj.* **1.** of or caused by allergy **2.** having an allergy

☆ **al·ler·gy** (al′ər jē) *n., pl.* -**gies** [< G. < Gr. *allos*, other + *ergeia* < *en*-, in + *ergon*, work] abnormal sensitivity to a specific substance (such as food, pollen, dust, etc.)

al·li·ance (ə lī′əns) *n.* [< OFr. < *alier*] a close association for a common goal, as of nations, parties, etc.

al·mond (ä′mənd, am′ənd, al′mənd) *n.* [< OFr. < L. < Gr. *amygdale*] the edible, nutlike kernel of a small, peachlike fruit

al·ter (ôl′tər) *v.* [< ML. *alterare* < L. *alter*, other] to make different; modify —**al′ter·a·ble** *adj.*

al·though (ôl thō′) *conj.* [ME < *all, al,* even (emphatic) + *though*] in spite of the fact that; though

am·a·teur (am′ə chər, -toor, -tyoor) *n.* [< Fr. < L. *amator*, a lover] a person who engages in some art, science, sport, etc. for pleasure rather than as a profession —*adj.* of or done by or as by an amateur or amateurs

a·maze (ə māz′) *v.* **a·mazed′**, **a·maz′ing** [< OE. *amasian*, to amaze + pp. *amasod*, puzzled] to fill with great surprise; astonish —**a·maz′ing·ly** *adv.*

a·maze·ment (ə māz′mənt) *n.* great surprise; astonishment

an·ar·chy (an′ər kē) *n., pl.* -**chies** [< Gr. < *an*-, without + *archos*, leader] **1.** the complete absence of government **2.** political disorder and violence

an·a·tom·i·cal (an′ə täm′i k'l) *adj.* of or connected with anatomy —**an′a·tom′i·cal·ly** *adv.*

a·nat·o·my (ə nat′ə mē) *n., pl.* -**mies** [< LL. < Gr. < *ana*-, up + *temnein*, to cut] **1.** the science of the structure of animals or plants **2.** the structure of a particular animal or plant [the *anatomy* of a frog]

-ance (əns, 'ns) *a suffix meaning* the act of or the state of being [*assistance, vigilance*]

an·cient (ān′shənt) *adj.* [< OFr., ult. < L. *ante*, before] **1.** of times long past, esp., of the time before the end of the Western Roman Empire in 476 A.D. **2.** very old

an·gel (ān′j'l) *n.* [< OFr. or OE. < L. *angelus* < Gr. *angelos*, messenger < Iran.] **1.** a supernatural being, with more power, intelligence, etc. than human beings **2.** a person regarded as beautiful, good, innocent, etc.

an·gel·ic (an jel′ik) *adj.* **1.** of an angel or angels **2.** like an angel in beauty, goodness, etc.

an·i·mat·ed (an′ə māt′id) *adj.* lively; spirited [an *animated* conversation] —**an′i·mat′ed·ly** *adv.*

an·ni·ver·sa·ry (an′ə vʉr′sər ē) *n., pl.* -**ries** [< L. < *annus*, year + pp. of *vertere*, to turn] the date on which some event occurred in an earlier year

an·noy·ance (ə noi′əns) *n.* a thing or person that irritates, bothers, or makes angry

an·nu·al (an′yoo wəl) *adj.* [< ME. + OFr. < L. *annus*, year] happening once a year; yearly [their *annual* picnic] —**an′nu·al·ly** *adv.*

an·swer (an'sər) *n.* [< OE. < *and-*, against +
swerian, to swear] something said or written in return
to a question, letter, etc. —*v.* to reply to in some
way

-ant (ənt, 'nt) *a suffix meaning:* **1.** that has, shows,
or does [*defiant*] **2.** a person or thing that [*occupant*]

an·thro·pol·o·gy (an'thrə päl'ə jē) *n.* the study of
human beings —**an'thro·po·log'i·cal** *adj.*
—**an'thro·po·log'i·cal·ly** *adv.*

an·tique (an tēk') *adj.* [< Fr. < L. *antiquus,* ancient < *ante,* before] of, or in the style of, a former
period —*n.* a piece of furniture, silverware, etc.
made in a former period, generally more than 100
years ago

an·y·time (en'ē tīm) *adj.* at any time

a·part·ment (ə pärt'mənt) *n.* [< Fr. < It. < *appar-
tare,* to separate < *parte,* part] a room or rooms to
live in

a·pol·o·gize (ə päl'ə jīz') *v.* **-gized', -giz'ing** to
make an apology; to state that one is aware of and
regrets a fault, wrong, etc.

a·pol·o·gy (ə päl'ə jē) *n., pl.* **-gies** [< LL. < Gr.
apologia, a speaking in defense < *apo-,* from +
logos, word] a statement that one is aware of having
committed a fault and asks for pardon

ap·pa·ra·tus (ap'ə rat'əs, ap'ə rāt'-) *n., pl.*
-ra'tus, -ra'tus·es [L., a making ready < *apparare*
< *ad-,* to + *parare,* to prepare] the instruments,
equipment, etc. for a specific use

ap·par·ent (ə per'ənt, -par'-) *adj.* [< OFr. < L.
prp. of *apparere,* appear] **1.** readily seen; visible
2. readily understood; obvious [it's *apparent* that he's
angry] —**ap·par'ent·ly** *adv.*

ap·peal (ə pēl') *v.* [< OFr. < L. *appellare,* to ac-
cost, appeal < *ad-,* to + *pellere,* drive] **1.** to make
an urgent request (*to* a person *for* help, sympathy,
etc.) **2.** to be attractive, interesting, etc.
—**ap·peal'ing** *adj.*—**ap·peal'ing·ly** *adv.*

ap·pe·tite (ap'ə tīt') *n.* [< ME + OFr. < L. *appe-
titus,* pp. of *appetere* < *ad-,* to + *petere,* to seek] a
desire for food

ap·pli·ance (ə plī'əns) *n.* a device or machine for a
specific task [irons are household *appliances*]

ap·pre·ci·ate (ə prē'shē āt') *v.* **-at'ed, -at'ing** [<
LL. pp. of *appretiare,* appraise] **1.** to think well of;
understand and enjoy [he *appreciates* the music of
Bach] **2.** to be grateful for [I *appreciate* your help]

ap·pro·pri·ate (ə prō'prē it') *adj.* [< LL. pp. of *ap-
propriare* < L. *ad-,* to + *proprius,* one's own] right
for the purpose; suitable —**ap·pro'pri·ate·ly** *adv.*
—**ap·pro'pri·ate·ness** *n.*

ap·prove (ə prōōv') *v.* **-proved', -prov'ing**
[< OFr. < L. *approbare* < *ad-,* to + *probare,* to
try, test] to have a favorable opinion (of) [does she
approve of your friends?] —**ap·prov'ing·ly** *adv.*

ap·prox·i·mate (ə präk'sə mit) *adj.* [< LL. pp. of
approximare < L. *ad-,* to + *prokimus,* near] not exact, but almost so [the *approximate* price is $10]
—*v.* **-mat'ed, -mat'ing** to come near; be almost the
same —**ap·prox'i·mate·ly** *adv.*

a·quar·i·um (ə kwer'ē əm) *n., pl.* **-i·ums, -i·a**
(-ē ə) [L., neut. of *aquarius,* of water < *aqua,*
water] a tank for keeping live water animals and
plants

a·quat·ic (ə kwät'ik, -kwat'-) *adj.* [< L. < *aqua,*
water] **1.** growing or living in or upon water
2. done in or upon water [*aquatic* sports]
—**a·quat'i·cal·ly** *adv.*

ar·che·ol·o·gy (är'kē äl'ə jē) *n.* [< Gr. *archaios,*
ancient < *archē,* the beginning + -logy (study of)]
the study of the life and culture of ancient peoples;
as by digging up the remains of ancient cities, etc.
—**ar'che·o·log'i·cal** *adj.* —**ar'che·o·log'i·cal·ly**
adv. —**ar'che·ol'o·gist** *n.*

ar·chi·tect (är'kə tekt') *n.* [< L. < Gr. < *archi-,*
chief + *tektōn,* carpenter] a person whose profession
is designing plans for buildings, bridges, etc.

ar·chives (är'kīvz) *n., pl.* [Fr. < L. < Gr. *archeion,*
town hall] **1.** a place where public records, documents, etc. are kept **2.** the public records,
documents, etc. kept there

a	fat	ir	here	ou	out	zh	leisure
ā	ape	ī	bite, fire	u	up	ŋ	ring
ä	car, lot	ō	go	ur	fur		a *in* ago
e	ten	ô	law, horn	ch	chin		e *in* agent
er	care	oi	oil	sh	she	ə	= i *in* unity
ē	even	oo	look	th	thin		o *in* collect
i	hit	ōō	tool	th	then		u *in* focus

ar·gu·ment (är′gyə mənt) *n.* [< Fr. < L. *argumentum* < *arguere*, to prove] discussion in which there is disagreement; dispute; debate

art·ist (är′tist) *n.* [ML. *artista*, craftsman < L. *ars*, art] a person who is skilled in any of the fine arts, esp. in painting, sculpture, etc.

ar·tis·tic (är tis′tik) *adj.* **1.** done skillfully and tastefully **2.** having a sensitive appreciation of art and beauty —**ar·tis′ti·cal·ly** *adv.*

as·pect (as′pekt) *n.* [< L. pp. of *aspicere* < *ad-*, to, at + *specere*, to look] any of the possible ways in which an idea, problem, etc. may be regarded [that's an *aspect* of the matter that I overlooked]

as·sem·ble (ə sem′b'l) *v.* -**bled**, -**bling** [< OFr. < L. < *ad-*, to + *simul*, together] **1.** to gather into a group **2.** to fit or put together the parts of —**as·sem′bler** *n.*

as·sist·ance (ə sis′təns) *n.* the act of giving help or the help given; aid

as·so·ci·ate (ə sō′shē āt′) *v.* -**at′ed**, -**at′ing** [< L. pp. of *associare* < *ad-*, to + *sociare*, to join < *socius*, companion] **1.** to join together; connect **2.** to bring (a person) into a relationship as partner or friend

as·so·ci·a·tion (ə sō′sē ā′shən; -shē-) *n.* **1.** companionship; partnership **2.** an organization of persons having the same interests

as·so·nance (as′ə nəns) *n.* [Fr. < L. prp. of *assonare* < *ad-*, to + *sonare*, to sound] a partial rhyme in which the stressed vowel sounds are alike but the consonant sounds are not, as is in *late* and *make* —**as′so·nant** *adj., n.*

as·sume (ə sōōm′, -syōōm′) *v.* -**sumed′**, -**sum′ing** [< L. *assumere*, to claim] **1.** to put on the appearance of **2.** to take over; seize [to *assume* control] **3.** to take for granted; suppose [we *assumed* that he was loyal] —**as·sum′a·ble** *adj.*

ath·let·ic (ath let′ik) *adj.* **1.** of, like, or proper to athletes or athletics **2.** physically strong, skillful, muscular, etc. —**ath·let′i·cal·ly** *adv.*

at·tain (ə tān′) *v.* [< OFr. < L. *attingere*, < *ad-*, to + *tangere*, to touch] to gain through effort; achieve [to *attain* fame] —**at·tain′a·bil′i·ty** *n.* —**at·tain′a·ble** *adj.*

at·tend (ə tend′) *v.* [< OFr. < L. *attendere*, to give heed to] to be present at [we *attend* school five days a week]

at·tend·ance (ə ten′dəns) *n.* being present at

at·ten·tion (ə ten′shən) *n.* **1.** the act of keeping one's mind closely on something **2.** notice or observation [her smile caught my *attention*]

at·ten·tive (ə ten′tiv) *adj.* paying attention [an *attentive* audience] —**at·ten′tive·ly** *adv.* —**at·ten′·tive·ness** *n.*

at·tract (ə trakt′) *v.* [< L. pp. of *attrahere* < *ad-*, to + *trahere*, to draw] **1.** to draw to itself or oneself [a magnet *attracts* iron] **2.** to get the admiration, attention, etc. of

au·di·ble (ô′də b'l) *adj.* [< ML. < L. *audire*, to hear] loud enough to be heard [an *audible* sigh] —**au′di·bil′i·ty** *n.* —**au′di·bly** *adv.*

Aug. August

au·then·tic (ô then′tik) *adj.* [< OFr. < LL. < Gr. *authentikos* < *authentēs*, one who does things himself] **1.** that can be believed; reliable [an *authentic* report] **2.** genuine; real [an *authentic* antique] —**au·then′ti·cal·ly** *adv.*

au·to·mat·ic (ôt′ə mat′ik) *adj.* [Gr. *automatos*, self-moving] moving, operating, etc. by itself [*automatic* machinery] —**au′to·mat′i·cal·ly** *adv.*

a·vail·a·ble (ə vā′lə b'l) *adj.* that can be got, had, or reached; accessible —**a·vail′a·bil′i·ty** *n.* —**a·vail′a·bly** *adv.*

Ave., ave. avenue

av·e·nue (av′ ə nōō′, -nyōō′) *n.* [Fr. < L. *advenire*, to come] **1.** a road, path, or drive, often one bordered with trees **2.** a way of approach to something [books are *avenues* to knowledge] ☆ **3.** a street, esp. a wide principal one

a·void (ə void′) *v.* [< Anglo-Fr. < OFr. *esvuidier*, to empty] to keep away from; shun [to *avoid* crowds] —**a·void′a·ble** *adj.* —**a·void′a·bly** *adv.* —**a·void′ance** *n.*

B

back·ache (bak′āk′) *n.* an ache or pain in the back

badge (baj) *n.* [ME. *bage*] a token, emblem, or sign worn to show rank, membership, etc.

bag (bag) *n.* [ON. *baggi*] a container made of fabric, paper, leather, etc., with an opening at the top that can be closed; sack

bag·gage (bag′ij) *n.* [< OFr. < *bagues,* baggage] the bags and other equipment of a traveler

bal·co·ny (bal′kə nē) *n., pl.* **-nies** [< It. < Gmc., akin to OHG. *balcho,* a beam] **1.** a platform projecting from a building and enclosed by a balustrade **2.** an upper floor of rows of seats in a theater, etc., often jutting out over the main floor

bal·let (bal′ā, ba lā′) *n.* [< Fr. < It. *balletto,* dim. < *ballo,* a dance] a style of dancing in which dancers in costume use graceful movements to tell a story

ban·quet (baŋ′kwit, ban′-) *n.* [Fr. < It. *banchetto,* dim. of *banca,* bank] an elaborate meal, feast

be·gin (bi gin′) *v.* **be·gan′, be·gun′, be·gin′ning** [< OE. *beginnan*] **1.** to start doing something; get under way **2.** to cause to start; commence

be·gin·ner (bi gin′ər) *n.* one just beginning to do or learn a thing; inexperienced person

be·lieve (bə lēv′) *v.* **-lieved′, -liev′ing 1.** to take as true or real. **2.** to suppose or think [I *believe* that I'll have tea] —**be·liev′a·bil′i·ty** *n.* —**be·liev′a·ble** *adj.* —**be·liev′a·bly** *adv.* —**be·liev′er** *n.*

ben·e·dic·tion (ben′ə dik′shən) *n.* [< L. < *bene,* well + *dicere,* to speak] a prayer asking for God's blessing

ben·e·fac·tor (ben′ə fak′tər) *n.* a person who has given help, esp. financial help; patron —**ben′e·fac′tress** (-tris) *n. fem.*

be·ret (bə rā′) *n.* [< Fr. < Pr. < LL. dim. of *birrus,* a hood] a soft, flat, round cap of felt, wool, etc.

bi·cy·cle (bī′ si k'l) *n.* [Fr.: bi- & cycle] a vehicle consisting of a metal frame mounted on two wheels, one behind the other, and equipped with handlebars, a saddlelike seat, and foot pedals or, sometimes, a gasoline engine —*v.* **-cled, -cling** to ride on a bicycle —**bi′cy·clist, bi′cy·cler** *n.*

big·ot (big′ət) *n.* [Fr. < OFr., a term of insult used of Normans < ? ME. *bi god,* by God] a narrow-minded person who is prejudiced against other religions, opinions, races, etc. —**big′ot·ed** *adj.*

bi·o·log·i·cal (bī′ə läj′i k'l) *adj.* of or connected with biology [*biological* drugs] —**bi′o·log′i·cal·ly** *adv.*

bi·ol·o·gy (bī äl′ə jē) *n.* [BIO + -LOGY] the science that deals with the origin, history, structure, etc. of plants and animals: it includes botany and zoology —**bi·ol′o·gist** *n.*

birth·place (bʉrth′plās′) *n.* **1.** the place of one's birth **2.** the place where something originated

block (bläk) *v.* [< MDu. or OFr. < LowG. *block,* log] **1.** to hinder passage or progress in; obstruct [grease *blocked* the drain] **2.** to stand in the way of [you're *blocking* my vision] —**block′age** *n.* —**block′er** *n.*

blue-eyed (blo͞o′ īd) *adj.* having blue eyes [Both children were *blue-eyed.*]

bough (bou) *n.* [OE. *bog,* shoulder; hence branch] a branch of a tree, esp. a main branch

bought (bôt) *pt.* + *pp. of* buy

bou·quet (bō kā′) *n.* [Fr.] a bunch of cut flowers

bou·tique (bo͞o tēk′) *n.* [Fr. < Gr. *apothēkē,* apothecary] a small shop, or a small department in a store, selling fashionable, expensive items

boy·cott (boi′kät) *v.* [after Captain C.C. *Boycott,* Irish land agent so treated in 1880] to refuse to buy, sell, or use [to *boycott* a newspaper] ☆ *n.* the act of boycotting

Braille (brāl) *n.* [after L. Braille (1809–52), Fr. teacher who devised it] [also **b-**] a system of printing and writing for the blind, using raised dots felt by the fingers

brake (brāk) *n.* [< MLowG. *brake* or ODu. *braeke* < *breken,* to break] any device for slowing or stopping the motion of a vehicle or machine, as by causing a block or band to press against a moving part —*v.* to slow down or stop as with a brake —**brake′less** *adj.*

a	fat	ir	here	ou	out	zh	leisure
ā	ape	ī	bite, fire	u	up	ŋ	ring
ä	car, lot	ō	go	ʉr	fur		a *in* ago
e	ten	ô	law, horn	ch	chin		e *in* agent
er	care	oi	oil	sh	she	ə = i *in* unity
ē	even	oo	look	th	thin		o *in* collect
i	hit	o͞o	tool	th	then		u *in* focus

bridge (brij) *n.* [OE. *brycge*] **1.** a structure built over a river, railroad, etc. to provide a way across **2.** a thing that provides connection or contact

bri·quet (bri ket′) *n.* [< Fr. dim of *brique*, brick] a brick made of compressed coal dust, etc., used for fuel

brought (brôt) *pt.* + *pp. of* bring

buf·fet¹ (buf′it) *n.* [< OFr. < *buffe*, a blow] a blow or shock —*v.* to thrust about [the waves *buffeted* the boat]

buf·fet² (bə fā′, boo-) *n.* [Fr. < OFr. *buffet*, a bench] **1.** a piece of furniture with drawers and cupboards **2.** a meal at which guests serve themselves

bump·er (bum′ pər) *n.* ☆ a device for absorbing some of the shock of a collision; specif., a bar across the front or back of an automobile

bu·reau (byoor′ō) *n., pl.* **-reaus, -reaux** (-ōz) [Fr., desk < OFr. *burel*, coarse cloth (as table cover)] ☆ **1.** a chest of drawers, often with a mirror, for clothing, etc. **2.** an agency providing services for clients [a travel *bureau*]

bur·glar·ize (bʉr′glə riz′) *v.* **-ized, -iz′ing** [Colloq.] to commit burglary in or upon; to steal from a home

but·ter·scotch (but′ ər skäch′) *n.* a hard, sticky candy made with brown sugar, butter, etc. —*adj.* having the flavor of butterscotch

C

CA California

cal·cu·la·tion (kal′kyə lā′shən) *n.* **1.** a determining by using mathematics **2.** an answer found by calculating

cal·is·then·ics (kal′ əs then′ iks) *n. pl.* [< Gr. *kallos*, beauty + *sthenos*, strength] **1.** exercises to develop a strong, trim body; simple gymnastics **2.** [with *sing. v.*] the art of developing bodily strength and gracefulness by such exercises —**cal′is·then′ic, cal′is·then′i·cal** *adj.*

cal·o·rie (kal′ ə rē) *n.* [Fr. < L. *calor*, heat < IE. base *kel-*, warm] **1.** the amount of heat needed to raise the temperature of one gram of water one degree centigrade: also **small calorie. 2.** [*occas.* C-] the amount of heat needed to raise the temperature of one kilogram of water one degree centigrade: also

large calorie 3. a unit equal to the large calorie, used for measuring energy produced by food in the body [one large egg produces about 100 *calories*] Also sp. **cal′o·ry,** *pl.* **-ries**

cam·paign (kam pān′) *n.* [Fr. *campagne*, open country < It. < LL. < L. *campus*, a field] a series of planned actions for a particular purpose, as for electing a candidate —*v.* to participate in a campaign —**cam·paign′er** *n.*

can·cel (kan′s'l) *v.* **-celed,** or **-celled, -cel·ing** or **-cel·ling** [< Anglo-Fr. < L. *cancellare*, to draw lines like a ladder across] to do away with; withdraw, etc. [to *cancel* an order]

ca·pac·i·ty (kə pas′ə tē) *n., pl.* **-ties** [< OFr. < L. < *capax*] the ability to contain, absorb, or receive

car·a·mel (kar′ ə m'l, -mel′; kär′ m'l) *n.* [Fr. < OFr., ult. < L. *canna mellis*, sugar cane] **1.** burnt sugar used to color or flavor food **2.** a chewy candy made from sugar, milk, etc.

care (ker) *n.* [< OE. *caru*, sorrow < IE. base, *gar-*, to cry out] **1.** a) worry or concern b) a cause of this **2.** a liking or regard (*for*) —*v.* **cared, car′ing** to feel concern about

care·ful (ker′fəl) *adj.* acting in a thoughtful way —**care′ful·ly** *adv.*

car·pet (kär′pit) *n.* [< OFr. < ML. *carpita*, woolen cloth] a heavy fabric for covering a floor, stairs, etc. —**roll out the red carpet** to welcome with great pomp and enthusiasm, entertain lavishly

car·ton (kärt′ 'n) *n.* [Fr. < It. *cartone* < *carta*, leaf of paper] **1.** a cardboard box or container **2.** a full carton or its contents

cash·mere (kazh′mir, kash′-) *n.* [< Kashmir, a region in southeast Asia] a fine carded wool from goats of Kashmir and Tibet

caught (kôt) *pt.* + *pp. of* catch

caulk (kôk) *v.* [< OFr. < L. *calcare*, to tread < *calix*, a heel] to stop up (cracks, seams, etc.) with a filler

cav·i·ty (kav′ə tē) *n., pl.* **-ties** [< Fr. < LL. *cavitas* < L. *cavus*, hollow] a hole, as one caused by decay in a tooth

cel·e·bra·tion (sel′ə brā′shən) *n.* that which is done to celebrate

cen·sus (sen′səs) *n.* [L., orig. pp. of *censere*, to tax, value] an official counting of all the people in a country or area to find out how many there are and of what sex, age, occupation, etc.

cen·ti·grade (sen′tə grād′) *adj.* [Fr. < L. *centum*, a hundred + *gradus*, a degree] consisting of or divided into 100 degrees

cen·ti·pede (sen′tə pēd′) *n.* [Fr. < L. *centum*, a hundred + *pes* (gen. *pedis*), a foot] a wormlike animal with many segments and a pair of legs to each segment

cer·tif·i·cate (sər tif′ə kit) *n.* [< OFr. < ML. < LL. pp. of *certificare*, certify] a written or printed statement that can be used as proof of something because it is official [a birth *certificate*]

cen·tu·ry (sen′chər ē) *n., pl.* **-ries** [L. *centuria* < *centum*, a hundred] any period of 100 years

chal·lenge (chal′ənj) *n.* [< OFr. < L. *calumnia*, calumny] **1.** a call or dare to take part in a fight, contest, etc. **2.** anything, as a difficult task, that calls for special effort —*v.* **-lenged, -leng·ing 1.** to call or dare to take part in a fight, contest, etc. ☆ **2.** to reject (a vote or voter) as not being valid or qualified —**chal′leng·er** *n.*

change·a·ble (chān′jə b'l) *adj.* **1.** that can change or be changed; alterable **2.** likely or tending to change; fickle —**change′a·bil′i·ty** *n.*

cha·teau (sha tō′) *n., pl.* **-teaux′** (-tōz′, -to′) **-teaus′** [Fr. < OFr. < L. *castellum*, castle] a French feudal castle or a large country house

chauf·feur (shō′fər, shō fur′) *n.* [< Fr. lit., stoker < *chauffer*, to heat] a person hired to drive a private automobile for someone else

chron·i·cle (krän′i k'l) *n.* [< Anglo-Fr. < OFr. < L. < Gr. *Chronika*, annals] a history or story; esp., a record or tale of things in the order in which they happened

cir·cu·lar (sur′kyə lər) *adj.* [L. *circularis*] **1.** in the shape of a circle; round **2.** moving in a circle or spiral —**cir′cu·lar·ly** *adv.*

cir·cu·la·tion (sur′kyə lā′ shən) *n.* **1.** a moving around, often in a complete circuit, as of blood through the veins. **2.** the passing of something from person to person

cir·cum·vent (sur′kəm vent′) *v.* [< L. pp. of *cir-cumvenire* < *circum-*, around + *venire*, to come] to surround or circle around —**cir′cum·ven′tion** *n.*

cir·cus (sur′kəs) *n.* [L. < G. *kirkos*, a circle] a show, esp. a traveling show, with acrobats, trained animals, clowns, etc.

clas·si·fi·ca·tion (klas′ə fi kā′shən) *n.* an arrangement according to some systematic division into classes or groups

clas·si·fy (klas′ə fī′) *v.* **-fied′, -fy′ing** to arrange in classes according to some system —**clas′si·fi′a·ble** *adj.* —**clas′si·fi′er** *n.*

clav·i·cle (klav′ə k'l) *n.* [< Fr. < L. *clavicula*, dim. of *clavis*, a key] a bone connecting the breastbone with the shoulder blade; collarbone

cli·mate (klī′mət) *n.* [< OFr. < L. < Gr. *klima*, region < IE. base *klei-*, to lean] **1.** the average weather conditions of a place over a period of years [Arizona has a mild, dry *climate*, but its weather last week was bad] **2.** a region with particular weather conditions [to move to a warm *climate*] —**cli·mat·ic** (klī mat′ ik) *adj.* —**cli·mat′i·cal·ly** *adv.*

clin·ic (klin′ik) *n.* [L. *clinicus*, physician who attends persons sick in bed < Gr. *klinikos*, of a bed < *klinē*, a bed] a place where patients are examined or treated by doctors

clin·i·cal (klin′i k'l) *adj.* **1.** of or connected with a clinic **2.** objective and impersonal in a scientific way —**clin′i·cal·ly** *adv.*

close¹ (klōs) *adj.* **clos′er, clos′est** [< OFr. *clos*, pp. of *clore:* see CLOSE²] **1.** shut; not open **2.** confining, narrow **3.** nearby **4.** very near in affection **5.** nearly equal or alike —**close′ly** *adv.* —**close′ness** *n.*

close² (klōz) *v.* **closed, clos′ing** [< OFr. < *clore* < L. *claudere*, to close] to shut (a door, lid, etc.)

a	fat	ir	here	ou	out	zh	leisure
ā	ape	ī	bite, fire	u	up	ŋ	ring
ä	car, lot	ō	go	ur	fur		a *in* ago
e	ten	ô	law, horn	ch	chin		e *in* agent
er	care	oi	oil	sh	she	ə = i *in* unity
ē	even	oo	look	th	thin		o *in* collect
i	hit	ōō	tool	*th*	then		u *in* focus

col·ic (käl′ik) *n.* [< OFr. < L. < Gr. < *kolon,* colon] sharp pain in the bowels —**col′ick·y** *adj.*

col·lapse (kə laps′) *v.* **-lapsed′, -laps′ing** [< L. pp. of *collabi* < *com-,* together + *labi,* to fall] **1.** to fall down or fall to pieces [the house *collapsed*] **2.** to fall down, as from exhaustion

col·lect (kə lekt′) *v.* [< L. *collectus,* pp. of *colligere* < *com-,* together + *legere,* to gather] to gather together; assemble

col·lec·tion (kə lek′shən) *n.* things collected [a *collection* of stamps]

col·lege (käl′ij) *n.* [< OFr. < L. *collegium,* a society, guild < *collega,* colleague] an institution of higher education that grants degrees

com- *a prefix meaning* with or together

com·bi·na·tion (käm′bə nā′shən) *n.* a uniting or being united; mixing; joining

co·me·di·an (kə mē′dē ən) *n.* an entertainer who tells jokes, sings comic songs, etc.

com·e·dy (käm′ə dē) *n., pl.* **-dies** [< OFr. < L. < Gr. *kōmōidia* < *kōmos,* festival + *aeidein,* to sing] any of various types of plays or motion pictures with a humorous treatment of characters and situations and a happy ending —**co·me·dic** (kə mē′dik, -med′ik) *adj.*

com·mand (kə mand′) *v.* [< OFr. < VL. < L. *com-,* very much + *mandare,* to commit] **1.** to give an order to [the police *commanded* the thief to halt] **2.** to have authority over; control [he *commands* a large crew] —*n.* an order; direction

com·mis·sion (kə mish′ən) *n.* [< L. pp. of *committere* < *com-,* together + *mittere,* to send] **1.** a committing or doing, as of a crime **2.** a group of people officially appointed to perform specified duties **3.** a percentage of money taken in on sales —*v.* to authorize or order (a person) to do a particular thing

com·mit (kə mit′) *v.* **-mit′ted, -mit′ting** [L. *committere* < *com-,* together + *mittere,* to send] **1.** to do or perpetrate (an offense or crime) **2.** to bind as by a promise; pledge [*committed* to the struggle]

com·mit·ment (kə mit′mənt) *n.* a committing or being committed

com·mit·tee (kə mit′ē) *n.* [< L. *committere:* see commit] a group of people chosen to consider or act on some matter

com·mon (käm′ən) *adj.* [< OFr. < L. *communis,* shared by all or many] **1.** of, from, by, or to all [the *common* interest] **2.** often seen, heard, used, etc.; widespread; familiar [a *common* saying]

com·mu·ni·cate (kə myoo′ni kāt′) *v.* **-cat′ed, -cat′ing** [< L. pp. of *communicare* < *communis,* common] to give or exchange information, etc. as by talk, writing, etc. —**com·mu′ni·ca′tor** *n.*

com·pan·ion (kəm pan′yən) *n.* [< OFr. < VL. *companio,* messmate < L. *com-,* with + *panis,* bread] one who spends much time with another or others —**com·pan′ion·ship′** *n.*

com·pa·ny (kum′pə nē) *n., pl.* **-nies** [< OFr. < VL. *compania,* lit., group sharing bread] **1.** a group associated for some purpose [a business *company*] **2.** a guest or guests [we had *company* for dinner]

com·pat·i·ble (kəm pat′ə b'l) *adj.* [< ML. < LL. *compassio,* ult. < L. *com-,* together + *pati,* to suffer] capable of living together in harmony or getting along well together —**com·pat′i·bil′i·ty** *n.* —**com·pat′i·bly** *adv.*

com·ple·tion (kəm plē′shən) *n.* the state of being completed

com·pli·cat·ed (käm′plə kāt′id) *adj.* quite involved; hard to untangle, solve, analyze, etc. —**com′pli·cat′ed·ly** *adv.*

com·pli·ca·tion (käm′plə kā′shən) *n.* **1.** a complicated condition or structure **2.** complicating factor

com·pli·ment (käm′plə mənt; *for v.* -ment′) *n.* [< Fr. < It. ult < L. *complere,* to complete] something said in praise —*v.* to pay a compliment to

com·pose (kəm pōz′) *v.* **-posed′, -pos′ing** [< OFr. *composer* < *com-,* with + *poser,* to place] **1.** to make up [mortar is *composed* of lime, sand, and water] **2.** create a musical or literary work

com·pos·er (kəm pō′zər) *n.* a person who composes

com·press (kəm pres′) *v.* [< OFr. < LL. < L. pp. of *comprimere* < *com-,* together + *premere,* to press] to press together; make more compact as by pressure [to *compress* medicine into tablets] —**com·pressed′** *adj.*

com·prise (kəm prīz′) *v.* **-prised′, -pris′ing** [< L. *comprehendere* < *com-,* with + *prehendere,* to seize] to make up; form

com·pro·mise (käm′prə mīz′) *n.* [< L. *compromit-tere* < *com-*, together + *promittere*, to promise] a settlement in which each side gives up part of what it wants —*v.* **-mised, -mis′ing** to settle by a compromise

con- *a prefix meaning* with or together. A form of the prefix *com-*

con·ceal (kən sēl′) *v.* [< OFr. < L. *concelare* < *com-*, together + *celare*, to hide] to keep from another's knowledge; keep secret [to *conceal* one's amusement] —**con·ceal′ment** *n.*

con·cede (kən sēd′) *v.* **-ced′ed, -ced′ing** [L. *concedere* < *com-*, with + *cedere*, to cede] to admit as true [to *concede* a point in an argument]

con·ceit·ed (kən sēt′id) *adj.* [< OFr. < L. *concipere*, to receive] having an exaggerated opinion of oneself, one's merits, etc.; vain —**con·ceit′ed·ly** *adv.*

con·cen·trate (kän′sən trāt′) *v.* **-trat′ed, -trat′ing** [< prec. + -ate] to focus (one's thoughts, efforts, etc.) or fix one's attention (*on* or *upon*)

con·ces·sion (kən sesh′ən) *n.* **1.** a conceding, or giving in **2.** the right to sell food, parking space, etc. on the lessor's premises

con·clude (kən klōōd′) *v.* **-clud′ed, -clud′ing** [< L. *concludere* < *com-*, together + *claudere*, to shut] **1.** to bring to a close; end **2.** to decide by reasoning; deduce [I *conclude* that no one is to blame]

con·fer (kən fʉr′) *v.* **-ferred′, -fer′ring** [< L. *conferre* < *com-*, together + *ferre*, to bear] to have a conference; meet for discussion

con·fer·ence (kän′fər əns, -frəns) *n.* a conferring or consulting on a serious matter

con·flict (kən flikt′; for n. kän′flikt) *v.* [< L. pp. of *confligere* < *com-*, together + *fligere*, to strike] to disagree sharply; clash [his ideas *conflict* with mine] —*n.* a fight, struggle, or strong disagreement

con·form·i·ty (kən fôr′mə tē) *n., pl.* **-ties** action in accordance with customs, rules, popular opinion, etc.

con·fuse (kən fyōōz′) *v.* **-fused′, -fus′ing** [< OFr. < L. pp. of *confundere*] to bewilder; perplex. —**con·fus′ed·ly** *adv.* —**con·fus′ing** *adj.*

con·fu·sion (kən fyōō′zhən) *n.* **1.** state of disorder **2.** bewilderment

con·grat·u·late (kən grach′ə lāt′) *v.* **-lat′ed, -lat′ing** [< L. pp. of *congratulari* < *com-*, together + *gratulari*, to wish joy] to express to (a person) one's pleasure at his good fortune, success, etc. —**con·grat′u·la·to′ry** *adj.*

con·junc·tion (kən junk′shən) *n.* an uninflected word used to connect words, phrases, clauses, or sentences

con·nec·tion (kə nek′shən) *n.* **1.** a joining or being joined; union **2.** a thing that joins; means of joining

con·quest (kän′kwest, kän′-) *n.* [< OFr. < ML. < L. pp. of *conquirere*, to procure] **1.** the act of winning; victory **2.** something won

con·science (kän′shəns) *n.* [OFr. < L. < prp. of *conscire* < *com-*, with + *scire*, to know] a sense of right and wrong, with an urge to do right

con·se·quence (kän′sə kwens′, -kwəns) *n.* [OFr. < L. < *com-*, with + *sequi*, to follow] a result of an action; effect—**take the consequences** to accept the results of one's actions

con·so·nant (kän′sə nənt) *n.* a letter representing a sound made by stopping the breath with the tongue, teeth, or lips, as p, t, k, m, l, f, etc.

con·stel·la·tion (kän′stə lā′shən) *n.* [< OFr. < LL. < L. *com-*, with + pp. of *stellare*, to shine < *stella*, star] a particular group of fixed stars, usually named after some object, animal, or mythological being that they supposedly suggest in outline

con·ta·gious (kən tā′jəs) *adj.* [< OFr. < LL. *contagiosus*] **1.** spread by contact: said of diseases **2.** carrying the agent causing such a disease —**con·ta′gious·ly** *adv.* —**con·ta′gious·ness** *n.*

con·tain (kən tān′) *v.* [< OFr. < L. *continere* < *com-*, together + *tenere*, to hold] to have in it; hold, enclose, or include

con·tain·er (kən tān′ər) *n.* a thing for holding something

a	fat	ir	here	ou	out	zh	leisure
ā	ape	ī	bite, fire	u	up	ŋ	ring
ä	car, lot	ō	go	ʉr	fur		a *in* ago
e	ten	ô	law, horn	ch	chin		e *in* agent
er	care	oi	oil	sh	she		ə = i *in* unity
ē	even	oo	look	th	thin		o *in* collect
i	hit	ōō	tool	*th*	then		u *in* focus

con·test·ant (kən tes′tənt) *n.* [Fr.] one that competes in a contest

con·ti·nent (känt′ ′n ənt) *n.* any of the main large land areas of the earth (Africa, Asia, Australia, Europe, N. America, S. America, and, sometimes, Antarctica)

con·tin·u·al (kən tin′yoo wəl) *adj.* going on without stopping —**con·tin′u·al·ly** *adv.*

con·tin·u·ous (kən tin′yōō wəs) *adj.* [< L. *continuus*] going on or extending without interruption —**con·tin′u·ous·ly** *adv.*

con·tract (kän′trakt *for n.,* kən trakt′ *for v.*) *n.* [OFr. < L. pp. of *contrahere* < *com-*, together + *trahere*, to draw] an agreement to do something —*v.* to reduce in size; draw together; shrink [cold *contracts* metals]

con·trol (kən trōl′) *v.* **-trolled′, -trol′ling** [< Anglo-Fr. < Fr. < ML. *contrarotulus*, a register] to have the power of ruling, guiding, or managing; regulate —*n.* **1.** power to direct or regulate [she has no *control* over her dog] **2.** the condition of being directed [the car went out of *control*] —**con·trol′la·bil′i·ty** *n.* —**con·trol′la·ble** *adj.*

con·ven·tion (kən ven′shən) *n.* [< L. < pp. of *convenire*, convene] a meeting of members from various places, held every year or so

co·op·er·a·tion (kō äp′ə rā′shən) *n.* joint effort or operation

cop·y (käp′ē) *n., pl.* **cop·ies** [< OFr. < ML. *copia*, copious transcript < L. *copia*, plenty] a thing made just like another; imitation —*v.* **cop′ied, cop′y·ing 1.** to make a copy or copies of; reproduce **2.** to act or be the same as; imitate

cop·y·right (käp′ē rīt′) *n.* [copy + right] the exclusive right to the publication, production, or sale of a literary, musical, or artistic work

cor·rec·tion (kə rek′shən) *n.* a change that corrects a mistake —**cor·rec′tion·al** *adj.*

cor·re·spond (kôr′ə spänd′, kär′-) *v.* [< Fr. < ML. *correspondere* < L. *com-*, together + *respondere*, to answer] to communicate (*with* someone) by letters, esp. regularly —**cor′re·spond′ing·ly** *adv.*

cor·rupt (kə rupt′) *adj.* [< L. < *com-*, together + *rumpere*, to break] changed from good to bad; having become evil, dishonest, etc.

cor·rup·tion (kə rup′shən) *n.* **1.** evil or wicked ways **2.** bribery or dishonest dealings

cor·sage (kôr säzh′, -säj′) *n.* [Fr., bodice] ☆ a small bouquet for a woman to wear, as at the waist or shoulder

coun·cil (koun′s'l) *n.* [< OFr. < L. *concilium*, meeting < *com-*, with + *calere*, to call] a group of people chosen to serve officially as administrators or advisers

coun·ty (koun′tē) *n., pl.* **-ties** [< OFr. < ML. *comitatus*, jurisdiction of a count] the largest local administrative subdivision of most states

cou·ra·geous (kə rā′jəs) *adj.* having or showing courage; brave —**cou·ra′geous·ly** *adv.*

cour·te·sy (kur′tə sē) *n., pl.* **-sies** [OFr. *curteisie*] **1.** courteous behavior; gracious politeness **2.** a polite or considerate act or remark

court·house (kôrt′hous′) *n.* a building in which law courts are held

cramp (kramp) *n.* [< OFr. *crampe*, bent, twisted < Frank < IE. base *ger-*, to twist] a sudden, painful tightening of a muscle due to chill, strain, etc. —*v.* to cause a cramp in

cra·zy (krā′zē) *adj.* **-zi·er, -zi·est** [< craze] **1.** mentally unbalanced or insane **2.** [Colloq.] foolish, wild, fantastic, etc. [a *crazy* idea] **3.** [Colloq.] very enthusiastic or eager [*crazy* about movies] —**cra′ zi·ly** *adv.* —**cra′zi·ness** *n.*

cre·a·tion (krē ā′shən) *n.* anything created; esp., something original created by the imagination

cre·a·tive (krē āt′iv) *adj.* showing imagination and ability [a *creative* mind] —**cre·a′tive·ly** *adv.*

cred·i·ble (kred′ə b'l) *adj.* [< L. < *credere*, believe] that can be believed; believable —**cred′i·bil′i·ty** *n.* —**cred′i·bly** *adv.*

cres·cent (kres′ 'nt) *n.* [< OFr. < L. *crescere*, to grow] the shape of the moon in its first or last quarter

crit·i·cize (krit′ə sīz′) *v.* **-cized, -ciz·ing 1.** to analyze and judge as a critic **2.** to find fault (with)

cro·chet (krō shā′) *n.* [Fr., small hook] needlework in which loops of thread or yarn are interwoven with a hooked needle —*v.* **-chet′ed** (-shād′), **-chet′ing** to do crochet or make by crochet

cro·quet (krō kā′) **n.** [Fr., dial. form of *crochet*, dim. < *croc.*, a hook] an outdoor game in which the players use mallets to drive a wooden ball through a series of hoops

cross (krôs) **v.** [< OE. *cros* & ON. *kross*, both < OIr. *cros* < L. *crux* (gen. *crucis*), a cross < IE. base *(s)ker-*, to turn, bend] **1.** to place across or crosswise [*cross* your fingers] **2.** to lie or cut across; intersect [where two streets *cross* one another] **3.** to extend across [the bridge *crosses* a river]

crumb (krum) **n.** [OE. *cruma*] a very small piece broken off something, as of bread or cake

cupboard (kub′ərd) **n.** a closet or cabinet with shelves for holding cups, plates, food, etc.

cur·a·ble (kyoor′ə b'l) **adj.** that can be cured

cur·few (kur′fyoo) **n.** [< OFr. *covrefeu* < *covrir*, to cover + *feu*, fire] a time in the evening set as a deadline beyond which children, etc. may not appear on the streets

cush·ion (koosh′ ən) **n.** [< OFr. *coissin* < ML. *coxinum* (infl. by L. *coxa*, hip) < L. *culcita*] **1.** a pillow or pad for sitting or kneeling on, or reclining against **2.** anything serving to absorb shock, as air or steam in some machines, the elastic inner rim of a billiard table, or a soft, padded insole —**v.** **1.** to provide with a cushion **2.** to act as a cushion as in protecting from injury, relieving distress, etc. [grass *cushioned* his fall]

cus·tom (kus′təm) **n.** [< OFr. < L. *consuetudo* < *com-*, very much + *suere*, to be accustomed] a social practice carried on by tradition

cyn·i·cal (sin′i k'l) **adj.** [< L. < Gr. *kynikos*, canine < *kyōn*, dog] doubting the sincerity of people's motives, or the value of living —**cyn′i·cal·ly adv.**

D

dam·age (dam′ij) **n.** [OFr. < L. *damnum*, loss, injury] injury or harm to something that makes it less valuable, useful, etc. —**v.** **-aged, -ag·ing** to do damage to —**dam′age·a·ble adj.**

damp (damp) **adj.** [MDu., vapor < IE. base *dhem-*, to smoke, mist] somewhat moist or wet; humid —**v.** to make damp; moisten —**damp′ ish adj.** —**damp′ ly adv.** —**damp′ ness n.**

daugh·ter (dôt′ər) **n.** [< OE. *dohtor*] a girl or woman as she is related to a parent or to both parents

D.C., DC District of Columbia

de- *a prefix meaning:* **1.** away from, off, down [*derail, decline*] **2.** undo [*defrost*]

de·bat·a·ble (di bāt′ə b'l) **adj.** that can be questioned or disputed; questionable

de·but (di byoo′, dā-) **n.** [Fr. < *debuter*, to lead off] the first appearance before the public, as of an actor

dec·ade (dek′ ād) **n.** [< OFr. < L. < Gr. < *deka*, TEN] **1.** a group of ten **2.** a period of ten years

de·ci·sion (di sizh′ən) **n.** the act of making up one's mind about something

dec·o·rate (dek′ə rāt′) **v.** **-rat′ed, -rat′ing** [< L. pp. of *decorare* < *decus*, an ornament] to add something to so as to make more attractive; ornament

dec·o·ra·tive (dek′ə rə tiv) **adj.** that which decorates —**dec′o·ra·tive·ly adv.**

de·fend·ant (di fen′dənt) **n.** *Law,* the person in a law court who is being sued or accused

de·fense (di fens′, dē′fens) **n.** [< L. pp. of *defendere*, < *de-*, away + *fendere*, to strike] **1.** a defending or being defended against attack or danger **2.** the side that is defending in any contest

de·fer (di fur′) **v.** **-ferred′, -fer′ring** [< OFr. < L. < *de-*, down + *ferre*, to bear] to give in or yield to the wish or judgment of another, as in showing respect

de·fi·ance (di fi′əns) **n.** a defying or opposing boldly a powerful person or thing

de·fi·cient (di fish′ənt) **adj.** [< L. *deficiens*, prp. of *deficere*, to fail] lacking in something essential; incomplete; defective —**de·fi′cient·ly adv.**

a	fat	ir	here	ou	out	zh	leisure
ā	ape	ī	bite, fire	u	up	ŋ	ring
ä	car, lot	ō	go	ur	fur		a *in* ago
e	ten	ô	law, horn	ch	chin		e *in* agent
er	care	oi	oil	sh	she	ə = i *in* unity
ē	even	oo	look	th	thin		o *in* collect
i	hit	oo	tool	th	then		u *in* focus

def·i·nite (def′ə nit) *adj.* [< L. pp. of *definire*, to limit < *de-*, from + *finis*, boundary] exact and clear —**def′i·nite·ly** *adv.*

de·lay (di lā′) *v.* [< OFr. < *de-*, entirely + *laier*, to leave, let < L. *laxare*, to loosen] 1. to put off to a later time; postpone 2. to make late —*n.* a delaying or being delayed

del·e·gate (del′ə gāt; *also for n.* -git) *n.* [< L. pp. of *delegare* < *de-*, from + *legare*, to send] a person sent to speak and act for his group or organization; representative —*v.* **-gat′ed, -gat′ing** to send or appoint as a representative

del·e·ga·tion (del′ə gā′shən) *n.* a group of representatives [the Iowa *delegation* voted as a unit]

de·li·cious (di lish′əs) *adj.* [< OFr. < L. *deliciae*, delight] very pleasing to taste or smell —**de·li′cious·ly** *adv.* —**de·li′cious·ness** *n.*

de·light·ful (di līt′fəl) *adj.* very pleasing; charming —**de·light′ful·ly** *adv.*

de·lin·quent (di liŋ′kwənt) *adj.* [< L. *delinquens*, prp. of *delinquere* < *de-*, from + *linquere*, to leave] 1. failing or neglecting to do what duty or law requires 2. overdue

de·moc·ra·cy (di mäk′rə sē) *n., pl.* **-cies** [< Fr. < ML. *democratia* < Gr. < *dēmos*, the people + *kratein*, to rule] 1. government in which the people hold the ruling power 2. a country, state, etc. with such government

dem·o·crat·ic (dem′ə krat′ik) *adj.* 1. of, belonging to, or upholding government by the people [a *democratic* nation] 2. treating people of all classes in the same way [a *democratic* employer] —**dem′o·crat′i·cal·ly** *adv.*

dem·on·strate (dem′ən strāt′) *v.* **-strat′ed, -strat′ing** [< L. pp. of *demonstrare* < *de-*, from + *monstrare*, to show] 1. to show by reasoning; prove 2. to show the operation or working of [the salesman *demonstrated* the vacuum cleaner to the housewife]

de·part (di pärt′) *v.* [< OFr. *departir* < VL. < L. < *dis-*, apart + *partire*, to divide] to go away (from); leave

de·plor·a·ble (di plôr′ə b'l) *adj.* that can be or should be deplored; very bad [a *deplorable* oversight] —**de·plor′a·bly** *adv.*

de·pres·sion (di presh′ən) *n.* 1. a hollow or low place 2. an emotional condition characterized by feelings of hopelessness, inadequacy, etc.

de·scend·ant (di send′ənt) *n.* one who is descended from a certain ancestor, family, group, etc.

de·scrip·tion (di skrip′shən) *n.* an account that gives a picture of [a *description* of the lost articles]

de·serve (di zurv′) *v.* **-served′, -serv′ing** [< OFr. *deservir* < L. < *de-*, entirely + *servire*, to serve] to be worthy of (reward, punishment, etc.); merit [he *deserves* a scolding]

de·sir·a·ble (di zīr′ə b'l) *adj.* worth wanting or having; excellent —**de·sir′a·bil′i·ty** *n.* —**de·sir′a·bly** *adv.*

de·sire (di zīr′) *v.* **-sired′, -sir′ing** [< OFr. < L. *desiderare* < *de-*, from + *sidus*, a star] to wish or long for —*n.* a strong wish or longing

de·spise (di spīz′) *v.* **-spised′, -spis′ing** [< OFr. < L. *despicere* < *de-*, down + *specere*, to look at] to regard with extreme dislike [he *despised* having to work nights]

des·sert (di zurt′) *n.* [< OFr. < *desservir*, to clear the table < *des-* (L. *de*), from + *servir* < L. *servire*, to serve] ☆ a course of pie, cake, ice cream, or the like, served at the end of a meal

de·tain (di tān′) *v.* [< OFr. < L. < *de-*, off + *tenere*, to hold] to keep from going on; hold back; confine [*detained* by government agents] —**de·tain′ment** *n.*

de·tect (di tekt′) *v.* [< L. *detectus*, pp. of *detegere* < *de-*, from + *tegere*, to cover] to discover (something hidden or not easily noticed) —**de·tect′a·ble, de·tect′i·ble** *adj.*

de·vise (di vīz′) *v.* **-vised′, -vis′ing** [< OFr. *deviser*, to distribute, direct] to work out (something) by thinking; plan; invent [to *devise* a filing system]

di·a·lect (dī′ə lekt′) *n.* [< Gr. *dialektos*, discourse] any of the forms of a language spoken in a particular region or community

di·a·mond (dī′ mənd, -ə mənd) *n.* [< OFr. < ML. *diamas* (gen. *diamantis*) < L. < Gr. *adamas*, adamant, diamond] 1. a mineral consisting of nearly pure carbon in crystalline form: it is the hardest mineral known and has great brilliance: unflawed stones are cut into precious gems; less perfect forms are used for phonograph needle tips, cutting tools, abrasives, etc. **2.** a gem cut from this mineral **3.** a lozenge-shaped figure (◇)

dic·ta·tion (dik tā′shən) **n.** the speaking of words for another to write down

die (dī) **v.** **died, dy′ing** [< ON. *deyja* < IE. base *dheu-*, to die] **1.** to stop living; become dead **2.** to cease existing or stop going, moving, acting, etc.; end **3.** to lose force or vitality; fade away [a *dying* culture]
SYN.—**die** is the basic, simple, direct word meaning to stop living or become dead; **decease** and **pass away** (or **pass on**) are euphemisms for the word *die*, **decease** being also the legal term and **pass away** and **pass on** being more common in informal usage; **perish** implies death by a violent means or in a disaster [twenty people *perished* in the fire]; **expire** means literally to breathe one's last breath

dif·fer (dif′ər) **v.** [< OFr. < L. *differe* < *dis-*, apart + *ferre*, to bear] to be unlike; be not the same

dif·fer·ence (dif′ər əns, dif′rəns) **n.** condition or quality of being different —**make a difference** to have an effect; matter —**split the difference** to share what is left over

dim (dim) **adj.** **dim′mer, dim′mest** [OE. *dimm* < IE. base *dhem-*, to smoke, mist] **1.** not bright; somewhat dark [the *dim* twilight] **2.** not clearly seen, heard, or understood; vague —**v.** **dimmed, dim′ming** to make or grow dim —**take a dim view of** to view without hope or enthusiasm —**dim′ly adv.** —**dim′ness n.**

dis·ci·pline (dis′ ə plin) **n.** [< OFr. < L. *disciplina* < *discipulus*, pupil] **1.** training that develops self-control or orderliness and efficiency **2.** strict control to enforce obedience [the *discipline* of the army] **3.** the result of such training or control; orderly conduct, obedience, etc. [the perfect *discipline* of the pupils studying] —**v.** **-plined, -plin·ing 1.** to train in discipline [soldiers *disciplined* to obey commands] **2.** to punish —**dis′ci·plin·a·ble, dis′ci·plin·ar·y adj.** —**dis′ci·plin·er n.**

dis·count (dis′kount) **n.** [< OFr. < ML. *discomputare*] a reduction from the usual price [sold at a 10% *discount*]

dis·miss (dis mis′) **v.** [< L < *dis-*, from + *mittere*, to send] to send away; cause or allow to leave [to *dismiss* a class] —**dis·miss′al n.**

dis·play (dis plā′) **v.** [< OFr. < L. *displicare* < *dis-*, apart + *plicare*, to fold] to put out to be

seen; exhibit [they *displayed* the flag on holidays] —**n.** a displaying; exhibition

dis·pos·a·ble (dis pō′zə b'l) **adj.** that can be thrown away after use [*disposable* bottles]

dis·prove (dis proov′) **v.** **-proved′, -prov′ing** to prove to be false or in error

dis·rupt (dis rupt′) **v.** [< L. < *dis-*, apart + *rumpere*, to break] to disturb the orderly course of (a meeting, etc.) —**dis·rup′tion n.** —**dis·rup′tive adj.**

dis·solve (di zälv′; -zôlv′) **v.** **-solved, -solving** [< L *dis-*, apart + *solvere*, to loosen] to make or become liquid; melt

dis·so·nance (dis′ə nəns) **n.** [< LL. < L. prp. of *dissonare* < *dis-*, apart + *sonare*, to sound] an inharmonious combination of sounds; discord

dis·tend (dis tend′) **v.** [< L. *distendere* < *dis-*, apart + *tendere*, to stretch] to expand; make or become swollen —**dis·ten′tion, dis·ten′sion n.**

dis·tin·guish (dis tiŋ′gwish) **v.** to perceive or show the difference in; differentiate [to *distinguish* right from wrong] —**dis·tin′guish·a·ble adj.**

dis·tract (dis trakt′) **v.** [< L. pp. of *distrahere* < *dis-*, apart + *trahere*, to draw] to draw (the mind, etc.) away in another direction; divert —**dis·tract′ed, adj.** —**dis·tract′ed·ly adv.** —**dis·tract′ing adj.** —**dis·tract′ing·ly adv.**

dis·traught (dis trôt′) **adj.** [< L. *distrahere* < *dis-*, apart + *trahere*, to draw] very troubled or confused

dodge (däj) **v.** **dodged, dodg′ing** [? akin to Scot. *dod*, to jog] to move or twist quickly aside, as to avoid a blow

does·n't (duz′ 'nt) does not

do·mes·tic (də mes′tik) **adj.** [< OFr. < L. *domesticus* < *domus*, house] **1.** of the home or family [*domestic* joys] **2.** of one's own country **3.** tamed; domesticated: said of animals —**do·mes′ti·cal·ly adv.**

a	fat	ir	here	ou	out	zh	leisure
ā	ape	ī	bite, fire	u	up	ŋ	ring
ä	car, lot	ō	go	ʉr	fur		a *in* ago
e	ten	ô	law, horn	ch	chin		e *in* agent
er	care	oi	oil	sh	she		ə = i *in* unity
ē	even	oo	look	th	thin		o *in* collect
i	hit	o͞o	tool	*th*	then		u *in* focus

dough·nut (dō′nut′) *n.* a small, usually ring-shaped cake, fried in deep fat

dra·mat·ic (drə mat′ik) *adj.* **1.** of or connected with drama **2.** full of action; vivid; striking, exciting, etc. —**dra·mat′i·cal·ly** *adv.*

dras·tic (dras′tik) *adj.* [Gr. *drastikos,* active < *dran,* to do] acting with force; having a violent effect; severe, harsh —**dras′ti·cal·ly** *adv.*

drive (drīv) *v.* **drove, driv′en, driv′ing** [OE. *drifan* < IE. base *dhreibh-,* to push] **1.** to control the movement of (a vehicle) **2.** to transport in a vehicle

driv·en (driv′ 'n) *pp.* of *drive*

drum (drum) *n.* [< Du. *trom*] a percussion instrument consisting of a hollow cylinder with a membrane stretched tightly over the end or ends —*v.* **drummed, drum′ming** to beat a drum

drum·mer (drum′ər) *n.* a drum player

du·pli·cate (dōō′plə kit, dyōō-; *for v.* -kāt) *adj.* [< L. pp. of *duplicare,* to double] exactly like each other [make a set of *duplicate* keys] —*n.* an exact copy; replica [the original letter and two *duplicates*] —*v.* **-cat′ed, -cat′ing** —**du′pli·ca′tion** *n.*

E

e·co·nom·i·cal (ē′kə näm′i k'l) *adj.* **1.** not wasting money, time, etc.; efficient [an *economical* stove] **2.** of economics —**e′co·nom′i·cal·ly** *adv.*

e·co·nom·ics (ē′kə näm′iks) *n., pl.* [*with sing v.*] the science dealing with the production, distribution, and consumption of wealth and related problems of labor, finance, taxation, etc.

ed·i·ble (ed′ə b'l) *adj.* [LL. *edibilis* < L. *edere,* eat] fit to be eaten

ed·i·tor (ed′i tər) *n.* [< L. pp. of *edere,* to publish] **1.** a person who edits **2.** the head of a department of a newspaper, magazine, etc.

ed·i·to·ri·al (ed′ə tôr′ē əl) *n.* a statement of opinion in a newspaper, etc. or on radio or TV that gives the views of the owner, publisher, etc. —**ed′i·to′ri·al·ly** *adv.*

ed·u·ca·tion (ej′e kā′shən) *n.* formal schooling

ef·fec·tive (ə fek′tiv, i-) *adj.* producing a desired effect [an *effective* remedy] —**ef·fec′tive·ly** *adv.* —**ef·fec′tive·ness** *n.*

ef·fi·cien·cy (ə fish′ən sē, i-) *n.* ability to produce a desired effect with the least effort or waste

ef·fi·cient (ə fish′ənt) *adj.* [< L. prp. of *efficere*] producing a desired effect with the least effort or waste [an *efficient* production method] —**ef·fi′cient·ly** *adv.*

ef·fort (ef′ərt) *n.* [OFr. < *esforcier,* to make an effort] use of energy to do something; a trying hard physically or mentally [rowing takes *effort;* he made no *effort* to be friendly]

eight·i·eth (āt′ē ith) *adj.* coming after seventy-nine others in a series; 80th

e·lec·tion (i lek′shən) *n.* a choosing or being chosen for office by vote

el·e·vate (el′ə vāt′) *v.* **-vat′ed, -vat′ing** [< L. pp. of *elevare* < *e-,* out + *levare,* to lift] to lift up; raise

e·lim·i·nate (i lim′ə nāt′) *v.* **-nat′ed, -nat′ing** [< L. pp. of *eliminare* < *e-,* out + *limen,* threshold] to take out; get rid of [to *eliminate* errors] —**e·lim′i·na′tion** *n.*

em·bar·rass (im ber′əs) *v.* [< Fr. < Sp. < It. < *imbarrare,* to impede < *in-* (L. *in-*) + *barra,* bar] to cause to feel self-conscious, confused, and ill at ease —**em·bar′rass·ing** *adj.* —**em·bar′rass·ing·ly** *adv.* —**em·bar′rass·ment** *n.*

SYN.—**embarrass** implies an uncomfortable feeling that one gets because of a sense of shyness, modesty, good manners, etc. [flattery *embarrasses* him]; **abash** suggests embarrassment that results from feeling ashamed of oneself [she was *abashed* by his kindness after she had insulted him]; **discomfit** implies that one's plans or hopes have been upset, resulting in a feeling of humiliation, embarrassment, etc. [*discomfited* when his proposals were rejected]; **disconcert** implies a sudden loss of poise that results in a confused state of mind [his interruptions were *disconcerting*]; **rattle** and **faze** are informal equivalents of **disconcert, faze** being commonly used in the negative [the barrage of criticism did not *faze* him] —***ANT.*** compose, assure

e·mit (i mit′) *v.* **e·mit′ted, e·mit′ting** [< L. *emittere* < *e-,* out + *mittere,* to send] to send out; give forth —**e·mit′ter** *n.*

e·mo·tion (i mō′shən) *n.* [Fr. (prob. after *motion*) < L. *emovere* < *e-,* out + *movere,* move] **1.** strong feeling; excitement [a voice choked with *emotion*] **2.** any specific feeling, as love, fear, etc.

e·mo·tion·al (i mō′shə n′l) *adj.* **1.** of the emotions or feelings [*emotional* problems] **2.** showing emotion, esp. strong emotion —**e·mo′tion·al·ly** *adv.*

em·pha·sis (em′fə sis) *n.*, *pl.* **-ses′** (sēz′) [L. < Gr. < *emphainein,* to indicate] **1.** special force given to a syllable, word, phrase, etc. in speaking **2.** special attention given to something so as to make it stand out

em·phat·ic (im fat′ik) *adj.* expressed, felt, or done with emphasis —**em·phat′i·cal·ly** *adv.*

emp·ty (emp′tē) *adj.* **-ti·er, -ti·est** [< OE. *aemettig,* unoccupied] containing nothing [an *empty* house] —*v.* **-tied, -tying** to make or become empty —*n., pl.* **-ties** an empty freight car, truck, bottle, etc. —**emp′ti·ly** *adv.* —**emp′ti·ness** *n.*

en·gine (en′ jən) *n.* [< OFr. < L. *ingenium,* genius < *in-,* & base of *gignere,* to produce] **1.** any machine that uses energy to develop mechanical power; esp., a machine for starting motion in some other machine **2.** a railroad locomotive

en·joy (in joi′) *v.* [< OFr. *enjoir* < *en-,* in + *joir* < L. *gaudere,* to be glad] to get joy or pleasure from [to *enjoy* family life]

en·ter (en′tər) *v.* [< OFr. *entrer* < L. *intra,* within < IE. base *en-,* in] **1.** to come or go into **2.** to become a participant in (a contest)

en·ter·prise (en′tər prīz′) *n.* [< OFr. < *entreprendre,* to undertake] an undertaking; project

en·ter·tain·ment (en′tər tān′mənt) *n.* something that is interesting, diverting, or amusing; a performance

en·vi·ous (en′vē əs) *adj.* [< OFr. < L. < *invidia,* envy] feeling or showing envy —**en′vi·ous·ly** *adv.*

en·vy (en′vē) *n. pl.* **-vies** [< OFr. < L. *invidia,* < *invidere,* to look askance at < *in-,* upon + *videre,* to look] a feeling of discontent and ill will because another has advantages, possessions, etc. that one would like to have —*v.* **-vied, -vy·ing** to feel envy toward, at, or because of

ep·i·sode (ep′ ə sōd′) *n.* [< Gr. < *epeisodios,* following upon the entrance < *epi-,* upon + *eis-,* into + *hodos,* a way] **1.** in a novel, poem, etc., any part of the story that is complete in itself; incident **2.** any installment of a serialized story or drama

e·qual·i·ty (i kwäl′ə tē, -kwôl′-) *n., pl.* **-ties** state or instance of being equal, esp. of having the same political, economic, and social rights

e·qua·tor (i kwāt′ər) *n.* [< ML. < LL. *aequator* < L. *aequare,* equate] an imaginary circle around the earth; it divides the earth into the Northern Hemisphere and Southern Hemisphere

e·quip (i kwip′) *v.* **e·quipped′, e·quip′ping** [< Fr. < OFr. *esquiper,* embark] to provide with what is needed; outfit

e·quip·ment (i kwip′mənt) *n.* whatever one is equipped with for some purpose; supplies [camping *equipment*]

e·rup·tion (i rup′shən) *n.* a bursting forth or out

es·cape (ə skāp′, e-) *v.* **-caped′, -cap′ing** [< L. *ex-,* out of + *cappa,* cloak] to get free [she *escaped* from prison] —*n.* **1.** the state of having escaped **2.** a means of escape [a fire *escape*]
SYN.—**escape** implies getting out of; **avoid** suggests using conscious effort to remain clear of something [to *avoid* crowds during a flu epidemic]; to **evade** is to escape or avoid by being clever [to *evade* pursuit]

es·pi·o·nage (es′pē ə näzh′, -nij′) *n.* [< Fr. < *espion,* a spy] the act of spying

es·say (es′ā) *n.* [< OFr. < LL. < L. *exagium,* a weighing < *ex-,* out of + *agere,* to do] a short piece of writing in which the writer attempts to analyze something in a personal way

et·i·quette (et′i kət, -ket′) *n.* [Fr. *etiquette,* a ticket] the forms, manners, and ceremonies established by general agreement as acceptable or required in social relations

e·vap·o·rate (i vap′ə rāt′) *v.* **-rat′ed, -rat′ing** [< L. pp. of *evaporare* < *e-,* out + *vapor,* vapor] **1.** to become vapor [the perfume *evaporated*] **2.** to disappear; vanish [his courage *evaporated* when he saw the lion] —**e·vap′o·ra′tion** *n.*

a	fat	ir	here	ou	out	zh	leisure
ā	ape	ī	bite, fire	u	up	ŋ	ring
ä	car, lot	ō	go	ʉr	fur		a *in* ago
e	ten	ô	law, horn	ch	chin		e *in* agent
er	care	oi	oil	sh	she	ə = i *in* unity
ē	even	oo	look	th	thin		o *in* collect
i	hit	o͞o	tool	th	then		u *in* focus

ev·er·y·where (ev'rē hwer', -wer') *adv.* in or to every place

ex- *a prefix meaning* from, out, beyond, out of [*expel, excess*]

ex·act (ig zakt') *adj.* [< L. pp. of *exigere*, to measure < *ex-*, out + *agere*, to do] very accurate; correct [an *exact* science]

ex·ceed (ik sēd') *v.* [< L. < *ex-*, out + *cedere*, to go] to go or be beyond (a limit, measure, etc.) [to *exceed* a speed limit]

ex·ces·sive (ik ses'iv) *adj.* being too much or too great —**ex·ces'sive·ly** *adv.* —**ex·ces'sive·ness** *n.*

ex·cit·a·ble (ik sīt'ə b'l) *adj.* that can be excited; easily excited

ex·claim (iks klām') *v.* [< Fr. < L. *exclamare* < *ex-*, out + *clamare*, to shout] to cry out; speak suddenly and excitedly

ex·cla·ma·tion (eks'klə mā'shən) *n.* something cried out suddenly

ex·clude (iks klōōd') *v.* **-clud'ed, -clud'ing** [< L. *excludere* < *ex-*, out + *claudere*, close] to refuse to admit

ex·cur·sion (ik skʉr'zhən) *n.* [< L. < pp. of *excurrere* < *ex-*, out + *currere*, to run] a short trip for pleasure

ex·cuse (ik skyōōz'; *for n.* -skyōōs') *v.* **-cused', -cus'ing** [< OFr. < L. *excusare* < *ex-*, from + *causa*, a charge] **1.** to pardon (a fault) [*excuse* me] **2.** to permit to leave —*n.* a plea in defense of some action; apology —**ex·cus'a·ble** *adj.*

ex·er·cise (ek'sər siz') *n.* [< OFr. < L. < pp. of *exercere*, to drive out (farm animals to work)] activity for training or developing the body or mind —*v.* **-cised', -cis'ing** to take exercise; do exercises

ex·pect (ik spekt') *v.* [< L. < *ex-*, out + *spectare*, to look] to look for as likely to occur or appear; look forward to [I *expected* you sooner]
SYN.—**expect** implies confidence that a particular thing will happen; **hope** implies a desire for something to happen [to *hope* for the best]; **await** implies a waiting for, or being ready for [a hearty welcome *awaits* you]

ex·pe·di·tion (ek'spə dish'ən) *n.* [< OFr. < L. < pp. of *expedire*, to free one caught by the feet] a journey, voyage, etc., as for exploration or battle

ex·pense (ik spens') *n.* [< Anglo-Fr. < LL. *expensa (pecunia)*, paid out (money)] **1.** financial cost; fee **2.** any cost or sacrifice

ex·pen·sive (ik spen'siv) *adj.* requiring much expense; high-priced —**ex·pen'sive·ly** *adv.* —**ex·pen'sive·ness** *n.*
SYN.—**expensive** implies a price that is greater than the article is worth or more than the customer is willing to pay [an *expensive* dress]; **costly** refers to something that costs much and usually implies richness, magnificence, rareness, etc.

ex·pe·ri·ence (ik spir'ē əns) *n.* [< L. < prp. of *experiri*, to try] **1.** anything or everything observed or lived through [an *experience* he'll never forget] **2.** activity that includes training, practice, and work —*v.* **-enced, -enc·ing** to have experience; undergo

ex·pert (ek'spərt; *also, for adj.*, ik spʉrt') *adj.* [< OFr. < L. pp. of *experiri*, to try] *n.* a person who is very skillful and informed in some field —**ex'pert·ly** *adv.* —**ex'pert·ness** *n.*

ex·pire (ik spīr') *v.* **-pired', -pir'ing** [< L. *exspirare* < *ex-*, out + *spirare*, to breathe] **1.** to breathe out air **2.** to come to an end; terminate

ex·port (ik spôrt') *v.* [< L. < *ex-*, out + *portare*, to carry] to carry or send (goods, etc.) to other countries, esp. for sale —**ex·port'a·ble** *adj.* —**ex·port'er** *n.*

ex·ten·sion (ik sten'shən) *n.* **1.** a part that forms an addition [building an *extension* onto the library] **2.** an extra period of time allowed for some purpose

ex·te·ri·or (ik stir'ē ər) *adj.* [L., compar. of *exter(us)*, on the outside] on the outside; outer —*n.* an outside or outside surface

ex·tinct (ik stiŋkt') *adj.* [< L. pp. of *exstinguere* < *ex-*, out + *stinguere*, to extinguish] no longer living; having died out [an *extinct* species]

ex·tin·guish (ik stiŋ'gwish) *v.* [< L. *exstinguere* < *ex-*, out + *stinguere*, to quench] to put out (a fire, light, etc.) —**ex·tin'guish·a·ble** *adj.* —**ex·tin'guish·er** *n.*

ex·trac·tion (ik strak'shən) *n.* a pulling out; specif., the pulling out of a tooth

ex·treme (ik strēm') *adj.* [< L. *extremus*, superl. of *exterus*, outer] to the greatest or an excessive degree; very great [*extreme* pain] —**ex·treme'ly** *adv.*

F

fac·sim·i·le (fak sim′ə lē) *n.* [L. *fac*, imper. of *facere*, do + *simile*, similar] an exact reproduction or copy

fac·to·ry (fak′tə rē, -trē) *n.*, *pl.* **-ries** [< OFr. < L. < pp. of *facere*, do] a building in which things are manufactured

fan·tas·tic (fan′tas′tik) *adj.* [< OFr. < ML. < LL.< Gr. *phantastikos*, able to present to the mind] **1.** strange and unusual; extravagant [a *fantastic* plan] **2.** seemingly impossible; incredible [*fantastic* progress] —**fan·tas′ti·cal·ly** *adv.*

fan·ta·sy (fan′tə sē, -zē) *n.*, *pl.* **-sies** [< OFr. < L. < Gr. *phantasia*, appearance < *phainein*, to show] a daydream or daydreaming; esp. about something one would like

fa·tigue (fə tēg′) *n.* [Fr. < L. *fatigare*, to weary] a tired feeling, as from hard work; physical or mental exhaustion; weariness

fi·let (fi lā′, fil′ā) *n.* [< OFr. dim. of *fil* < L. *filum*, a thread] a boneless, lean piece of meat or fish

fire·proof (fīr′proof′) *adj.* that does not burn

floor (flôr) *n.* [OE. *flor* < IE. base *pele-*, flat and broad] **1.** the inside bottom surface of a room **2.** any bottom surface [the ocean *floor*] **3.** a level or story in a building [an office on the fifth *floor*] —*v.* to cover or furnish with a floor

fluc·tu·ate (fluk′choo wāt′) *v.* **-at′ed, -at′ing** [< L. pp. of *fluctuare* < *fluctus*, a wave] to move back and forth or up and down —**fluc′tu·a′tion** *n.*

flu·ent (floo′ənt) *adj.* [< L. prp. of *fluere*, to flow] flowing smoothly and easily [*fluent* verse] —**flu′en·cy** *n.* —**flu′ent·ly** *adv.*

flu·id (floo′id) *adj.* [< L. *fluidus* < *fluere*, to flow] that can flow; not solid —*n.* any substance that can flow; liquid or gas —**flu·id′i·ty, flu′id·ness** *n.* —**flu′id·ly** *adv.*

flu·o·res·cence (floo res′ ′ns) *n.* [< L. *fluere*, to flow + -escence] light produced by radiant energy, such as ultraviolet rays or X-rays —**flu′o·res′cent** *adj.*

folk·lore (fōk′lôr′) *n.* the traditional beliefs, legends, sayings, customs, etc. of a people

fore- *a prefix meaning* before in time, place, order, or rank [*forenoon*]

fore·cast (fôr′kast′) *v.* **-cast′** or **-cast′ed, -cast′ing** to predict —*n.* a prediction —**fore′cast′er** *n.*

for·eign (fôr′in, fär-) *adj.* [< OFr. *forain* < LL. < L. *foras*, out-of-doors] of or from another country [a *foreign* language]

fore·warn (fôr wôrn′) *v.* to warn ahead of time [*"forewarned* is forearmed"]

for·get (fər get′, fôr-) *v.* **-got′, -got′ten** or **-got′, -get′ting** [OE. *forgietan*] **1.** to be unable to remember **2.** to fail to do without meaning to [to *forget* to lock the door] **3.** to overlook [Let's *forget* our differences] —**forget it** don't trouble to think about it —**forget oneself** to behave in an improper or unseemly manner —**for·get′ta·ble** *adj.*

for·get·ful (fər get′f′l, fôr-) *adj.* apt to forget; having a poor memory —**for·get′ful·ly** *adv.* —**for·get′ful·ness** *n.*

for·give (fər giv′, fôr-) *v.* **-gave′, -giv′en, -giv′ing** [OE. *forgiefan*] to give up being angry with; pardon —**for·giv′a·ble** *adj.*

forty-eight (fôr′tē āt′) *adj.* one more than forty-seven [my father is *forty-eight* years old] *n.* eight and forty [the total number of rooms was *forty-eight*]

for·give·ness (fər giv′ nis) *n.* a forgiving; pardon

for·mu·la (fôr′myə lə) *n.*, *pl.* **-las, -lae′** (-lē′) [L., dim. of *forma*, form] **1.** a rule or method for doing something **2.** a set of symbols and figures expressing a mathematical fact or chemical composition

fought (fôt) *pt.* + *pp.* of fight

frag·ile (fraj′′l) *adj.* [< OFr. < L. *fragilis* < *frangere*, break] easily damaged or destroyed; delicate [*fragile* china] —**fra·gil·i·ty** (frə jil′ə tē) *n.*

fran·chise (fran′chīz) *n.* [< OFr. < *franc*, free] the right to sell a product or provide a service in an area, as granted by a manufacturer or company —*v.* **-chised, -chis·ing** to grant a franchise to

a fat	**ir** here	**ou** out	**zh** leisure
ā ape	**ī** bite, fire	**u** up	**ŋ** ring
ä car, lot	**ō** go	**ur** fur	a *in* ago
e ten	**ô** law, horn	**ch** chin	e *in* agent
er care	**oi** oil	**sh** she	**ə** = i *in* unity
ē even	**oo** loók	**th** thin	o *in* collect
i hit	**ōo** tool	**th** then	u *in* focus

fran·tic (fran′tik) *adj.* wild with anger, pain, worry, etc.; frenzied —**fran′ti·cal·ly** *adv.*

freight (frāt) *n.* [< MDu. *vracht,* a load] **1.** a method or service for transporting goods **2.** the goods transported; cargo

fre·quent (frē′kwənt) *adj.* [< OFr. < L. *frequens,* crowded] happening often, time after time [his *frequent* requests for help] —**fre′quent·ly** *adv.*

fright·en (frīt′'n) *v.* to cause to feel fear; make suddenly afraid; scare

frol·ic (fräl′ik) *n.* [< Du. < MDu. *vrō,* merry] merriment; fun —*v.* **-icked, -ick·ing** to make merry, have fun; play or romp about

fu·gi·tive (fyoo′jə tive) *n.* [< OFr. < L. pp. of *fugere,* to flee] a person who flees or has fled from danger, justice, etc.

-ful (fəl, f'l; fool) [OE. < *full,* full] *a suffix meaning:* **1.** full of, having [*joyful*] **2.** able or tending to [*helpful*]

fu·se·lage (fyoo′sə läzh′, -läj′, -lij) *n.* [Fr. < *fuselé,* tapering] the body of an airplane not including the wings, tails, and engines

G

gadg·et (gaj′it) *n.* any small mechanical device

gal·lop (gal′əp) *v.* [< OFr. *galoper* < Frank.] **1.** to go at a gallop **2.** to move fast; hurry —*n.* the fastest gait of a horse

ga·rage (gə räzh′, -räj′) *n.* [< Fr. < *garer,* to guard] **1.** a closed shelter for automobiles **2.** a business establishment where automobiles are repaired, stored, etc.

ge·ne·al·o·gy (jē′nē äl′ə jē, -al′ə jē) *n., pl.* **-gies** [< Gr. < *genea,* race, stock + *logia,* -logy (study of)] the study of family descent —**ge′ne·a·log′i·cal** *adj.* —**ge′ne·a·log′i·cal·ly** *adv.* —**ge′ne·al′o·gist** *n.*

gen·e·sis (jen′ə sis) *n., pl.* **-ses** (sēz′) [< L. < Gr. < *gignesthai,* to be born] a beginning, origin

ge·net·ics (jə net′iks) *n., pl.* [*with sing v.*] [genetic] the branch of biology that deals with heredity —**ge·net′i·cist** *n.*

ge·nius (jen′yəs, jē′nē əs) *n., pl.* **ge′nius·es** a person with great mental and inventive ability

ge·o·graph·i·cal (jē ə graf′i k'l) *adj.* of or having to do with geography

ge·o·gra·phy (jē äg′rə fē) *n., pl.* **-phies** [< L. < Gr. < *geō-,* the earth + *graphein,* to write] the science dealing with the surface of the earth —**ge·og′ra·pher** *n.*

gi·gan·tic (jī gan′tik) *adj.* huge; enormous; immense —**gi·gan′ti·cal·ly** *adv.*

gnarled (närld) *adj.* [ult. < ME. *knur,* a knot] knotty and twisted [a *gnarled* tree, *gnarled* hands]

gold·en (gōl′ d'n) *adj.* **1.** of, containing, or yielding gold **2.** bright-yellow, like gold —**gold′ en·ly** *adv.* —**gold′ en·ness** *n.*

good·na·tured (good nā′chərd) *adj.* pleasant and friendly —**good′na′tured·ly** *adv.*

gor·geous (gôr′jəs) *adj.* [< OFr. *gorgias,* beautiful] beautiful, wonderful, delightful, etc. —**gor′geous·ly** *adv.* —**gor′geous·ness** *n.*

gour·met (goor′mā; Fr. gōōr me′) *n.* [Fr.< OFr. *gourmet,* wine taster] a person who likes and is an excellent judge of fine foods and drinks

grab (grab) *v.* **grabbed, grab′bing** to seize or snatch suddenly

grad·u·al (graj′oo wəl) *adj.* [< ML. < L. *gradus,* a step] taking place little by little, not sharply or suddenly —**grad′u·al·ly** *adv.*

grad·u·a·tion (graj′oo wā′shən) *n.* a completion of school, college, or course of study

gram·mar (gram′ər) *n.* [< OFr. < L. < Gr. *grammatikē (technē),* (art) of grammar] a body of rules for speaking and writing a given language

gram·mat·i·cal (grə mat′i k'l) *adj.* of or according to grammar or the rules of grammar [a *grammatical* sentence] —**gram·mat′i·cal·ly** *adv.*

gran·deur (gran′jər, -joor) *n.* [Fr. < *grand* < L. *grandis,* large] great size, beauty, dignity, etc.; splendor; magnificence [the *grandeur* of the Swiss Alps]

great-aunt (grāt′ant′) *n.* a sister of any of one's grandparents

griev·ance (grē′vəns) *n.* complaint or resentment, or a statement expressing this, against a real or imagined wrong

guar·an·tee (gar'ən tē', gär'-) *n.* [altered < guaranty] a pledge that something will be replaced or repaired if it is not as represented [a thirty-day *guarantee* on the clock] —*v.* **-teed', -tee'ing** to give a guarantee for

guid·ance (gīd' 'ns) *n.* the act of guiding; direction; leadership

gym·nas·tics (jim nas'tiks) *n., pl.* exercises that develop and train the body and the muscles, esp. those exercises that can be done in a gymnasium

H

hap·pen (hap' 'n) *v.* [ME. *happenen*] to take place; occur [what *happened* at the party?]

hatch·et (hach'it) *n.* [< OFr. dim. of *hache*, an ax] a small ax with a short handle —**bury the hatchet** to stop fighting; make peace

hate (hāt) *v.* **hat'ed, hat'ing** [OE. *hatian* < IE. base *kad*-] **1.** to have strong dislike or ill will for; despise [to *hate* an enemy] **2.** to dislike or wish to avoid; shrink from [to *hate* arguments] —*n.* a strong feeling of dislike or ill will; hatred —**hate'a·ble, hat'a·ble** *adj.* **hat'er** *n.*

haul (hôl) *v.* [< OFr. *haler*, to draw < ODu. *halen*, fetch < IE. base *kel*-] **1.** to move by pulling or drawing; tug; drag [we *hauled* the boat up on the beach] **2.** to transport by wagon, truck, etc. [to *haul* coal] —*n.* **1.** the distance or route covered in transporting or traveling [it's a long *haul* to town] **2.** a load transported

heap (hēp) *v.* [OE. *heap*, a troop < IE. base *keu-*, bend, hollow] **1.** to make a heap of [toys *heaped* in the corner] **2.** to fill (a plate, etc.) full or to overflowing **3.** to pile up in a heap

heaven (hev' 'n) *n.* [OE. *heofon*] **1.** [usually pl.] the space surrounding the earth; the sky (in pl. used with *the*) **2.** *Theol.* [often **H-**] the place where God and his angels are and where the blessed go after death **3.** any place or condition of great beauty or happiness [it's *heaven* to be home again]

height (hīt) *n.* [OE. *heigthu* < *heah*, high] **1.** the topmost point of anything **2.** the distance from the bottom to the top [a man six feet in *height*]

here's (hirz) here is

hes·i·ta·tion (hez'ə tā'shən) *n.* a pausing or delaying because of doubt, fear, etc.

hi·er·ar·chy (hī'ə rär'kē) *n., pl.* **-chies** [< OFr. < ML < Gr. *hieros*, sacred + *archos*, ruler] a group of persons or things arranged in order of rank, grade, etc.

high·way (hī'wā') *n.* a main road; thoroughfare

his·tor·ic (his tôr'ik, -tär'-) *adj.* historical; esp., famous in history [a *historic* site]

his·tor·i·cal (his tôr'i k'l) -tär'i k'l) *adj.* **1.** of or concerned with history **2.** that really existed or happened in history; factual [*historical* persons and events] —**his·tor'i·cal·ly** *adv.*

hol·i·day (häl'ə dā) *n.* a day set aside, as by law, when work and business are not carried on, to commemorate some event [Thanksgiving is a *holiday* in the United States]

☆ **honk** (hôŋk, häŋk) *v.* [echoic] to make or cause to make the sound like the call of a wild goose or any similar sound, as of an automobile horn —**honk'er** *n.*

hope (hōp) *n.* [OE. *hopa*] a feeling that what is wanted will happen —*v.* **hoped, hop'ing** to want and expect

hope·ful (hōp'fəl) *adj.* **1.** feeling or showing hope **2.** giving hope [a *hopeful* sign] —**hope'ful·ness** *n.*

hos·tile (häs't'l) *adj.* [< L. < *hostis*, enemy] having or showing dislike or ill will; unfriendly [a *hostile* gesture] —**hos'tile·ly** *adv.*

hos·til·i·ty (häs til'ə tē) *n., pl.* **-ties** a feeling of dislike, ill will; unfriendliness

hu·man (hyōo'mən) *n.* [< OFr. < L. *humanus*, related to *homo*, man] a person —**hu'man·ness** *n.*

hu·man·i·ty (hyōo man'ə tē) *n., pl.* **-ties 1.** the fact of being human; human nature **2.** the human race; people [atomic warfare threatens *humanity*]

hu·mid (hyōo' mid, yōo'-) *adj.* [< Fr. < L. *humidus*, ult. < *umere*, to be moist] full of water vapor; damp; moist [*humid* air, a *humid* day] —**hu'mid·ly** *adv.*

a	fat	**ir**	here	**ou**	out	**zh**	leisure
ā	ape	**ī**	bite, fire	**u**	up	**ŋ**	ring
ä	car, lot	**ō**	go	**ʉr**	fur		a *in* ago
e	ten	**ô**	law, horn	**ch**	chin		e *in* agent
er	care	**oi**	oil	**sh**	she	**ə** = i *in* unity
ē	even	**oo**	look	**th**	thin		o *in* collect
i	hit	**ōo**	tool	**th**	then		u *in* focus

☆ **hy·drant** (hī′drənt) *n.* [< Gr. *hydōr*, water] a large discharge pipe with a valve for drawing water from a water main; fireplug

hy·dro·gen (hī′drə jən) *n.* [< Fr. < Gr., *hydōr*, water + base of *gignesthai*, to be born] a flammable, colorless, odorless, gaseous chemical element

hy·dro·pho·bi·a (hī′drə fō′bē ə) *n.* [< Gr. *hydro*, water + *phobos*, fear] an abnormal fear of water

hys·ter·i·cal (his ter′i k'l) *adj.* showing wild, uncontrolled excitement, such as fits of laughing and crying —**hys·ter′i·cal·ly,** *adv.*

hys·ter·ics (his ter′iks) *n.* [< L. < Gr. *hysterikos*, suffering in the womb < *hystera*, uterus] *usually pl., occas. with sing. v.* a fit of uncontrolled laughing, crying, etc.

I

☆ **ice cream** [orig., *iced cream*] *n.* a sweet, creamy frozen food made from variously flavored cream and milk products and often containing gelatin, eggs, fruits, etc.—**ice′-cream′** *adj.*

ig·no·rance (ig′nə rəns) *n.* the condition of being ignorant; lack of knowledge

IL, Ill. Illinois

il·le·gal (i lē′gəl) *adj.* not lawful; against the law or against the rules —**il·le·gal·i·ty** (il′ē gal′ə tē)*n., pl.* -ties —**il·le′gal·ly** *adv.*

il·lus·tra·tion (il′ə strā′shən) *n.* an explanatory or decorative picture, diagram, etc.

im·bal·ance (im bal′əns) *n.* lack of balance, as in proportion, force, functioning, etc.

im·ma·ture (im′ə toor′, -choor′, -tyoor′) *adj.* not mature or ripe; not completely grown —**im′ma·ture′ly** *adv.* —**im′ma·tu′ri·ty** *n.*

im·meas·ur·a·ble (i mezh′ər ə b'l) *adj.* too large or too much to be measured; boundless; vast [the *immeasurable* space of the universe] —**im·meas′ur·a·bil′i·ty** *n.* —**im·meas′ur·a·bly** *adv.*

im·mo·bile (i mō′b'l, -bēl, bil) *adj.* not movable or moving; stable; motionless —**im′mo·bil′i·ty** *n.*

im·par·tial (im pär′shəl) *adj.* not favoring one side more than another; fair —**im·par′ti·al′i·ty** *n.* —**im·par′tial·ly** *adv.*

im·per·son·ate (im pur′sə nāt′) *v.* -at′ed, -at′ing to act the part of; to pretend to be —**im·per′son·a′tion** *n.* —**im·per′son·a′tor** *n.*

im·port (im pôrt′) *v.* [< L < *in-*, in + *portare*, to carry] to bring (goods) from another country, esp. for selling —**im·port′a·ble** *adj.* —**im·port′er** *n.*

im·pos·si·bil·i·ty (im päs′ə bil′ə tē) *n.* **1.** the fact or quality of being impossible **2.** *pl.* -ties something that is impossible

im·pres·sion (im presh′ən) *n.* **1.** a mark, imprint, etc. made by physical pressure [a fingerprint *impression*] **2.** an effect produced on the mind or senses [the play made a great *impression* on her]

im·pres·sion·a·ble (im presh′ən ə b'l) *adj.* easily affected or influenced; sensitive —**im·pres′sion·a·bil′i·ty** *n.* —**im·pres′sion·a·bly** *adv.*

im·prove (im proov′) *v.* —**proved, -prov′ing** [< Anglo-Fr. < *en-*, in + *prou*, gain < LL. < L. *prodesse*, to be of advantage] to make better —**im·prov′a·ble** *adj.*

im·prove·ment (-mənt) *n.* a making or becoming better

im·prov·i·sa·tion (im präv′ə zā′shən, im′prəvi-) *n.* an improvising or something improvised —**im·prov′i·sa′tion·al** *adj.*

im·pro·vise (im′prə viz′) *v.* -vised′, vis′ing [< Fr. < It. < *improvisso*, unprepared] to compose and perform at the same time without any preparation —**im′pro·vis′er, im′pro·vi′sor** *n.*

im·pulse (im′puls) *n.* [< L. pp. of *impeller*, impel] a sudden feeling that makes one want to act [she had an *impulse* to scream]

im·pul·sive (-pul′siv) *adj.* acting or likely to act on impulse [an *impulsive* person]

in- *a prefix meaning* in, into, within, on [*induct*]

in·an·i·mate (in an′ə mit) *adj.* not animate, without life [a rock is an *inanimate* object]

inc. **1.** inclosure **2.** incorporated

in·ci·dent (in′si dənt) *n.* [< OFr. < ML. < prp. of L. *incidere* < *in-*, on + *cadere*, to fall] something that happens; occurrence

in·ci·den·tal (in′si den′t'l) *adj.* secondary or minor, but usually associated [*incidental* expenses]

in·ci·den·tal·ly (in′si dent′lē, -den′t'l ē) *adv.*
1. in an incidental way; along with something else
2. by the way [*incidentally*, what time is it?]

in·ci·sion (in sizh′ən) *n.* a cut made with a sharp tool, as in surgery

in·clude (in klōōd′) *v.* **-clud′ed, -clud′ing**
[< L. < *in-,* in + *claudere,* close] to take into account; put in a total, category, etc. [to be *included* as a candidate]

in·cu·bate (iŋ′kyə bāt′, in-) *v.* **-bat′ed, -bat′ing**
[< L. pp. of *incubare* + *in-,* on + *cubare,* to lie] to keep (eggs, embryos, etc.) in a favorable environment for hatching or developing

in·cu·ba·tion (iŋ′kyə bā′shən, in′-) *n.* an incubating or being incubated

in·dent (in dent′) *v.* [< OFr. < ML. < L. *in-,* in + *dens,* tooth] to space (a line or column) in from the regular margin

in·di·vis·i·ble (in′di viz′ə b'l) *adj.* that cannot be divided —**in′di·vis′i·bil′i·ty** *n.* —**in′di·vis′i·bly** *adv.*

in·dulge (in dulj′) *v.* **-dulged′, -dulg′ing 1.** to yield to or satisfy (a desire) [to *indulge* a craving for sweets] **2.** to gratify the wishes of; humor

in·dus·tri·ous (in dus′trē əs) *adj.* characterized by earnest, steady effort; hardworking

in·fec·tion (in fek′shən) *n.* a disease resulting from contamination by bacteria, viruses, etc.

in·fi·nite (in′fə nit) *adj.* [< L. *in-,* not + *finis,* an end] lacking limits or bounds; extending beyond measure or comprehension; without beginning or end [is the universe *infinite?*] —**in′fi·nite·ly** *adv.*

in·fin·i·ty (in fin′ə tē) *n., pl.* **-ties 1.** endless or unlimited space, time, distance, amount, etc. **2.** an indefinitely large number or amount

in·flict (in flikt′) *v.* [< L. pp. of *infligere* < *in-,* against + *fligere,* to strike] to cause (pain, wounds, etc.) as by striking

in·flu·ence (in′floo wəns) *n.* [< OFr. < ML. < L. prp. of *influere* < *in-,* in + *fluere,* to flow] the power of persons or things to affect others —*v.* **-enced, -enc·ing** to affect the nature, behavior, or thought of [her advice *influenced* my decision]

in·hab·it·ant (in hab′i tənt) *n.* a person or animal that inhabits some specified region, house, etc.

in·ju·ry (in′jə rē) *n., pl.* **-ries** [< L. *injuria,* ult. < *in-,* not + *jus,* right] harm or damage done to a person or thing

in·no·cence (in′ə səns) *n.* freedom from sin or guilt

in·nu·mer·a·ble (i nōō′mər ə b'l, -nyōō′-) *adj.* too numerous to be counted; countless —**in·nu′mer·a·bly** *adv.*

in·scrip·tion (in skrip′shən) *n.* something marked or engraved, as on a coin, book, monument, etc. —**in·scrip′tion·al** *adj.*

in·sist (in sist′) *v.* [< MFr. < L. *insistere* < *in-,* in + *sistere,* to stand] to declare firmly [I *insist* that I saw her there] —**in·sist′ing·ly** *adv.*

in·spec·tion (in spek′shən) *n.* careful examination

in·stall (in stôl′) *v.* **-stalled′, -stall′ing** [< ML. < *in-,* in + *stallum* < OHG. *stal,* a place) to establish in a place or fix in a position [to *install* new fixtures]

in·stinct (in′stiŋkt) *n.* [< L. pp. of *instinguere,* to impel] **1.** an inborn tendency to behave in a way characteristic of a species **2.** a natural ability; talent; knack [an *instinct* for doing the right thing] —**in·stinc′tu·al** *adj.*

in·sur·ance (in shoor′əns) *n.* an insuring or being insured against loss by fire, accident, death, etc.

in·sure (in shoor′) *v.* **-sured′, -sur′ing** to take out or issue insurance on [she *insured* her jewels against theft] —**in·sur′a·ble** *adj.*

in·te·grate (in′tə grāt′) *v.* **-grat′ed, -grat′ing** [< L. pp. of *integrare* < *integer,* whole] **1.** to make whole or complete **2.** to do away with the segregation of (racial groups) —**in′te·gra′tion** *n.*

in·tel·lect (in′t'l ekt′) *n.* [< L. < *inter-,* between + *legere,* to choose] the ability to reason or understand

a	fat	ir	here	ou	out	zh	leisure
ā	ape	ī	bite, fire	u	up	ŋ	ring
ä	car, lot	ō	go	ʉr	fur		a *in* ago
e	ten	ô	law, horn	ch	chin		e *in* agent
er	care	oi	oil	sh	she	ə	= i *in* unity
ē	even	oo	look	th	thin		o *in* collect
i	hit	ōō	tool	th	then		u *in* focus

in·tel·li·gence (in tel′ə jens) *n.* [< OFr. < L. *intelligentia* < prp. of *intelligere*] the ability to learn or understand or to respond successfully to a new situation; cleverness; shrewdness

in·ten·sive (in ten′siv) *adj.* of or characterized by intensity; thorough; exhaustive [an *intensive* search] —**in·ten′sive·ly** *adv.*

in·ten·tion (in ten′shən) *n.* determination to do a specified thing; aim or purpose

in·ter·mis·sion (in′tər mish′ən) *n.* an interval of time between periods of activity; pause, as between acts of a play

in·ter·rupt (in′tə rupt′) *v.* to make a break in; obstruct; cut off [to *interrupt* the speaker is rude]

in·ter·rup·tion (in′tə rup′shən) *n.* a break, pause, or halt

in·ter·sec·tion (in′tər sek′shən) *n.* a place of intersecting; specif., the point, line, or place where two lines, surfaces, or streets meet or cross

in·ter·vene (in′tər vēn′) *v.* -**vened′**, -**ven′ing** [< L. < *inter-*, between + *venire*, to come] to come or be between [two weeks *intervened* between semesters]

in·trigue (in trēg′; *for n. also* in′trēg) *v.* to stir up the interest or curiosity of; fascinate [movies *intrigue* her] —*n.* a secret or underhanded plot or scheme

in·ven·tion (in ven′shən) *n.* a new device, plan, etc. [the many *inventions* of Edison]

in·ves·ti·ga·tion (in ves′tə gā′shən) *n.* a careful examination or inquiry

in·vin·ci·ble (in vin′sə b'l) *adj.* [< MFr. < L. *in-*, not + *vincere*, conquer] that cannot be defeated or overcome; unconquerable —**in·vin′ci·bil′i·ty** *n.* —**in·vin′ci·bly** *adv.*

in·volve (in välv′) *v.* -**volved**, -**volv′ing** [L. < *in-*, in + *volvere*, to roll] **1.** to entangle in difficulty, trouble, etc. [repairs on his house *involved* him in debt] **2.** to draw or hold within itself [a rally that *involved* thousands] —**in·volve′ment** *n.*

ir·i·des·cent (ir′ə des′'nt) *adj.* [< L. *iris* (< Gr. *iris*), rainbow + -escent] having or showing shifting changes in color or a play of rainbowlike colors [soap bubbles are *iridescent*] —**ir′i·des′cence** *n.* **ir′i·des′cent·ly** *adv.*

ir·reg·u·lar (i reg′yə lər) *adj.* **1.** not according to an established rule, method, etc.; out of the ordinary **2.** uneven in occurence [at *irregular* intervals] —**ir·reg′u·lar′i·ty** —*n.*, *pl.* -**ties** —**ir·reg′u·lar·ly** *adv.*

ir·ri·ga·tion (ir′ə gā′shən) *n.* [< L. pp. of *irrigare* < *in-*, in + *rigare*, to water, moisten] artificial application of water to land

ir·ri·tate (ir′ə tāt′) *v.* -**tat′ed**, -**tat′ing** [< L. pp. of *irritare*, to excite] **1.** to annoy **2.** to make (a part of the body) inflamed or sore [harsh soaps *irritate* her skin] —**ir′ri·ta′tive** *adj.*

it's (its) **1.** it is **2.** it has

J

jack·et (jak′it) *n.* [< OFr. dim of *jaque* < Sp. *jaco*, coat] **1.** a short coat ☆ **2.** a cardboard holder for a phonograph record

jag·uar (jag′wär, -yoo wär′) *n.*, *pl.* -**uars**, -**uar** a large cat, yellowish with black spots

jar·gon (jär′gən) *n.* [MFr., a chattering] the specialized vocabulary and idioms of those in the same work, profession, etc.

jaun·dice (jôn′dis, jän′-) *n.* [< OFr. *jaunisse*, ult. < L. *galbinus*, greenish yellow] a condition in which the eyeballs, skin, and urine become abnormally yellow —*v.* -**diced**, -**dic·ing** to cause to have jaundice

jeal·ous (jel′əs) *adj.* [< OFr. *gelos* < ML. *zelosus*, zeal] unhappy because another has something one would like [he was *jealous* of her good fortune] —**jeal′ous·ness** *n.*

jeop·ard·y (jep′ər dē) *n.*, *pl.* -**ard·ies** [< OFr. *jeu parti*, lit., a game with even chances] great danger; peril [a miner's life is often in *jeopardy*]

☆ **jinx** (jiŋks) *v.* [< L. *iynx* < Gr. *iynx*, the wryneck (bird used in black magic)] [Colloq.] to bring bad luck to

jog[1] (jäg) *v.* **jogged**, **jog′ging** [ME. *joggen*, to spur] to shake up or revive (a person's memory); to move along at a slow, steady pace —*n.* **1.** a little shake or nudge **2.** a slow, steady pace —**jog′ger** *n.*

jog[2] (jäg) *n.* [var. of *jag*] a sharp, temporary change of direction, as in a road —*v.* **jogged**, **jog′ging** to form or make a jog [turn left where the road *jogs*]

jour·nal (jʉr′n'l) *n.* [< OFr., daily] a daily record of happenings, as a diary

jour·ney (jʉr′nē) *n., pl.* **-neys** [< OFr. *journee* < LL. < L. *diurnus,* daily] a traveling from one place to another; trip —*v.* **-neyed, -ney·ing** to go on a trip; travel

ju·bi·lee (jo͞o′bə lē′, jo͞o′bə lē′) *n.* [< OFr. < LL. < Gr. < Heb. *yōbēl,* a ram's horn (trumpet: infl. by L. *jubilum,* wild shout)] **1.** a 50th or 25th anniversary **2.** a time or occasion of rejoicing

judge (juj) *n.* [< OFr. < L. *judex* < *jus,* law + *dicere,* to say] a public official with authority to hear and decide cases in a court of law —*v.* **judged, judg′ing** to hear and pass judgment (on) in a court of law

ju·di·cial (jo͞o dish′əl) *adj.* [< OFr. < L. *judicialis* < *judex,* a judge] of judges, law courts, or their duties —**ju·di′cial·ly** *adv.*

juice (jo͞os) *n.* [< OFr. < L. *jus*] the liquid part of a plant, fruit, or vegetable —*v.* **juiced, juic′ing** ☆ to squeeze juice from

Jul. July

☆ **jum·bo** (jum′bō) *n., pl.* **-bos** [< Gullah *jamba,* elephant; orig. Afr.; infl. by P.T. Barnum's use of it for his elephant, *Jumbo*] a very large person, animal, or thing —*adj.* very large; larger than usual of its kind

jus·tice (jus′tis) *n.* fairness; impartiality

ju·ven·ile (jo͞o′və n'l, -nīl′) *adj.* [< L. < *juvenis,* young] **1.** a) young; youthful b) immature; childish **2.** of, characteristic of, or suitable for children

K

kick (kik) *v.* [ME. *kiken* < ?] to strike out with the foot or feet —*n.* a blow with a foot —**get a kick out of** be delighted or stimulated by

knead (nēd) *v.* [O.E. *cnedan* < IE. base *gen-,* to press together, from which also come knot + knob] to keep pressing and squeezing (dough, clay, etc.) with the hands until it is easy to shape

knife (nīf) *n., pl.,* **knives** [OE. *cnif*] a cutting or stabbing instrument with a blade set in a handle

knock (näk) *v.* [OE. *cnocian*] **1.** to rap on a door **2.** to hit; strike

knoll (nōl) *n.* [OE. *cnoll*] a small, rounded hill

L

la·bor (lā′bər) *n.* [< OFr. < L. *labor*] physical or mental exertion; work —*v.* **1.** to work; toil **2.** to move slowly and with difficulty [the car *labored* up the hill]

lane (lān) *n.* [OE. *lanu*] **1.** a narrow way between hedges, walls, etc.; narrow country road or city street ☆ **2.** a marked strip of road wide enough for a single lane of cars, trucks, etc.

lan·guage (laŋ′gwij) *n.* [< OFr. < *langue,* tongue] **1.** human speech **2.** all the words and ways of combining them common to a particular nation, tribe, etc. [the French *language*]

league¹ (lēg) *n.* [< OFr. < L. *ligare,* to bind] **1.** an agreement made by nations, groups, or individuals for promoting common interests, etc. **2.** an association formed by such an agreement

league² (lēg) *n.* [< OFr. < LL. *leuga,* Gallic mile] an old measure of distance, usually about 3 miles

left-hand·ed (left′ han′ did) *adj.* using the left hand more skillfully than the right [he won the game with a *left-handed* throw] —*adv.* with the left hand [she wrote *left-handed*]

leg·a·cy (leg′ə sē) *n., pl.* **-cies** [< OFr. *legacie* < L. *legatus,* bequest] money or property left to someone by a will

leg·i·ble (lej′ə b'l) *adj.* [< LL. *legibilis* < *legere,* to read] that can be read or read easily [*legible* handwriting] —**leg′i·bil′i·ty** *n.* —**leg′i·bly** *adv.*

leg·is·late (lej′is lāt′) *v.* **-lat′ed, -lat′ing** [< legislator] to make or pass a law or laws

le·git·i·mate (lə jit′ə mit) *adj.* [< ML. pp. of *legitimare,* to make lawful] allowed by law or custom; lawful [a *legitimate* claim] —**le·git′i·mate·ly** *adv.*

life·time (līf′tīm′) *n.* the length of time that someone lives

a	fat	ir	here	ou	out	zh	leisure
ā	ape	ī	bite, fire	u	up	ŋ	ring
ä	car, lot	ō	go	ʉr	fur		a *in* ago
e	ten	ô	law, horn	ch	chin		e *in* agent
er	care	oi	oil	sh	she	ə	= i *in* unity
ē	even	oo	look	th	thin		o *in* collect
i	hit	o͞o	tool	th	then		u *in* focus

lik·a·ble (līk′ə b'l) *adj.* having qualities that make one liked —**lik′a·bil′i·ty** *n.*

like (līk) *v.* **liked, lik′ing** [OE. *lician*] **1.** to be pleased with; enjoy **2.** to want or wish

like·ness (-nis) *n.* something that is like; copy

limb (lim) *n.* [OE. *lim*] **1.** an arm, leg, or wing **2.** a large branch of a tree —☆ **out on a limb** in a dangerous position —**limb′less** *adj.*

lin·er¹ (lī′ nər) *n.* a steamship, passenger airplane, etc. in regular service for a specific lane

lin·er² (lī′ nər) *n.* a lining or something that suggests a lining by fitting inside something else [a helmet *liner*]

lit·er·a·ture (lit′ər ə chər, lit′rə choor′) *n.* [< OFr. < L. *litteratura* < *littera*, a letter] all the writings of a particular time, country, etc., esp. those of lasting value

lo·cal·ize (lō′kə līz′) *v.* **-ized′, -iz′ing** to make local, limit, confine, or trace to a particular area [the pain is *localized* in his hand] —**lo′cal·i·za′tion** *n.*

lo·ca·tion (lo kā′shən) *n.* position, place, situation [a fine *location* for a restaurant]

log·i·cal (läj′i k'l) *adj.* according to the principles of logic, or correct reasoning [a *logical* explanation] —**log′i·cal·ly** *adv.*

-ly (lē) [OE. *-lice* < *-lic*] *a suffix used to form adjectives or adverbs, meaning:* **1.** in a specified manner, to a specified extent or direction, in or at a specified time or place [*harshly, outwardly, hourly*] **2.** in the specified order [*secondly*] **3.** like or suitable to [*fatherly*]

M

mag·nan·i·mous (mag nan′ə məs) *adj.* [< L. < *magnus*, great + *animus*, soul] great in soul; generous in overlooking injury or insult; rising above pettiness or meanness —**mag·nan′i·mous·ly** *adv.*

mag·ni·fy (mag′nə fī′) *v.* **-fied′, -fy′ing** [< OFr. < L. *magnificare*, < *magnus*, great] **1.** to make look larger than actual size [using a microscope to *magnify* bacteria] **2.** to make seem greater, more important, than is really so —**mag′ni·fi′er,** *n.*

mag·ni·tude (mag′nə tood′, -tyood′) *n.* [< L. < *magnus*] greatness, as of size, extent, or influence

main·tain (mān tān′) *v.* [< OFr. *maintenir*, ult. < L. *manu tenere*, to hold in the hand] to keep in a certain condition, as of repair [to *maintain* roads]

make·up, make-up (māk′up′) *n.* **1.** the way in which something is put together [the *makeup* of the atom] **2.** cosmetics

man·age·a·ble (man′ij ə b'l) *adj.* that can be managed —**man′age·a·bil′i·ty** *n.* —**man′age·a·bly** *adv.*

man·i·cure (man′ə kyoor′) *n.* [Fr. < L. *manus*, a hand + *cura*, care] trimming, polishing, etc. of the fingernails —*v.* **-cured′, -cur′ing** to trim, polish, etc. (the fingernails) —**man′i·cur′ist** *n.*

ma·nip·u·late (mə nip′yə lāt′) *v.* **-lat′ed, -lat′ing** to work, operate, or treat with or as with the hands —**ma·nip′u·la′tor** *n.*

man·u·al (man′yoo wəl) *adj.* [< OFr. < L. < *manus*, a hand] **1.** made, done, worked, or used by the hands [*manual* controls] **2.** involving or doing hard physical work requiring use of the hands [*manual* labor] —*n.* a handy book of facts, instructions, etc.; handbook —**man′u·al·ly** *adv.*

man·u·fac·ture (man′yə fak′chər) *v.* **-tured, -tur′ing** [Fr. < ML. < L. < *manus*, a hand + *factura*, a making] to make by hand or, esp., by machinery, often on a large scale

man·u·script (man′yə skript′) *n.* [< L. < *manus*, a hand + pp. of *scribere*, to write] a written or typewritten book, article, etc.

mar·riage (mar′ij) *n.* [OFr. < *marier* < L. < *maritus*, a husband] **1.** the state of being married; wedlock **2.** the act or rite of marrying; wedding

marsh·mal·low (marsh′mel′ō, -mal′ō) *n.* a soft, spongy confection of sugar, starch, corn syrup, and gelatin

mar·vel·ous (mär′v'l əs) *adj.* **1.** causing wonder; extraordinary; incredible **2.** [Colloq.] fine; splendid

mas·ter·piece (mas′tər pēs′) *n.* **1.** a thing made or done with masterly skill **2.** the greatest work made or done by a person or group: also **mas′ter·work′**

mat·tress (mat′ris) *n.* [< OFr. < It. *materasso* < Ar. *matrah*, cushion] a casing of strong cloth filled with cotton, hair, foam rubber, etc., and usually coiled springs, and used on or as a bed

ma·tu·ri·ty (mə toor′ə tē, mə choor′ə tē, mə tyoor′ə tē) *n.* a being full-grown, ripe, or fully developed

mean·while (mēn′hwīl′) *adv.* at the same time

meas·ure (mezh′ər, mā′zhər) *v.* **-ured, -ur·ing**
[< OFr. *mesure* < L. *mensura* < pp. of *metiri,* to
measure] to get or take measurements

meas·ure·ment (-mənt) *n.* quantity determined by
measuring [a waist *measurement* of 32 inches]

me·dic·i·nal (mə dis′ ′n ′l) *adj.* of, or having the
properties of, medicine; curing, relieving
—**me·dic′i·nal·ly** *adv.*

med·i·cine (med′ə s'n) *n.* [< OFr. < L. < *medi-
cus,* physician] **1.** the science of diagnosing,
treating, and preventing disease **2.** any substance, as
a drug, used in treating disease, relieving pain, etc.

Med·i·ter·ra·ne·an (med′i tə rā′nē ən) *adj.* of the
Mediterranean Sea or nearby regions

me·lo·di·ous (mə lō′dē əs) *adj.* pleasing to hear;
tuneful —**me·lo′di·ous·ly** *adv.*
—**me·lo′di·ous·ness** *n.*

mel·o·dy (mel′ə dē) *n.,* *pl.* **-dies** [< OFr. < LL.
< Gr. *melōidia* < *melos,* song + *aeidein,* to sing] a
tune, song, or other pleasing sound

mem·o·rize (mem′ə rīz′) *v.* **-rized′, -riz′ing** ☆ to
fix in one's memory, learn word for word
—**mem′o·ri·za′tion** *n.*

me·nag·er·ie (mə naj′ə rē, -nazh′-) *n.* [< Fr.
< *ménage* < *manoir,* to dwell] a collection of wild
animals kept for exhibit

-ment (mənt, mint) [< OFr. < L. *-mentum*] *a suffix
meaning:* **1.** a result or product [*improvement*] **2.** a
means or instrument [*adornment*] **3.** the act, state, or
art [*movement*]

mer·ci·ful (mur′si fəl) *adj.* full of mercy; having or
showing mercy —**mer′ci·ful·ly** *adv.*

mer·cy (mur′sē) *n.,* *pl.* **-cies** [< OFr. < L. *merces,*
payment, reward] kind or compassionate treatment
[acts of *mercy* were frequent during the flood] —**at
the mercy of** completely in the power of

meth·od (meth′əd) *n.* [< Fr. < L. < Gr.
methodos, pursuit < *meta,* after + *hodos,* a way]
1. a way of doing anything; mode; process; esp., a
regular, orderly procedure or way of teaching, inves-
tigating, etc. **2.** a system in doing things or handling
ideas **3.** regular, orderly arrangement
SYN.—**method** implies a regular, orderly, logical series of
actions for getting something done [a *method* of vulcanizing
rubber]; **manner** applies to a special, often personal,

method [her *manner* of speech]; **mode** refers to a custom-
ary, established, or usual method or manner [the Amish
mode of dress]; **way** is a simple, common, but more general synonym for any of the preceding words [a *way* of
walking, preparing something, etc.]; **fashion,** also a general term, is often used specifically to refer to ways of
dressing, living, etc. that are in style [it is the *fashion* to
wear bright colors]; **system** implies a highly developed,
complicated method [a *system* of government]

mi·gra·tion (mī grā′shən) *n.* **1.** a moving from one
place to another **2.** a group of people, or of birds,
etc., migrating together

☆ **mile·age** (mīl′ij) *n.* **1.** total number of miles trav-
eled, recorded, etc. **2.** the number of miles a motor
vehicle will go on a gallon of fuel, a tire will run
before it wears out, etc.

mim·ic (mim′ik) *n.* [< L. < Gr. < *mimos,* a mime]
a person or thing that imitates —*v.* **mim′icked,
mim′ick·ing** to imitate in speech or action, to copy
closely [parakeets *mimic* human voices]
—**mim′ick·er** *n.*

mi·rage (mi räzh′) *n.* [Fr. < (se) *mirer,* to be re-
flected] an optical illusion in which the image of a
distant object, as an oasis, is made to appear nearby

mis·sile (mis′′l) *n.* [L. *missilis* < pp. of *mittere,* to
send] an object designed to be thrown or shot toward
a target

mis·sion·ar·y (mish′ən er′ē) *n.,* *pl.* **-ar′ies** a person sent out by a church to spread its religion

mis·spell (mis spel′) *v.* **-spelled′** or **-spelt′,
-spell′ing** to spell incorrectly

mo·lec·u·lar (mə lek′yə lər) *adj.* of, produced by,
or existing between molecules —**mo·lec′u·lar·ly** *adv.*

mol·e·cule (mäl′ə kyōōl′) *n.* [< Fr. < Mod L.
molecula, dim. of L. *moles,* a mass] the smallest
particle of an element or compound that can exist in
the free state and still retain the characteristics of the
element or compound

a	fat	ir	here	ou	out	zh	leisure
ā	ape	ī	bite, fire	u	up	ŋ	ring
ä	car, lot	ō	go	ur	fur		a *in* ago
e	ten	ô	law, horn	ch	chin		e *in* agent
er	care	oi	oil	sh	she	ə = i *in* unity
ē	even	oo	look	th	thin		o *in* collect
i	hit	ōō	tool	th	then		u *in* focus

197

mo·men·tous (mō men′təs) *adj.* of great importance [a *momentous* decision]

Mon. Monday

mon·ar·chy (män′ər kē) *n., pl.* **-ar′chies** a government headed by a hereditary ruler, such as a king or queen

mon·o·cle (män′ə k'l) *n.* [Fr. < LL. *monoculus*, one-eyed < Gr. *monos*, single + L. *oculus*, eye] an eyeglass for one eye only

mon·o·logue (män′ə lôg′, -läg′) *n.* [Fr. < Gr. < *monos*, alone + *legein*, to speak] a poem, story, or part of a play in which one character speaks alone

mon·u·ment (män′yə mənt) *n.* [OFr. < L. *monumentum* < *monere*, to warn] something set up to keep alive the memory of a person or event, as a tablet, statue, building, etc.

moon (mōōn) *n.* [OE. *mona*] the satellite of the earth, that revolves around it once in 29½ days and shines at night —**once in a blue moon** very seldom; hardly ever [I watch TV *once in a blue moon*]

mort·gage (môr′gij) *n.* [< OFr. < *mort*, dead + *gage*, gage] an agreement in which a person borrowing money gives the lender a claim to a certain piece of property as a pledge that the debt will be paid

mos·qui·to (mə skēt′ ō, -ə) *n., pl.,* **-toes, -tos** [Sp. & Port., dim. of *mosca* < L. *musca*, a fly] a two-winged insect, the female of which has skin-piercing, bloodsucking mouthparts

mound (mound) *n.* [< ? MDu. *mond*, protection] **1.** a heap or bank of earth, sand, etc., whether built or natural; small hill **2.** any heap or pile ☆ **3.** *Baseball* the slightly raised area on which the pitcher must stand when pitching

mov·a·ble (mōō′ və b'l) *adj.* that can be moved from one place to another

move (mōōv) *v.* **moved, mov′ing** [< Anglo-Fr. < OFr. < L. *movere* < IE. base *mew-*, to push away] **1.** to change the place or position of **2.** to arouse the emotions of **3.** to change the place where one lives

move·ment (mōōv′mənt) *n.* **1.** an action or motion **2.** organized action by people working toward some goal **3.** tendency; trend

mug·gy (mug′ē) *adj.* **-gi·er, -gi·est** [prob. < or akin to ON. *mugga*, a drizzle < IE. base *meuk-*, slippery] hot, damp, and close [*muggy* weather] —**mug′ gi·ness** *n.*

mul·ti·ply (mul′tə plī′) *v.* **-plied′, -ply′ing** [< OFr. < L. *multiplicare* < *multiplex* < *multus*, many + *-plex*, -fold] **1.** to cause to increase in number **2.** *Math* to find the product of by multiplication

mur·mur (mur′mər) *n.* [< OFr. < L.: echoic word] **1.** a low, indistinct, continuous sound, as of a stream, far-off voices, etc. **2.** a mumbled complaint —*v.* to make a murmur —**mur′mur·ing** *adj.*

mus·cle (mus′'l) *n.* [Fr. < L. *musculus*, dim. of *mus*, mouse] **1.** any of the fleshy parts of the body made up of bundles of cells or fibers that can be contracted and expanded to produce bodily movements **2.** the tissue making up such a fleshy part

mu·sic (myōō′zik) *n.* [OFr. < L. < Gr. *mousiké* (*technē*), musical (art) < *mousa*, a Muse] any rhythmic sequence of pleasing sounds ☆ **face the music** to accept the consequences

mu·si·cal (myōō′zi k'l) *adj.* **1.** of or for the creation or performance of music **2.** melodious **3.** fond of or skilled in music —**mu′si·cal·ly** *adv.*

my·self (mī self′, mə self′) *pron.* a form of the first person singular pronoun

mys·ti·fy (mis′tə fī′) *v.* **-fied′, -fy′ing** [< Fr. < *mystère*, mystery + *-fier*, -fy] to puzzle or perplex —**mys′ti·fi·ca′tion** *n.*

N

name (nām) *n.* [OE. *nama* < IE. base (o) *nomn-*, from which also come L. *nomen* + Gr. *onoma*] a word or phrase by which a person or thing is known —*v.* **named, nam′ing** to give a name to —**name′a·ble, nam′a·ble** *adj.*

name·ly (nām′lē) *adv.* that is to say [a choice of two desserts, *namely*, cake or pie]

nar·ra·tion (na rā′shən) *n.* **1.** a telling of a story **2.** a story or account —**nar·ra′tion·al** *adj.*

nar·ra·tive (när′ə tiv) *n.* a story; account; tale

na·tion (nā′shən) *n.* [< OFr. < L. *natio* < pp. of *nasci*, to be born] people with a territory, history, culture, and language in common

na·tion·al (nash′ə n′l) *adj.* of a nation or the nation [the *national* anthem] —**na′tion·al·ly** *adv.*

naugh·ty (nôt′ē) *adj.* **-ti·er, -ti·est** [< obs. *naught,* wicked] not behaving properly; mischievous or disobedient —**naugh′ti·ly** *adv.*

NE, N.E., n.e. 1. northeast **2.** northeastern

neg·lect·ful (ni glekt′fəl) *adj.* neglecting; heedless; negligent (often with *of*) —**neg·lect′ful·ly** *adv.*

neigh·bor·hood (nā′bər hood′) *n.* **1.** a district or area of a city, town etc. (an old *neighborhood*] **2.** people living near one another; community [the whole *neighborhood* helped]

-ness (nis, nəs) [OE. *-nes(s)*] *a suffix meaning* state, quality, or instance of being [*greatness, sadness*]

news·cast (nōōz′kast′, nyōōz′-) *n.* [news + (broad) cast] a program of news that is broadcast over radio or TV —**news′cast′er** *n.* —**news′cast′ing** *n.*

night·time (nīt′tīme′) *n.* the period of darkness from sunset to sunrise

ninety-four (nīn′tē fôr) *adj.* one more than ninety-three [this book has been around for *ninety-four* years] *n.* four and ninety [the final count was *ninety-four*]

north·east (nôrth′ēst′) *n.* the direction halfway between north and east —*adj.* **1.** in, of, to, or toward the northeast **2.** from the northeast [there was a *northeast* wind] —☆ **the Northeast** the northeastern part of the U.S., esp. New England

no·tice·a·ble (nōt′is ə b′l) *adj.* readily noticed; easily seen; conspicuous —**not′tice·a·bly** *adv.*

no·ti·fy (nōt′ə fī′) *v.* **-fied′, -fy′ing** [< MFr. < L. < *notus* + *facere,* to make] to give notice to; inform

N.Y., NY New York

O

o·blige (ə blīj′, ō-) *v.* **o·bliged′, o·blig′ing** [< OFr. < L. *obligare* < *ob-,* to + *ligare,* to bind] to make indebted for a kindness, do a favor for [I am much *obliged* for your help]

ob·serv·ance (əb zur′vəns, äb-) *n.* the act or practice of observing a law, duty, custom, etc.

ob·tain (əb tān′, äb-) *v.* [< OFr. < L. *obtinere* < *ob-* + *tenere,* to hold] to get possession of by effort —**ob·tain′a·ble** *adj.*

oc·cur (ə kur′) *v.* **-curred′, -cur′ring** [< L. *occurrere* < *ob-,* against + *currere,* to run] **1.** to present itself; come to mind [an idea *occurred* to him] **2.** to take place; happen [the accident *occurred* last week]

oc·cur·rence (ə kur′əns) *n.* something that occurs; event; incident

o·cean (ō′shən) *n.* (< OFr. < L. *oceanus* < Gr. *Ōkeanos*] **1.** the great body of salt water that covers about 71% of the earth's surface **2.** any of its five principal divisions: the Atlantic, Pacific, Indian, Arctic, or Antarctic Ocean —**o·ce·an·ic** (ō′shē an′ik) *adj.*

of·fense (ə fens′; ô′fens, ä′-) *n.* **1.** a breaking of the law; sin or crime **2.** the side that is seeking to score in any contest

of·fer (ôf′ər, äf′-) *v.* [OE. *offrian* < LL. *offerre,* to sacrifice] to present for acceptance or consideration [to *offer* one's services]

o·mit (ō mit′) *v.* **o·mit′ted, o·mit′ting** [< L. *omittere* < *ob-* + *mittere,* to send] to fail to include; leave out [to *omit* a name from the roster]

one-half (wun haf′) *n.* one of the two equal parts of a whole

o·paque (ō pāk′) *adj.* [L. *opacus,* shady] not letting light through; not transparent [an *opaque* screen] —**o·paque′ly** *adv.*

op·er·a·tion (äp′ə rā′shən) *n.* **1.** the condition of being in action or at work **2.** a treatment by surgery

op·po·nent (ə pō′nənt) *n.* [< L. prp. of *opponere* < *ob-,* against + *ponere,* to set] one who opposes, as in a fight, game, etc.; adversary

op·por·tu·ni·ty (äp′ər tōō′nə tē, tyōō′-) *n. pl.* **-ties** a good chance or occasion, as to advance oneself

a	fat	ir	here	ou	out	zh	leisure
ā	ape	ī	bite, fire	u	up	ŋ	ring
ä	car, lot	ō	go	ur	fur		a *in* ago
e	ten	ô	law, horn	ch	chin		e *in* agent
er	care	oi	oil	sh	she	ə = i *in* unity
ē	even	oo	look	th	thin		o *in* collect
i	hit	ōō	tool	*th*	then		u *in* focus

op·ti·cal (äp′tik ′l) *adj.* **1.** of the sense of sight; visual [an *optical* illusion] **2.** for aiding vision [eyeglasses are *optical* instruments] —**op′ ti·cal·ly** *adv.*

op·ti·mism (ap′tə miz'm) *n.* [< Fr. < L. *optimus,* best] the tendency to take the most hopeful or cheerful view of matters —**op′ti·mist** (-mist) *n.* —**op′ti·mis′tic, op′ti·mis′ti·cal** *adj.* —**op′ti·mis′ti·cal·ly** *adv.*

or·a·tor·i·cal (ôr′ə tôr′i k′l, är′-) *adj.* of or characteristic of orators or oratory —**or′a·tor′i·cal·ly** *adv.*

or·a·to·ry (ôr′ə tôr′ē, är′-) *n., pl.* **-ries** [L. *oratoria*] the art of an orator; skill in public speaking

or·bit (ôr′bit) *n.* [< MFr. < ML. < L. *orbita,* path < *orbis,* a circle] the path of a heavenly body, satellite, or spacecraft revolving around another body —**or′bit·al** *adj.*

ought (ôt) *v.* [orig., pt. of *owe*] to be probable or expected [it *ought* to be over soon]

out·ra·geous (out rā′jəs) *adj.* so wrong or uncontrolled as to be shocking [to charge *outrageous* prices] —**out·ra′geous·ly** *adv.*

P

pa·ja·mas (pə jam′əz, -jä′məz) *n. pl.* [< Hindi < Per. *pāi,* a leg + *jāma,* garment] a loosely fitting sleeping or lounging suit consisting of a jacket, or pullover blouse, and trousers —**pa·ja′ma** *adj.*

palm¹ (päm; *occas.* pälm) *n.* [OE. < L. *palma:* from its handlike fronds] any of a family of tropical or subtropical trees with a tall, branching trunk and large leaves at the top

palm² (päm; *occas.* pälm) *n.* [< OFr. < L. *palma* < IE *pele-,* flat and broad] the inner surface of the hand between fingers and wrist

pa·per·weight (pā′pər wāt′) *n.* any small, heavy object set on papers to keep them from being scattered

par·ent (per′ənt, par′-) *n.* [OFr. < L. *parens,* parent, orig. prp. of *parere,* to beget] a father or mother —**pa·ren·tal** (pə ren′t′l) *adj.* —**pa·ren′tal·ly** *adv.* —**par′ent·hood′** *n.*

par·ti·cle (pär′ti k′l) *n.* [< MFr. < L. *particula,* dim. of *pars,* part] a tiny fragment; speck

par·ti·san (pärt′ə z'n, -s'n) *n.* [MFr. < It. *partigiano* < L. *pars,* part] a strong supporter of a side

par·ti·tion (pär tish′ən, pər-) *n.* [< L. *partitio*] something that divides, as a wall separating rooms —**par·ti′tioned** *adj.*

pas·teur·ize (pas′chə rīz′, pas′tə-) *v.* **-ized, -iz′ing** [after L. Pasteur (1822–95), Fr. chemist who invented it] to subject (milk, beer, etc.) to heating in order to destroy bacteria

pa·ter·nal (pə tʉr′n′l) *adj.* [< L. < *pater,* father] of or like a father; fatherly —**pa·ter′nal·ly** *adv.*

pa·tri·arch (pā′trē ärk′) *n.* [< L. < Gr., ult, < *patēr,* father + *archein,* to rule] **1.** the father and ruler of a family or tribe **2.** a person thought of as the founder of a religion, business, etc. —**pa′tri·ar′chal** *adj.*

pa·trol (pə trōl′) *v.* **-trolled′, -trol′ling** [Fr. *patrouiller,* to paddle] to make regular, repeated trips around (an area, camp, etc.), as in guarding —*n.* a person or group patrolling —**pa·trol′ler** *n.*

☆ **pe·can** (pi kan′, -kän′; pē′kan, -kän) *n.* [< Algonquian *pakan*] **1.** an oval, edible nut with a thin, smooth shell **2.** the N. American tree on which it grows

ped·es·tal (ped′is t'l) *n.* [< Fr. < It. < *piè,* a foot + *di,* of + *stal,* a rest] the bottom support of a column, statue, etc.

pe·des·tri·an (pə des′trē ən) *adj.* [< L. *pedester* < *pedis,* genitive of *pes,* a foot + -*ian*] of or for pedestrians [a *pedestrian* crossing] —*n.* one who goes on foot; a walker

per- *a prefix meaning* through, throughout, thoroughly [*perceive, persuade*]

per·cent (pər sent′) *adv., adj.* [< It. < L. *per centum*] in or for every hundred [a 20 *percent* rate means 20 in every hundred]

per·fo·rate (pʉr′fə rāt′) *v.* **-rat′ed, -rat′ing** [< L. pp. of *perforare* < *per,* through + *forare,* to bore] to make a hole through, as by punching

per·fo·ra·tion (pʉr′fə rā′shən) *n.* any of a series of punched holes

per·form (pər fôrm′) *v.* **1.** to act on so as to complete; do (a task, etc.) **2.** to play or enact (a piece of music, a dramatic role, etc.) —**per·form′er** *n.*

pe·ri·od·ic (pir′ē äd′ik) *adj.* appearing or coming again at regular intervals [a *periodic* fever]

pe·ri·od·i·cal·ly (pir′ē äd′ik ′l ē, -ik lē) *adv.* at regular intervals

per·mis·si·ble (pər mis′ə b′l) *adj.* that can be permitted; allowable —**per·mis′si·bil′i·ty** *n.*

per·mit (pər mit′; *for n., usually* pʉr′mit) *v.*
-mit′ted, -mit′ting [< L. *per*, through + *mittere*, to send] to allow; consent to [smoking is not *permitted*] —*n.* a document granting permission; license

per·son·al·ize (pʉr′s′n ə līz′) *v.* **-ized′, -iz′ing** to have marked with one's name or initials [*personalized* checks]

per·tain (pər tān′) *v.* [< OFr. < L. *pertinere*, to reach < *per-*, thoroughly + *tenere*, to hold] to belong; be connected or associated [lands *pertaining* to an estate]

phi·lan·thro·py (fi lan′thrə pē) *n.* [< LL. < Gr. < *philein*, to love + *anthrōpos*, man] a desire to help mankind, as by gifts to charitable institutions —**phi·lan′thro·pist** *n.*

phil·o·soph·ic (fil′ ə säf′ik) *adj.* calm, as in a difficult situation, reasonable [she was *philosophic* about losing her purse] also **phil′o·soph′i·cal** —**phil′o·soph′i·cal·ly** *adv.*

phi·los·o·phy (fi läs′ə fē) *n., pl.* **-phies** [< OFr. < L. < Gr. *philos*, loving + *sophos*, wise] **1.** the study of the basic nature of conduct, thought, knowledge, existence, and reality **2.** a particular system of principles for the conduct of life [Plato's *philosophy*]

pho·bi·a (fō′bē ə) *n.* [< Gr. *phobos*, a fear] a strong, unreasonable, continuing fear of some particular thing or situation —**pho′bic, *adj.***

phy·si·cian (fə zish′ən) *n.* [< OFr. < L. *physica*, natural science] a person licensed to practice medicine; doctor of medicine

phy·sique (fi zēk′) *n.* [Fr.] the form or build of one's body [a muscular *physique*]

pic·nic (pik′nik) *n.* [< Fr., prob. < *piquer*, to pick + *nique*, a trifle] an outing during which a meal is eaten outdoors —*v.* **-nicked, -nick·ing** to hold or go on a picnic —**pic′nick·er** *n.*

pic·tur·esque (pik′chə resk′) *adj.* **1.** like a picture; having natural beauty; quaint [a *picturesque* village] **2.** suggesting a mental picture; vivid [a *picturesque* description]

pier (pir) *n.* [ML. *pera*, ult. < ? or akin to L. *petra*, stone] a structure built out over water and supported by pillars: used as a landing place, a walk, etc.

pi·lot (pī′lət) *n.* [< MFr. < It. *pilota*, ult. < Gr. *pēdon*, oar blade] a person who handles the controls of an aircraft, spacecraft, or ship —*v.* to act as a pilot of, on, in, or over —**pi′lot·less** *adj.*

pine·ap·ple (pīn′ ap′ ′l) *n.* [ME. *pinappel*, pine cone] **1.** a juicy tropical fruit looking somewhat like a pine cone **2.** the plant it grows on, with spiny-edged leaves

place (plās) *n.* [OFr. < L. *platea* < Gr. *plateria*, a street] **1.** the part of space occupied by a person or thing **2.** a city, town, or village **3.** a dwelling **4.** a spot or part of something [a sore *place* on the leg] —*v.* **placed, plac′ing** to put in a particular place or condition

place·ment (plās′mənt) *n.* location or arrangement

plan (plan) *n.* [Fr., plan < MFr. *plant* < It. *pianta* < L. *planta*, sole of the foot] a scheme, program, or diagram for making, doing, or arranging something —*v.* **planned, plan′ning** to think of a way of doing, making, etc. —**plan′ner** *n.*

plaque (plak) *n.* [Fr. < MDu. *placke*, a disk] any thin, flat piece of metal, wood, etc. with a design, etc., used to decorate or to commemorate something

pla·teau (pla tō′) *n., pl.* **-teaus′, -teaux′** (-tōz′) [Fr. < OFr. < *plat*, flat object] an elevated area of more or less level land

play·wright (plā′rīt′) *n.* a writer of plays; dramatist

pleas·ure (plezh′ər, plā′zhər) *n.* a pleased feeling; enjoyment; delight

pledge (plej) *n.* [< OFr. or ML., prob. < OS. *plegan*, to guarantee] **1.** a token or symbol of something [he gave her a locket as a *pledge* of his love] **2.** a promise or agreement [the *pledge* of allegiance to the flag ☆ **3.** a person serving a trial period before he is initiated into a fraternity —*v.* to bind by a promise

a	fat	ir	here	ou	out	zh	leisure
ā	ape	ī	bite, fire	u	up	ŋ	ring
ä	car, lot	ō	go	ʉr	fur		a *in* ago
e	ten	ô	law, horn	ch	chin		e *in* agent
er	care	oi	oil	sh	she	ə = i *in* unity
ē	even	oo	look	th	thin		o *in* collect
i	hit	oō	tool	th	then		u *in* focus

plight (plīt) *n.* [< Anglo-Fr. *plit*, for OFr. *pleit*, a fold] an awkward, sad, or dangerous situation

po·lice (pə lēs′) *n.* [Fr. < LL. <Gr. *politeia*, the state < *politēs*, citizen < *polis*, city < IE. base *pel-*, fortress] **1.** the governmental department (of a city, state, etc.) for keeping order, enforcing the law, making arrests, and preventing crimes **2.** [*with pl. v.*] the members of such a department, or of a private organization like this [security *police*] —*v.* **-liced′, -lic′ing** to control, protect, etc. with police or the like [to *police* the streets]

pol·i·tic (päl′ə tik) *adj.* [< MFr. < L. < Gr. < *politēs*, citizen < *polis*, city] having practical wisdom; prudent —*v.* **-ticked, -tick·ing** to engage in political campaigning

po·lit·i·cal (pə lit′i k′l) *adj.* **1.** of or concerned with government, politics, etc. [*political* science] **2.** engaged in politics [*political* parties] —**po·lit′i·cal·ly** *adv.*

pol·i·tics (päl′ə tiks) *n., pl.* [*with sing. or pl. v.*] **1.** the science of government; political science **2.** political affairs

port·a·ble (pôr′tə b′l) *adj.* [< L. *portare*, to carry] that can be carried —**port′a·bil′i·ty** *n.*

pos·si·ble (päs′ə b′l) *adj.* [OFr. < L. < *posse*, to be able] that can be

post- *a prefix meaning* after, following [*postwar*]

post·date (pōst′dāt′) *v.* **-dat′ed, -dat′ing** to put a date on that is later than the actual date

post·pone (pōst pōn′, pōs-) —*v.* **-poned′, -pon′ing** [< L. *post*, after + *ponere*, to put] to put off until later; delay [I *postponed* my trip because of illness] —**post·pon′a·ble** *adj.* —**post·pone′ment** *n.*

post·script (pōst′skript′, pōs′-) *n.* [< ModL. < L. pp. of *postscribere* < *post-*, after + *scribere*, to write] a note added below the signature of a letter

post·war (pōst′wôr′) *adj.* after war

pre- *a prefix meaning* before in time, place, or rank [*prewar*]

pre·cau·tion (pri kô′shən) *n.* [< Fr. < LL. < L. pp. of *praecavere* < *prae-*, before + *cavere*, to take care] care taken beforehand; careful foresight —**pre·cau′tion·ar′y** *adj.*

pre·cede (pri sēd′) *v.* **-ced′ed, -ced′ing** [< MFr. < L. < *prae-*, before + *cedere*, to go] to be, come, or go before in time, order, rank, importance, etc. [she *preceded* him into the room; a colonel *precedes* a major]

pre·ci·sion (pri sizh′ən) *n.* exactness; accuracy [the *precision* of a watch]

pre·dic·tion (pri dik′shən) *n.* something foretold; prophecy

pre·fer (pri fur′) *v.* **-ferred′, -fer′ring** [< MFr. < L. < *prae-*, before + *ferre*, to bear] to choose first; like better [he *prefers* baseball to football]

pref·er·ence (pref′ər əns, pref′rəns) *n.* a preferring; greater liking [a *preference* for lively music]

pre·med·i·tate (pri med′ə tāt′) *v.* **-tat′ed, -tat′ing** to think out or plan beforehand [a *premeditated* murder] —**pre·med′i·tat′ed** *adj.*

pre·scrip·tion (pri skrip′shən) *n.* **1.** an order, rule, or direction **2.** a doctor's written direction

pres·sure (presh′ər) *n.* [OFr. < L. *pressura* < pp. of *premere*, to press] **1.** a pressing or being pressed **2.** a state of trouble or strain that is hard to bear [overcome by *pressure*] *v.* **-sured, -sur·ing**

pre·tend (pri tend′) *v.* [< L. < *prae-*, before + *tendere*, to stretch] **1.** to claim or profess falsely [to *pretend* illness] **2.** to make believe, as in play [to *pretend* to be astronauts]

pre·ven·tion (pri ven′shən) *n.* a keeping from happening [*prevention* of crime]

priv·i·lege (priv′′l ij, priv′lij) *n.* [< OFr. < L. *privilegium*, a law for or against an individual] a right, advantage, favor, etc. specially granted to a certain person, group, or class

pro- *a prefix meaning:* **1.** forward or ahead [*progress*] **2.** forth [*produce*]

pro·ceed (prə sēd′, prō-) *v.* [< L. < *pro-*, forward + *cedere*, to go] to advance or go on, esp. after stopping

proc·ess (präs′es) *n.* [< OFr. < L. pp. of *procedere* < *pro-*, forward + *cedere*, to go] a particular method of making or doing something, in which there are a number of steps —*v.* to prepare by or subject to a process

pro·ces·sion (prə sesh′ən, prō-) *n.* [< L. < *procedere* < *pro-*, forward + *cedere*, to go] a number of persons or things moving forward, as in a parade, in an orderly way

pro·cras·ti·nate (prō kras′tə nāt′, prə-) *v.* **-nat′ed, -nat′ing** [< L. pp. of *procrastinare*, ult. < *pro-*, forward + *cras*, tomorrow] to put off doing [something] until later; delay —**pro·cras′ti·na′tion** *n.* —**pro·cras′ti·na′tor** *n.*

pro·fes·sion (prə fesh′ən) *n.* **1.** an occupation requiring advanced education, as medicine, law, or teaching **2.** loosely, any occupation

pro·fes·sion·al (prə fesh′ən′l) *adj.* of, engaged in, or worthy of the standards of, a profession —*n.* person who does something with great skill —**pro·fes′sion·al·ism** *n.* —**pro·fes′sion·al·ly** *adv.*

pro·fi·cient (prə fish′ənt) *adj.* [< L. prp. of *proficere*, to advance] highly competent; skilled [a *proficient* golfer] —**pro·fi′cien·cy** (-ən sē) *n., pl.* **-cies** —**pro·fi′cient·ly** *adv.*

pro·gram (prō′gram, -grəm) *n.* [< Fr. < LL. < Gr. *programma*, an edict] the acts, speeches, musical pieces, etc. that make up an entertainment, ceremony, etc. —*v.* **-grammed**, or **-gramed**, **-gram·ming** or **-gram·ing** to schedule in a program —**pro′gram·mer, pro′gram·er** *n.*

pro·gres·sion (prə gresh′ən) *n.* a moving forward or onward

pro·logue (prō′lôg, -läg) *n.* [< MFr. < L. < Gr. < *pro-*, before + *logos*, a discourse] introductory lines spoken by an actor before a dramatic performance

pro·long (prə lôŋ′) *v.* [< MFr. < LL. < L. *pro-*, forth + *longus*, long] to lengthen in time or space [we *prolonged* our visit by another day]

proof·read (proof′rēd′) *v.* to read and mark corrections on —**proof′read′er** *n.*

pro·pel (prə pel′) *v.* **-pelled′, -pel′ling** [< L. < *pro-*, forward + *pellere*, to drive] to push, drive, or make go forward [a rocket *propelled* by liquid fuel]

pro·pel·ler (prə pel′ər) *n.* a device consisting of rotating blades used for driving a ship or aircraft

pro·pose (prə pōz′) *v.* **-posed′, -pos′ing** [< OFr. < L. pp. of *proponere*] to put forth for consideration or acceptance [we *propose* that the city build a zoo]

pros·pect (präs′pekt) *n.* [L. *prospectus*, lookout] **1.** the view from any particular point; outlook **2.** something hoped for —*v.* ☆ to explore or search (*for*) [to *prospect* for gold]

psy·chic (sī′kik) *adj.* [< Gr. < *psychē*, the soul] of the psyche, or mind [*psychic* processes]

psy·chol·o·gy (sī käl′ə jē) *n., pl.* **-gies** [< ModL < Gr. *psychē*, soul + *-logy* (study of)] the science that studies the mind and the reasons for the ways people think and act

pulse (puls) *n.* [< OFr., ult. < L. pp. of *pellere*, to beat < IE. base *pel-*, to beat] **1.** the regular beating in the arteries, caused by the contractions of the heart **2.** any regular or rhythmical beat, signal, etc. —*v.* **pulsed, puls′ing** to beat or throb [the music *pulsed* in his ears] —**puls′er** *n.*

punc·tu·a·tion (puŋk′choo wā′shən) *n.* the use of standardized marks in writing and printing to separate sentences or parts of a sentence or to make meaning clearer

Q

quad·ran·gle (kwäd′raŋ′g′l) *n.* [< MFr. < LL. < fem. of L. base of *quattuor*, four + *angulus*, angle] a plane figure with four angles and four sides

quad·ru·ped (kwäd′roo ped′) *n.* [< L.< *quadru-*, four + *pes*, a foot] an animal, esp. a mammal, with four feet

quad·ru·ple (kwä droo′p′l, -drup′′l, kwäd′roo-) *n.* [MFr. < L. < *quadru-*, four + *-plus*, -fold] —*n.* an amount four times as much or as many —*v.* **-pled, -pling** to make or become four times as much or as many

quar·rel (kwôr′əl, kwär′-) *n.* [< OFr. < L. *querela*, complaint] a dispute, esp. one marked by anger and resentment —*v.* **-reled, -rel·ing** to dispute heatedly —**quar′rel·er, quar′rel·ler** *n.*

quar·ter (kwôr′tər) *n.* [< OFr. < L. *quartarius*, a fourth < *quartus*, fourth] **1.** any of the four equal parts of something; fourth **2.** a coin of the U.S. and Canada equal to 25 cents or one fourth of a dollar

a	fat	ir	here	ou	out	zh	leisure
ā	ape	ī	bite, fire	u	up	ŋ	ring
ä	car, lot	ō	go	ʉr	fur		a *in* ago
e	ten	ô	law, horn	ch	chin		e *in* agent
er	care	oi	oil	sh	she	ə = i *in* unity
ē	even	oo	look	th	thin		o *in* collect
i	hit	ōo	tool	th	then		u *in* focus

quar·ter·ly (kwôr′tər lē) *adj.* occurring or appearing at regular intervals four times a year

quick (kwik) *adj.* [OE. *cwicu,* living] rapid in action; swift [a *quick* walk] —**quick′ly** *adv.* —**quick′ness** *n.*

qui·et (kwī′ət) *adj.* [< OFr. < L. *quietus,* pp. of *quiescere,* to keep quiet] **1.** still, calm, motionless **2.** not speaking, silent —**qui′et·ly** *adv.* —**qui′et·ness** *n.*

quilt (kwilt) *n.* [< OFr. < L. *culcita,* a bed] a bedcover made of two layers of cloth filled with down, wool, etc. and stitched together in lines or patterns —*v.* to stitch as or like a quilt [*quilt* a potholder]

quin·tet (kwin tet′) *n.* [< Fr. < It. dim of *quinto* < L. *quintus,* a fifth] any group of five

quin·tu·plet (kwin tup′lit, -tōō′plit, -tyōō′-; kwin′too plit) *n.* any of five offspring born at a single birth

quip (kwip) *n.* [< L. *quippe,* indeed] a witty or sarcastic remark, jest —*v.* **quipped, quip′ping** to utter quips

quite (kwīt) *adv.* [ME form of quit] **1.** completely; entirely [not *quite* done] **2.** really; truly [*quite* a hero]

quot·a·ble (kwōt′ə b′l) *adj.* worthwhile quoting or suitable for quotation

quo·ta·tion (kwō tā′shən) *n.* **1.** the act of quoting **2.** the words or passage quoted

quote (kwōt) *v.* **quot′ed, quot′ing** [< ML. *quotare,* to number (chapters, etc.) < L. *quotus,* of what number] to repeat a passage from or statement of

quo·tient (kwō′shənt) *n.* [< L. *quoties,* how often < *quot,* how many] the result obtained when one number is divided by another [in 32 ÷ 8 = 4, the number 4 is the *quotient*]

R

ral·ly (ral′ē) *v.* **-lied, -ly·ing** [< Fr. < OFr. < *re-,* again + *alier,* to join] to come together for a common purpose [the students *rallied* to cheer the football team] —*n., pl.* **-lies 1.** a rallying or being rallied; specif., a mass meeting [a political *rally*]

rap·port (ra pôr′, -pôrt′) *n.* [Fr. < OFr. < *re-,* again + *aporter,* to carry] relationship, esp. of a sympathetic kind; agreement; harmony

rare (rer) *adj.* **rar′er, rar′est** [MFr. < L. *rarus*] not often seen, done, found, etc.; uncommon [radium is a *rare* element] —**rare′ness** *n.*

SYN.—**rare** is applied to something of which there are not many examples and usually suggests great value [a *rare* gem]; **infrequent** applies to that which occurs only once in a long while [his *infrequent* trips]; **uncommon** and **unusual** refer to that which does not ordinarily happen and is therefore remarkable [her *uncommon* generosity; this *unusual* heat]; **scarce** applies to something of which there is, at the moment, not enough [potatoes are *scarce* these days]

rare·ly (rer′lē) *adv.* not often; seldom

rar·i·ty (rer′ə tē) *n.* uncommonness; scarcity

rasp·ber·ry (raz′ber′ē, -bər ē) *n., pl.* **-ries** [earlier *raspis berry* < *raspis,* raspberry] a small, juicy, edible fruit having a cluster of red, purple, or black drupelets

re- *a prefix meaning:* **1.** back [*repay*] **2.** again [*reappear*]

re·al·ize (rē′ə līz′) *v.* **-ized′, -iz′ing 1.** to make real; bring into being [to *realize* one's ambitions] **2.** to understand fully or clearly [only then did he *realize* he was lost] —**re′al·i·za′tion** *n.*

reb·el (reb′'l; for *v.* ri bel′) *n.* [< OFr. < L. < *re-,* again + *bellare,* to war < *bellum*] a person who resists any authority or controls —*v.* **-elled′, -el′ling** to resist any authority or controls

re·bel·lion (ri bel′yən) *n.* [< MFr. < L.] a fight or struggle against any authority or controls

re·cede (ri sēd′) *v.* **-ced′ed, -ced′ing** to go or move back

re·cent (rē′s'nt) *adj.* [MFr. < L. *recens* < *re-,* again + base akin to Gr. *kainos,* new] of a time just before the present —**re′cent·ly** *adv.*

re·ces·sion (ri sesh′ən) *n.* [L. *recessio* < pp. of *recedere,* to recede] **1.** a going backward; withdrawal **2.** a temporary falling off of business activity

rec·om·mend (rek′ə mend′) *v.* [< ML. *re-,* back + *commendare* < *com-,* very much + *mandare,* to command] **1.** to suggest, favorably [to *recommend* a book] **2.** to advise; counsel [I *recommend* that we stop here]

re·cur (ri kur′) *v.* **-curred′, -cur′ring** [< L. *re-,* back + *currere,* to run] to happen or appear again or from time to time [his fever *recurs* every few months]

re·dou·ble (rē dub′′l) *v.* **-bled, -bling** [MFr. *redoubler* < ML. *re-*, back + OFr. *duble, doble* < L. *duplus*, lit., twofold] **1.** to make twice as much or twice as great **2.** to make much greater [to *redouble* one's efforts]

re·fer (ri fʉr′) *v.* **-ferred′, -fer′ring** [< MFr. < L. *referre* < *re-*, back + *ferre*, to bear] to direct (to someone or something) for aid, information, etc.

ref·er·ence (ref′ər əns, ref′rəns) *n.* **1.** the direction of attention to a person or thing **2.** a source of information: often used like an adjective [*reference* book]

re·form (ri fôrm′) *v.* [< OFr. < L. *reformare* < *re-*, again + *forma*, form] to make better by removing faults; stopping wrongs —**re·formed′** *adj.*

re·frig·er·ate (ri frig′ə rāt′) *v.* **-at′ed, -at′ing** [< L. pp. of *refrigerare* < *re-*, thoroughly + *frigerare*, to cool < *frigus*, cold] to make or keep cool or cold; chill —**re·frig′er·a′tion** *n.*

re·fus·al (ri fyōo′z′l) *n.* the act of refusing

re·gres·sion (ri gresh′ən) *n.* a going back; movement backward

re·gret (ri gret′) *v.* **-gret′ted, -gret′ting** [< OFr. *regreter*, to mourn] to feel troubled or guilty over —*n.* a troubled feeling or guilt —**re·gret′ful** *adj.* —**re·gret′ful·ly** *adv.* —**re·gret′ta·ble** *adj.* —**re·gret′ta·bly** *adv.*

reg·u·la·tion (reg′yə lā′shən) *n.* **1.** an adjusting or being adjusted **2.** a rule or law by which conduct is controlled [safety *regulations*]

re·hears·al (ri hʉr′s′l) *n.* a practice performance of a play, concert, etc.

re·hearse (ri hʉrs′) *v.* **-hearsed′, -hears′ing** [< OFr. < *re-*, again + *herser*, to harrow] to perform (a play, concert, etc.) for practice

reign (rān) *n.* [< OFr. < L. *regnum* < *regere* to rule] the period of rule, influence, etc. —*v.* to rule as a sovereign [Henry VIII *reigned* for 38 years]

re·joice (ri jois′) *v.* **-joiced′, -joic′ing** [< OFr. *rejoir* < *re-*, again + *joir* < L. *gaudere*, to rejoice] to be glad or happy [we *rejoiced* at the news]

re·lapse (ri laps′; *for n.,* also rē′laps) *v.* **-lapsed′ -laps′ing** [< L. pp. of *relabi*, to slip back] to slip back into a former condition, —*n.* the reappearance of a disease after apparent improvement

re·lat·ed (ri lāt′id) *adj.* connected or associated by kinship, marriage, etc., of the same family or kind [oranges, lemons, and *related* fruits; a man *related* to the king]

rel·a·tive (rel′ə tiv) *adj.* related each to the other; referring to each other [to stay in the same *relative* positions] —*n.* a person related to others by blood or marriage; member of the same family

re·li·ance (ri lī′əns) *n.* trust, dependence, or confidence [air travelers put complete *reliance* in the pilot]

re·li·gion (ri lij′ən) *n.* [< OFr. < L. *religio* < *re-*, back + *ligare*, to bind] belief in a superhuman power or powers to be obeyed and worshiped

re·me·di·al (ri mē′dē əl) *adj.* **1.** providing, or intended to provide, a remedy **2.** of or being a course for helping students who are having difficulty in the subject [*remedial* reading] —**re·me′di·al·ly** *adv.*

rem·e·dy (rem′ə dē) *n., pl.* **-dies** [< Anglo-Fr. < OFr. < L. *remedium* < *re*, again + *mederi*, to heal] any medicine or treatment that cures or relieves a disease or restores health

re·peal (ri pēl′) *v.* [< OFr. *rapeler*] to withdraw; revoke; cancel [to *repeal* a law]

re·pel (ri pel′) *v.* **-pelled′, -pel′ling** [< L. < *re-*, back + *pellere*, to drive] to drive back or force back [to *repel* an attack] —**re·pel′ler** *n.*

re·ply (ri plī′) *v.* **-plied′, -ply′ing** [< OFr. < L. < *re-*, back + *plicare*, to fold] to answer in speech or writing [to *reply* to a question] —*n., pl.* **plies′** an answer in speech or writing

re·port·er (ri pôrt′ər) *n.* a person who gathers information and writes reports for a newspaper, magazine, etc.

re·press (re pres′) *v.* [< L. pp. of *reprimere*] **1.** to hold back [to *repress* a sigh] **2.** to put down, subdue [to *repress* an uprising] —**re·pres′sive** *adj.* —**re·pres′sive·ly** *adv.*

re·quire (ri kwīr′) *v.* **-quired′, -quir′ing** [< OFr. < L. *requirere* < *re-*, again + *quaerere*, to ask] **1.** to insist upon; demand **2.** to be in need of [to *require* help]

a	fat	ir	here	ou	out	zh	leisure
ā	ape	ī	bite, fire	u	up	ŋ	ring
ä	car, lot	ō	go	ʉr	fur		a *in* ago
e	ten	ô	law, horn	ch	chin		e *in* agent
er	care	oi	oil	sh	she	ə = i *in* unity
ē	even	oo	look	th	thin		o *in* collect
i	hit	ōo	tool	th	then		u *in* focus

re·quire·ment (-mənt) *n.* something required or de-manded, as a condition [to meet the *requirements* for the job]

re·sem·ble (ri zem′b'l) *v.* **-bled, -bling** [< OFr. < *re-*, again + *sembler* < L. *simulare*] to be like or similar to in appearance or nature [rabbits *resemble* hares but are smaller]

re·sign (ri zīn′) *v.* [< MFr. < L. < *re-*, back + *signare*, to sign] to give up or relinquish esp. by for-mal notice [he *resigned* from the club]

re·sist (ri zist′) *v.* [< MFr. < L. < *re-*, back + *sistere*, to set < *stare*, to stand] **1.** to withstand; fend off [stainless steel *resists* rust] **2.** to refuse to cooperate with or submit to [to *resist* a police officer] —**re·sist′er** *n.*

re·sist·ance (ri zis′təns) *n.* a resisting; opposition

re·solved (ri zälvd′, -zôlvd′) *adj.* with one's mind made up; determined

re·spell (rē spel′) *v.* to spell again

re·sume (ri zōōm′, -zyōōm′) *v.* **-sumed′, -sum′ing** [< L. < *re-*, again + *sumere*, to take] to begin again or go on with again after interruption [to *re-sume* a conversation]

re·tract (ri trakt′) *v.* [< L. ult. < *re-*, back + *trahere*, to draw] **1.** to draw back or in [the cat *re-tracted* its claws] **2.** to withdraw or take back (a statement, promise, etc.)

ret·ro·spect (ret′rə spekt′) *n.* [< L. < *retro-*, back + *specere*, to look] a looking back on or thinking about things past —**ret′ro·spec′tion** *n.*

rev·e·nue (rev′ə nōō, -nyōō) *n.* [< MFr. < *re-*, back + *venir* < L. *venire*, to come] the income or return from property, investment, taxes, etc.

re·vi·sion (ri vizh′ən) *n.* act or work of revising

re·viv·al (ri vī′v'l) *n.* **1.** a new presentation of an earlier play, movie, etc. **2.** restoration to life or activity

re·vive (ri vīv′) *v.* **-vived′, -viv′ing** [< OFr. < L. < *re-*, again + *vivere*, to live] **1.** to come or bring back to life or health **2.** to present (a play or movie) again after a time

ri·dic·u·lous (ri dik′yə ləs) *adj.* deserving ridicule; absurd —**ri·dic′u·lous·ly** *adv.*
—**ri·dic′u·lous·ness** *n.*

rob (räb) *v.* **robbed, rob′bing** [OFr. *rober* < IE. base *rev-*, to tear apart] to steal something from —**rob′ber** *n.*

rob·ber·y (räb′ə rē) *n. pl.* **-ber·ies** a robbing; stealing

ro·man·tic (rō man′tik) *adj.* **1.** of, like, or charac-terized by romance **2.** describing or having to do with loving or wooing in an idealized way —**ro·man′ti·cal·ly** *adv.*

roof (rōōf, roof) *n., pl.* **roofs** [OE. hrof] the out-side top covering over a house or building —**raise the roof** to be very noisy, as in anger or joy —**roof′less** *n.*

rope (rōp) *n.* [OE. *rap*] a thick strong cord made of strands of fiber, wires, etc. twisted together —**the end of one's rope** the end of one's endurance, re-sources, etc.

rub (rub) *v.* **rubbed, rub′bing** [ME. *rubben*] to move (one's hand, a cloth, etc.) back and forth over —**rub the wrong way** to annoy or irritate

rup·ture (rup′chər) *n.* [< L. < pp. of *rumpere*, to break] a breaking apart or being broken apart —*v.* **-tured, -tur·ing** to break apart or burst

S

S, S., s, s. 1. south **2.** southern

sab·o·tage (sab′ə täzh′) *n.* [Fr. < *saboter*, to damage < *sabot* + age: from damage done to ma-chinery by wooden shoes] deliberate harm or damage done to an object, cause, effort, etc. —*v.* **-taged′, -tag′ing** to injure or destroy by sabotage

sad (sad) *adj.* **sad′der, sad′dest** [OE. *saed*, sated < IE. base *sa-*, satisfied] having or expressing low spir-its or sorrow; unhappy —**sad′ly** *adv.* —**sad′ness** *n.*

sal·a·ry (sal′ə rē) *n., pl.* **-ries** [< L. *salarium*, orig., part of a Roman soldier's pay for buying salt < *sal*, salt] a fixed amount of money paid at regular times for work done

sar·cas·tic (sär kas′tik) *adj.* of, using, or full of mocking or sneering; jeering —**sar·cas′ti·cal·ly** *adv.*

sau·na (sou′nə *or* sô′nə) *n.* **1.** a kind of Finnish bath, in which the body is exposed to very hot, rela-tively dry air, and the skin is beaten lightly with birch or cedar branches **2.** the room or other en-closure for such a bath

scarce (skers) *adj.* [ONormFr. *escars,* ult. < L. *ex-cerpere,* to select] **1.** not common; rarely seen **2.** not plentiful; hard to get

scarce·ly (skers′lē) *adv.* hardly; barely [I can *scarcely* hear you]

scar·ci·ty (sker′sə tē) *n., pl.* **-ties** the condition of being scarce; inadequate supply

sci·ence (sī′əns) *n.* [< OFr. < L. < prp. of *scire,* to know, orig., to distinguish, separate] knowledge made up of an orderly system of facts gotten by means of observation, study, and experimentation

scoop (skoōp) *n.* [MDu. *schope,* bailing vessel & *schoope,* a shovel < IE. base *(s)kep-,* to cut] **1.** any of various tools shaped like a small shovel; specif., a kitchen utensil used to take up sugar, flour, etc. or a small utensil with a round bowl, for dishing up ice cream, mashed potatoes, etc. **2.** the deep shovel of a dredge or steam shovel, which takes up sand, dirt, etc. **3.** the amount taken up at one time by a scoop [two *scoops* of ice cream] —*v.* to take up or out as with a scoop —**scoop′er** *n.*

se·cede (si sēd′) *v.* **-ced′ed, -ced′ing** [< L < *se-,* apart + *cedere,* to go] to withdraw formally from membership in a group

se·ces·sion (si sesh′ən) *n.* an act of seceding

se·cure (si kyoor′) *adj.* [< L. < *se-,* free from + *cura,* care] **1.** free from fear, doubt [to feel *secure* about the future] **2.** free from danger [a *secure* hiding place] —*v.* **-cured′, -cur′ing 1.** to make secure or safe —**se·cure′ly** *adv.*

se·cu·ri·ty (si kyoor′ə tē) *n., pl.* **-ties** the state of being free from fear, danger, doubt, etc.

se·lec·tion (sə lek′shən) *n.* **1.** a selecting or being selected **2.** a group of things to choose from [a *selection* of colors]

self-ad·dressed (self′ə drest′) *adj.* addressed to oneself [a *self-addressed* envelope]

sen·ti·ment (sen′tə mənt) *n.* [< L. prp. of *sentire,* to feel] feelings, esp. tender feelings, as apart from reason or judgment [he claims there is no room for *sentiment* in business]

sen·ti·men·tal (sen′tə men′t'l) *adj.* **1.** having or showing tender, gentle feelings **2.** influenced more by feeling than reason —**sen′ti·men′tal·ism** *n.* —**sen′ti·men′tal·ly** *adv.*

sep·a·rate (sep′ə rāt) *v.* **-rat′ed, -rat′ing** [< L. pp. of *separare* < *se-,* apart + *parare,* to arrange]

1. to set apart into groups; divide **2.** to keep apart by being between —**sep′a·rate·ly** *adv.*

se·quence (sē′kwəns) *n.* [< MFr. < LL. < L. *sequens,* sequent] the following of one thing after another; succession or continuity [the *sequence* of events in his life]
SYN.—**sequence** emphasizes a relationship through logical connection, numerical order, etc. [the *sequence* of events]; **series** applies to a number of similar, related things following one another in time or place [a *series* of concerts]; **chain** refers to a series that is connected physically or logically [a *chain* of ideas]; **succession** merely implies a following of one thing after another, without any necessary connection between them [a *succession* of errors]

set·tle (set′'l) *v.* **-tled, -tling** [OE. < *setl,* a seat < base of *sit*] **1.** to set in place comfortably [to *settle* oneself in a chair] **2.** to establish as a resident [he *settled* in London] **3.** to end a dispute

set·tle·ment (set′'l mənt) *n.* **1.** a new colony **2.** an agreement, adjustment [to reach a *settlement* in a dispute]

shel·lac (shə lak′) *n.* a thin varnish containing resin and alcohol —*v.* **-lacked′, -lack′ing** to apply shellac to

sher·bet (shur′bət) *n.* [< Turk. < Ar. *sharbah,* a drink] a frozen dessert like an ice but with gelatin and, often, milk added

ship (ship) *n.* [OE. *scip*] any large vessel for traveling on deep water —*v.* **shipped, ship′ping** to send by any carrier [to *ship* coal by rail] —**when** (or **if,** etc.) **one's ship comes in** when (or if, etc.) one becomes rich —**ship′pa·ble** *adj.*

ship·ment (ship′mənt) *n.* **1.** the shipping or transporting of goods **2.** goods shipped

sight·see·ing (sīt′sē′iŋ) *n.* the act of visiting places and things of interest —**sight′se′er** *n.*

sign (sīn) *n.* [< OFr. < L. *signum*] **1.** a gesture that tells something [a nod is a *sign* of approval] **2.** a publicly displayed board, etc. bearing information, advertising, etc. —*v.* to write one's name on [to *sign* a contract] —**sign′er** *n.*

a	fat	ir	here	ou	out	zh	leisure
ā	ape	ī	bite, fire	u	up	ŋ	ring
ä	car, lot	ō	go	ur	fur		a *in* ago
e	ten	ô	law, horn	ch	chin		e *in* agent
er	care	oi	oil	sh	she	ə = i *in* unity
ē	even	oo	look	th	thin		o *in* collect
i	hit	oō	tool	th	then		u *in* focus

sin·cere (sin sir′) *adj.* **-cer′er, -cer′est** [< MFr. < L. *sincerus,* clean] **1.** truthful; honest [*sincere* in wanting to help] **2.** genuine; real [*sincere* grief] —**sin·cere′ly** *adv.*

sin·cer·i·ty (sin ser′ə tē) *n., pl.* **-ties** a being sincere; honesty

si·nus (sī′nəs) *n.* [L., a bent surface] any air cavity in the skull opening into a nasal cavity

skep·tic (skep′tik) *adj.* [< L. < Gr. *skeptikos,* inquiring] one who habitually doubts or questions matters that most people accept

skep·ti·cal (skep′ti k'l) *adj.* not easily convinced; doubting; questioning —**skep′ti·cal·ly** *adv.*

skin (skin) *n.* [ON. *skinn*] the outer covering of the body —**jump out of one's skin** to shudder or start in fear

sky·scrap·er (skī′skrā′pər) *n.* ☆ a very tall building

slight (slīt) *adj.* [OE. *sliht,* level] **1.** light in build; slender **2.** small in amount, extent, or importance [a *slight* fever] —**slight′ly** *adv.* —**slight′ness** *n.*

slip (slip) *v.* **slipped, slip′ping** [MLowG. *slippen*] **1.** to shift or slide from position [the plate *slipped* from my hand] **2.** to slide accidentally [to *slip* on ice] —**let slip** to say without meaning to

slip·per·y (slip′ər ē, slip′rē) *adj.* **-per·i·er, -per·i·est** [OE. *slipur*] causing or liable to cause slipping, as a wet surface —**slip′per·i·ness** *n.*

☆ **smoke·stack** (smōk′stak′) *n.* a pipe for the discharge of smoke from a steamship, factory, etc.

snake (snāk) *v.* **snaked, snak′ing** [OE. *snaca*] to move, twist, etc. like a snake [a soldier *snaking* along on his belly]

so·ci·e·ty (sə sī′ə tē) *n. pl.* **-ties** [< MFr. < L. *societas* < *socius,* companion] a group of persons who have the same customs, beliefs, etc. or live under a common government

some·one (sum′wun′, -wən) *pron.* a person unknown or not named —*n.* a person of importance

so·nar (sō′när) *n.* [*so(und) n(avigation) a(nd) r(anging)*] an apparatus that transmits high-frequency sound waves through water and registers the vibrations reflected back from an object

son·net (sän′it) *n.* [Fr. < It. < Pr. dim of *son,* a song < L. *sonus,* sound] a poem of fourteen lines in any of several fixed verse and rhyme schemes, usually in iambic pentameter

spe·cif·ic (spi sif′ik) *adj.* [LL. *specificus* < L. *species,* appearance, shape, kind + *-ficus,* -fic] definite; exact [no *specific* plans for the trip] —**spe·cif′i·cal·ly** *adv.*

spec·tac·u·lar (spek tak′yə lər) *adj.* of or like a spectacle; strikingly grand or unusual [a *spectacular* display of roses] —**spec·tac′u·lar·ly** *adv.*

spec·ta·tor (spek′tāt ər, spek tāt′-) *n.* [L. < pp. of *spectare,* to behold] a person who watches something without taking part; onlooker [*spectators* at a sports event]

spell¹ (spel) *n.* [OE., a saying] **1.** a word or words supposed to have some magic power **2.** power or control that seems magical; charm; fascination —**cast a spell on** to enchant or charm by or as by magic —**under a spell** held in a spell

spell² (spel) *v.* **spelled** or **spelt, spell′ing** [< OFr. *espeller,* to explain < Frank. *spellōn*] to say, write, or signal in order the letters of (a word, etc.) —**spell out 1.** to read letter by letter or with difficulty ☆ **2.** to explain in detail [the supervisor *spelled out* his duties]

spell³ (spel) *v.* **spelled, spell′ing** [OE. *spelian*] [Colloq.] to work in place of (another) while he rests; relieve —*n.* **1.** a turn of working in place of another **2.** any period of work, duty, etc. [a two-year *spell* as reporter] **3.** a period (of being in some state) [a *spell* of gloom]

split (split) *v.* **split, split′ting** [MDu. *splitten*] **1.** to separate, cut, or divide along the grain or length into two or more parts [to *split* a wiener bun] **2.** to break or rip apart by force [the crash *split* the wing off the plane] **3.** to divide into parts or shares [to *split* the cost] —*n.* **1.** a break, crack, or tear [a *split* in the seam of her dress] **2.** a division in a group, between persons, etc. —*adj.* **1.** separated along the length or grain **2.** divided; separated —**split′ter** *n.*

spon·ta·ne·i·ty (spän′tə nē′ə tē, -nā′-) *n.* the state or quality of being spontaneous

spon·ta·ne·ous (spän tā′nē əs) *adj.* [< LL. < L. *sponte,* of free will] acting or done in a free, natural way, without effort or much thought [the audience broke into *spontaneous* applause] —**spon·ta′ne·ous·ly** *adv.*

spoon·ful (spoon′ fool′) *n., pl.* **-fuls′** as much as a spoon will hold

spray (sprā) *n.* [< or akin to MDu. *spraeien,* to spray] a cloud or mist of fine liquid particles, as of water from breaking waves —*v.* to direct a spray (upon) —**spray′er** *n.*

squash (skwäsh, skwôsh) *v.* [< OFr. *esquasser,* ult. < L. *ex-,* thoroughly + pp. of *quatere,* to shake] to crush into a soft or flat mass

squir·rel (skwɵr′əl) *n., pl.* **-rels, -rel** [< OFr., ult < L. *sciurus* < Gr. < *skia,* a shadow + *oura,* tail] any of a group of small rodents that have a long, bushy tail and live in trees

stalk (stôk) *n.* [akin to OE. *stela,* a stalk] the main stem of a plant

stall (stôl) *v.* [OE. *steall* < IE. base *stel-,* to place] to stop, as from failure to work properly [the car *stalled* when the motor got wet]

star (stär) *n.* [OE. *steorra* < IE. base *ster-,* a star] **1.** any heavenly body seen as a point of light in the night sky **2.** a leading actor or actress or other person outstanding in some field —*v.* to have a leading role [she *stars* in his new movie]

stead·y (sted′ē) *adj.* **stead′i·er, stead′i·est** [OE. *stede* + -y] **1.** that does not shake, totter, etc.; firm; stable [a *steady* table] **2.** constant, regular, or continuous; not faltering [a *steady* gaze] —*v.* **stead′ied, stead′y·ing** to make or become steady ☆ **go steady** to date only one person and do so regularly —**stead′i·ly** *adv.* —**stead·i·ness** *n.*

steel (stēl) *n.* [OE. *stiele*] **1.** a hard, tough metal composed of iron alloyed with a small percentage of carbon and often with other metals, as nickel, chromium, etc., to produce hardness, resistance to rust, etc. **2.** great strength or hardness [muscles of *steel*] —*adj.* of or like steel

ster·e·o (ster′ē ō′, stir′-) *n., pl.* **-os′** ☆ a stereophonic record player, radio, record, tape, etc.

ster·e·o·phon·ic (ster′ē ə fän′ik, stir′-) *adj.* [stereo + phonic] describing sound reproduction using two or more channels

ster·e·o·type (ster′ē ə tīp′, stir′-) *n.* a fixed idea or popular conception, as about how a certain type of person looks, acts, etc. —*v.* **-typed′, -typ′ing** to make a stereotype of

stir (stɵr) *v.* **stirred, stir′ring** [OE. *styrian*] **1.** to mix (a liquid, etc.) by moving it around **2.** to incite or provoke (often with *up*) [to *stir* up trouble] —**stir′rer** *n.*

stop (stäp) *v.* **stopped, stop′ping** [< OE. < Gr. *styppē,* tow fibers] **1.** to cause to cease motion, activity, etc. **2.** to come to an end [the noise *stopped*] —*n.* a finish; end —**pull out all (the) stops** to make an all-out effort

stor·age (stôr′ij) *n.* **1.** a storing or being stored **2.** a place for storing goods

straight (strāt) *adj.* [< ME. pp. of *strecchen,* to stretch] not crooked, bent, wavy, etc. —*adv.* without detour, delay, etc. [go *straight* home]

straight·en (strāt′′n) *v.* to make or become straight —**straight′en·er** *n.*

sub- a prefix meaning: **1.** under, beneath [*subsoil*] **2.** somewhat [*subtropical*] **3.** by or forming a smaller part [*subsection*]

sub·con·scious (sub kän′shəs) *adj.* occurring with little or no awareness on the part of the individual [a *subconscious* desire] —**sub·con′scious·ly** *adv.* —**sub·con′scious·ness** *n.*

sub·di·vi·sion (sub′di vizh′ən, sub′di vizh′ən) *n.* **1.** a dividing (or being divided) into smaller parts **2.** one of the parts resulting from dividing **3.** an area of land divided into smaller lots

sub·merge (səb mɵrj′) *v.* **-merged′, -merg′ing** [< L. < *sub-,* under + *mergere,* to plunge] to sink, plunge, or place under or as under water, etc.

sub·mit (səb mit′) *v.* **-mit′ted, -mit′ting** [< L. < *sub-,* under + *mittere,* to send] to present to others for them to look over, decide about, etc. —**sub·mit′ter** *n.*

sub·or·di·nate (sə bôr′də nit) *adj.* [< ML. pp. of *subordinare* < L. *sub-,* under + *ordinare,* to order] below another in rank, power, importance, etc.; secondary [a *subordinate* job] —**sub·or′din·ate·ly** *adv.* —**sub·or′di·na′tion** *n.*

sub·ter·ra·ne·an (sub′tə rā′nē ən) *adj.* [< L. < *sub-,* under + *terra,* earth] being, living, or working beneath the earth's surface; underground [a *subterranean* river]

a	fat	ir	here	ou	out	zh	leisure
ā	ape	ī	bite, fire	u	up	ŋ	ring
ä	car, lot	ō	go	ɵr	fur	ə	*a in* ago
e	ten	ô	law, horn	ch	chin		e *in* agent
er	care	oi	oil	sh	she	ə = i *in* unity
ē	even	oo	look	th	thin		o *in* collect
i	hit	o͞o	tool	*th*	then		u *in* focus

sub·ur·ban (sə bʉr′bən) *adj.* of or living on the outskirts of a city

suc·ceed (sək sēd′) *v.* [L. < *sub-*, under + *cedere*, to go] to manage to do something planned or tried [to *succeed* in convincing someone]

suc·cess·ful (sək ses′fəl) *adj.* **1.** turning out to be as was hoped for **2.** having gained wealth, fame, etc. —**suc·cess′ful·ly** *adv.* —**suc·cess′ful·ness** *n.*

suf·fer (suf′ər) *v.* [< Anglo-Fr. < L. *suffere* < *sub-*, under + *ferre*, to bear] to undergo (something painful or unpleasant, as injury, a loss, etc.) —**suf′fer·er** *n.* —**suf′fer·ing** *n.*

suf·fi·cient (sə fish′′nt) *adj.* [< OFr. < L. *sufficere* < *sub-*, under + *facere*, to make] as much as is needed; enough [*sufficient* supplies to last through the month] —**suf·fi′cient·ly** *adv.*

☆ **sun·dae** (sun′dē, -dā) *n.* [prob. < Sunday] a dish of ice cream covered with syrup, fruit, nuts, etc.

sun·set (sun′set) *n.* **1.** the daily disappearance of the sun below the western horizon **2.** the time of this **3.** the color of the sky at this time

su·per- *a prefix meaning* over, above, beyond, superior to, surpassing [*superstructure, superintendent*]

su·per·in·tend·ent (sōō′pər in ten′dənt) *n.* a person in charge of a department, institution, etc.; supervisor

su·per·la·tive (sə pʉr′lə tiv, soo-) *adj.* [< MFr. < LL. < L. *super-*, above + *latus*, pp. of *ferre*, to carry] of the highest kind; supreme

su·per·mar·ket (sōō′pər mär′kit) *n.* a large, self-service food store, often one of a chain

su·per·nat·u·ral (sōō′pər nach′ər əl) *adj.* existing outside normal experience or the known laws of nature —**su′per·nat′u·ral** *adv.*

su·per·son·ic (sōō′pər sän′ik) *adj.* moving at a speed greater than that of sound

su·per·vise (sōō′pər vīz′) *v.* -**vised′**, -**vis′ing** [< ML. pp. of *supervidere* < L. *super-*, over + *videre*, to see] to oversee or manage —**su′per·vi′sion** *n.*

sup·port (sə pôrt′) *v.* [< MFr. < LL. < L. < *sub-*, under + *portare*, to carry] **1.** to carry or bear the weight of; hold up [the ladder will *support* you] **2.** to give approval to or be in favor of; uphold [to *support* a cause]

sup·pose (sə pōz′) *v.* -**posed′**, **pos′ing** [< L. *sub-*, under + *ponere*, to place] **1.** to believe, think,

guess, etc. [I *suppose* you're right] **2.** to expect: always in the passive [she's *supposed* to telephone]

sur·geon (sʉr′jən) *n.* a doctor who specializes in surgery

sur·plus (sʉr′plus, -pləs) *n.* <OFr. < *sur-*, above + L. *plus*, more] a quantity over and above what is needed or used; excess [a grain *surplus* stored in silos]

sur·ren·der (sə ren′dər) *v.* [< MFr. < *sur-*, over + *rendre*, to render] to give oneself up, esp. as a prisoner; yield [the troops *surrendered*] —**sur·ren′der·er** *n.*

sur·round (sə round′) *v.* [< OFr. < LL. < L. *super*, over + *undare*, to rise < *unda*, a wave] to encircle on all or nearly all sides; enclose [trees *surround* the house]

sur·vey (sər vā′; *also, & for n. usually,* sʉr′vā) *v.* [< Anglo-Fr. < OFr. < *sur-* + *veoir* < L. *videre*, to see] to examine or inspect carefully —*n.,* *pl.* -**veys** a detailed study made by gathering and analyzing information [a *survey* of public opinion]

sur·viv·al (sər vī′v'l) *n.* the act or fact of surviving

sus·cep·ti·ble (sə sep′tə b'l) *adj.* [< ML. < L. pp. of *suscipere*, to receive] easily affected emotionally; having sensitive feelings

sweat (swet) *v.* **sweat** or **sweat′ed**, **sweat′ing** [OE. *swaetan* < *swat*, sweat < IE. base *sweid-*, to sweat] to give out a salty liquid through the pores of the skin; perspire [running fast made him *sweat*]

swim (swim) *v.* **swam, swum, swim′ming** [OE. *swimman*] to move through water by movements of the arms and legs, or of flippers, fins, etc. —*n.* an act, time, or distance of swimming [a short *swim*] —**in the swim** doing what is popular at the moment —**swim′ma·ble** *adj.* —**swim′mer** *n.*

swirl (swʉrl) *v.* [ME. *swyrl*, prob. < Norw. dial. *sverra*, to whirl] to move with a whirling motion [the snow kept *swirling* down] —**swirl′ing·ly** *adv.* —**swirl′y** *adj.*

sword (sôrd) *n.* [Oe. *sweord*] a hand weapon having a long, sharp, pointed blade, set in a hilt

sym·pa·thize (sim′pə thīz′) *v.* -**thized′**, -**thiz′ing** to share or understand the feelings or ideas of another; be in sympathy —**sym′pa·thiz′er** *n.*

sys·tem·at·ic (sis′tə mat′ik) *adj.* according to a system, method, or plan; orderly [a *systematic* search] —**sys′tem·at′i·cal·ly** *adv.*

T

tan·gi·ble (tan′jə b'l) *adj.* [< LL. *tangibilis* < L. *tangere,* to touch] that can be touched or felt by touch; having actual form and substance —**tan′gi·bil′i·ty** *n.* —**tan′gi·bly** *adv.*

taught (tôt) *pt.* + *pp. of* teach

tech·ni·cal (tek′ni k'l) *adj.* [< Gr. *technē,* an art + -al] of or used in a specific science, art, craft, etc. [*technical* terms] —**tech′ni·cal·ly** *adv.*

tech·nique (tek nēk′) *n.* [Fr. < Gr. *technē,* an art] the method of procedure in creating an artistic work or carrying out a scientific or mechanical operation

tech·nol·o·gy (tek näl′ə jē) *n.* [Gr. *technologia,* systematic treatment] **1.** the science or study of the practical or industrial arts, applied sciences, etc. **2.** science as it is put to use in actual practice or to work out practical problems —**tech·nol′o·gist** *n.*

tel·e·vise (tel′ə vīz′) *v.* -vised′, -vis′ing to send pictures of by television —**tel′e·vi′sor** *n.*

tel·e·vi·sion (tel′ə vizh′ən) *n.* [tele < Gr. < *telē,* far off + vision < L. *videre,* to see] **1.** the process of sending pictures by radio waves or wire **2.** a television set

tem·per·a·ment (tem′prə mənt, -pər ə mənt, -pər mənt) *n.* [L. *temperamentum,* proper mixing] one's usual frame of mind or natural disposition

tem·per·a·men·tal (tem′prə ment′t'l, -pər ə men′t'l, -pər men′t'l) *adj.* having a nature that is easily upset or excited —**tem′per·a·men′tal·ly** *adv.*

tend·en·cy (ten′dən sē) *n., pl.* -cies an inclination to move or act in a particular direction or way; leaning [a *tendency* to criticize]

ten·sion (ten′shən) *n.* mental or nervous strain; tense feeling

ter·race (ter′əs) *n.* [OFr., walled platform < It. *terrazzo* < L. *terra,* earth] **1.** an unroofed, paved area next to a house and overlooking a lawn or garden **2.** a balcony or deck outside an apartment

ter·rain (tə rān′, ter′ān) *n.* [Fr. < L. < *terra,* earth] an area of land, esp. with regard to its special features or its fitness for some use [hilly *terrain*]

ter·rar·i·um (tə rer′ē əm) *n. pl.* -i·ums, -i·a (-ə) [ModL. < L. *terra,* earth + -*arium* as in *aquarium*] an enclosure for keeping small animals or small plants

ter·rif·ic (tə rif′ik) *adj.* [< L < base of *terrere,* to frighten + -fic] **1.** causing great fear; terrifying; dreadful [a *terrific* storm] **2.** [Colloq.] a) unusually great, intense, etc. [a *terrific* burst of energy] b) unusually fine, admirable, enjoyable, etc. [a *terrific* actor] —**ter·rif′i·cal·ly** *adv.*

ter·ri·fy (ter′ə fī′) *v.* -fied′, -fy′ing [L. *terrificare* < *terrificus,* terrific] < to fill with terror; frighten greatly —**ter′ri·fy′ing·ly** *adv.*

ter·ri·to·ry (ter′ə tôr′ē) *n. pl.* -ries [L. *territorium* < *terra,* earth] the land and waters under the control of a nation, state, ruler, etc.

there's (*th*erz) **1.** there is **2.** there has

thor·ough (thʉr′ō, -ə) *prep., adv.* [ME. *thoruh,* a var. of *through*] complete in every way; with nothing left out, undone, etc. [a *thorough* checkup] —**thor′ough·ly** *adv.* —**thor′ough·ness** *n.*

thor·ough·bred (thʉr′ə bred′) *adj.* of pure or unmixed breed, as a horse or dog; pedigreed —*n.* a thoroughbred animal

thought·less (thôt′lis) *adj.* **1.** not stopping to think; careless; rash **2.** not considerate of others —**thought′less·ly** *adv.* —**thought′less·ness** *n.*

through·out (thro͞o out′) *prep.* all the way through; in or during every part of [*throughout* the week]

Thurs., Thur. Thursday

time·ta·ble (tīm′tā′b'l) *n.* a schedule of the times when certain things are to happen, esp. the arrival and departure of planes, buses, etc.

tim·id (tim′id) *adj.* [< L. *timere,* to fear] easily frightened; shy —**ti·mid·i·ty** (tə mid′ə tē), **tim′id·ness** *n.* —**tim′id·ly** *adv.*

tongue (tuŋ) *n.* [OE. *tunge*] **1.** the movable muscular part attached to the floor of the mouth **2.** something like a tongue in shape, position, motion, or use —**hold one's tongue** to keep oneself from speaking

a	fat	ir	here	ou	out	zh	leisure
ā	ape	ī	bite, fire	u	up	ŋ	ring
ä	car, lot	ō	go	ʉr	fur		a *in* ago
e	ten	ô	law, horn	ch	chin		e *in* agent
er	care	oi	oil	sh	she	ə	= i *in* unity
ē	even	oo	look	th	thin		o *in* collect
i	hit	o͞o	tool	*th*	then		u *in* focus

top·ping (täp′iŋ) *n.* something that forms the top of, or is put on top of, something else, as a sauce on food

tow (tō) *v.* [OE. *togian*] to pull as by a rope or chain

track (trak) *n.* [MFr. *trac*, a track] **1.** a mark or marks left by a person, animal, or thing in passing, as a footprint or rut **2.** a path or circuit laid out for running, horse racing, etc. **3.** a pair of parallel metal rails on which the wheels of trains, etc. run **4.** athletic sports performed on a track, as running, hurdling, etc.

☆ **trac·tor** (trak′tər) *n.* [ModL. < L. *tractus*, pp. of *trahere*, to draw] a powerful vehicle with large rear wheels, for pulling farm machinery, hauling loads, etc.

tra·di·tion (trə dish′ən) *n.* [< MFr. < L. < pp. of *tradere*, to deliver] any long-established custom or practice

tra·di·tion·al (trə dish′ən'l) *adj.* of, handed down by, or conforming to tradition; conventional —**tra·di′tion·al·ly** *adv.*

traf·fic (traf′ik) *n.* [< Fr. < It. < *trafficare*, to trade < L. *trans*, across + It. *ficcare*, to bring] the movement or numbers of cars along a street, pedestrians along a sidewalk, etc. —*adj.* of traffic or its regulation [a *traffic* light]

trag·e·dy (traj′ə dē) *n., pl.* **-dies** [< MFr. < L. < Gr. *tragōidia* < *tragos*, goat + *ōidē*, song] a very sad or unfortunate event

trail·er (trā′lər) *n.* ☆ **1.** a cart or van designed to be pulled by an automobile or truck, for hauling freight, animals, a boat, etc. ☆ **2.** a closed vehicle designed to be pulled by a motor vehicle and equipped as a place to live or work in

tram·po·line (tram′pə lēn′, -lin; tram′pə lēn′) *n.* [< It. *trampolino*, a springboard] ☆ a sheet of strong canvas stretched tightly on a frame, used as a kind of springboard in acrobatic tumbling —**tram′po·lin′er, tram′po·lin′ist** *n.*

tran·quil (traŋ′ kwəl, tran′-) *adj.* [L. < *tranquillus*] calm, quiet, peaceful, etc. [*tranquil* waters] —**tran′quil·ly** *adv.*

tran·quil·li·ty (traŋ kwil′ə tē, tran-) *n.* the quality or state of being tranquil; calmness

trans- *a prefix meaning* over, across, through [*transatlantic*]

trans·con·ti·nen·tal (trans′ kän tə nen′t'l) *adj.* that crosses a continent [a *transcontinental* flight]

trans·fer (trans fur′, *also, & for n. always,* trans′fər) *v.* **-ferred′, -fer′ring** [< L. < *trans-*, across + *ferre*, to bear] **1.** to move, carry, send, etc. from one person or place to another **2.** to change from one school, college, etc. to another **3.** to change from one bus, train, etc. to another —*n.* a ticket allowing the bearer to change from one bus, train, etc. to another

trans·for·ma·tion (trans′fər mā′shən) *n.* a changing of form or appearance —**trans′for·ma′tion·al** *adj.*

trans·fu·sion (trans fyo͞o′zhən) *n.* a transferring or introducing, esp. of blood into a blood vessel

trans·la·tion (trans lā′shən) *n.* writing or speech put into the words of another language

trans·mis·sion (trans mish′ən) *n.* **1.** a sending or being sent; conveying **2.** the part of an automobile that sends power from the engine to the wheels

trans·mit (trans mit′) *v.* **-mit′ted, -mit′ting** [< L. < *trans-*, over + *mittere*, to send] to send or cause to go from one person or place to another; convey [to *transmit* a letter]

trans·plant (trans plant′) *v.* to dig up (a growing plant) from one place and put it in another —**trans·plant′a·ble** *adj.* —**trans′plan·ta′tion** *n.*

trans·por·ta·tion (trans′pər tā′shən) *n.* a means or system of carrying things

tri·an·gle (trī′aŋ′g'l) *n.* [< MFr. < L.] **1.** a plane figure having three angles and three sides **2.** any three-sided or three-cornered figure, area, etc.

trib·al (trī′b'l) *adj.* of a tribe or tribes —**tri′bal·ly** *adv.*

tribe (trīb) *n.* [L. *tribus*, any of the divisions of the ancient Romans] a group of persons living together under a leader

trip (trip) *v.* **tripped, trip′ping** [OFr. *treper* < Gmc.] **1.** to stumble **2.** to make stumble —*n.* a going to or from a place; journey, esp. a short one

trou·ble (trub′'l) *v.* **-bled, -bling** [OFr. *trubler*, ult. < LL. *turbidare*, to trouble] **1.** to worry; perturb **2.** cause inconvenience to —*n.* **1.** worry **2.** a difficult situation

trou·ble·some (-səme) *adj.* full of or causing difficulty [a *troublesome* cough]

trous·seau (tro͞o′sō, tro͞o sō′) *n. pl.* **-seaux** (-sōz), **-seaus** [Fr. < OFr., dim of *trousse*, a bundle] a bride's outfit of clothes

tug·boat (tug′bōt′) *n.* a small, powerful boat used for towing or pushing ships, barges, etc.

tur·quoise (tʉr′koiz, -kwoiz) *n.* [< MFr. fem. of OFr. *turqueis*, Turkish] **1.** a greenish-blue, semi-precious stone **2.** a greenish-blue —*adj.* greenish-blue

two-thirds (to͞o thʉrdz′) *n.* two of the three equal parts of a whole

typ·i·cal (tip′i k'l) *adj.* belonging to a type; characteristic [a snail moving with *typical* slowness] —**typ′i·cal·ly** *adv.*

U

u·nan·i·mous (yoo nan′ə məs) *adj.* [< L. < *unus*, one + *animus*, the mind] agreeing completely; united in opinion —**u′na·nim′i·ty** *n.* —**u·nan′i·mous·ly** *adv.*

u·ni·form (yo͞o′nə fôrm′) *adj.* [< MFr. < L. < *unus*, one + *-formis*, -form] always the same; not varying in form, rate, degree, manner, etc. —*n.* the special clothes worn by members of a particular group —**u′ni·form′ly** *adv.*

u·nit·ed (yoo nīt′id) *adj.* **1.** combined; joined [the *united* armies of the allies] **2.** in agreement [we are *united* on that point]

u·ni·ver·sal (yo͞o′nə vʉr′s'l) *adj.* [< OFr. < L. *universum* < *unus*, one + pp. of *vertere*, to turn] present or occurring everywhere

up·set (up set′) *v.* **-set′**, **-set′ting 1.** to tip over, overturn [to *upset* a vase] **2.** to disturb mentally, emotionally, or physically [the bad news *upset* him]

us·a·ble, use·a·ble (yo͞o′zə b'l) *adj.* that can be used; ready for use —**us′a·bly** *adv.*

us·age (yo͞o′sij, -zij) *n.* **1.** the extent of using; treatment **2.** the way in which a word or phrase is used in speaking or writing

V

Va., VA, Virginia

va·ca·tion (və kā′shən, vā-) *n.* [< MFr. < L. *vacatio*] a period of time when one stops working or going to school in order to rest

vague (vāg) *adj.* **va′guer, va′guest** [Fr. < L. *vagus*, wandering] not definite in shape or form [*vague* figures in the fog] —**vague′ly** *adv.* —**vague′ness** *n.*

val·ley (val′ē) *n. pl.* **-leys** [< OFr. < L. *vallis*] a stretch of low land lying between hills or mountains

val·u·a·ble (val′yoo b'l, -yoo wə b'l) *adj.* having value; esp., having great value [a *valuable* diamond, *valuable* knowledge]

ve·hi·cle (vē′ə k'l, vē′hi-) *n.* [< Fr. < L. *vehiculum*, carriage < *vehere*, to carry] **1.** a means of carrying persons or things, esp. over land or in space, as an automobile, bicycle, sled, spacecraft, etc. **2.** a means by which something is expressed, passed along, etc. [television as a *vehicle* for advertising]

ven·tril·o·quism (ven tril′ə kwiz'm) *n.* [< L. < *venter*, belly + *loqui*, to speak + ism] the practice of speaking so that the voice seems to come from some source other than the speaker —**ven·tril′o·quist** *n.*

ven·ture (ven′chər) *n.* [< ME. *aventure*] an action or undertaking involving a risk [her *venture* into a stage career] —*v.* **-tured, -tur·ing** to risk; hazard [to *venture* one's fortune]

ven·ture·some (-səm) *adj.* willing to take chances; daring

vi·rus (vī′ rəs) *n.* [L., a poison] **1.** a form of matter that can multiply in living cells and cause disease **2.** a disease caused by a virus

vis·i·ble (viz′ə b'l) *adj.* [< OFr. < L. *visibilis* < pp. of *videre*, to see] that can be seen, evident [a barely *visible* scar] —**vis′i·bly** *adv.*

vis·it (viz′it) *v.* [< OFr. < L. *visere*, to go to see] to go or come to see (someone) —*n.* the act of visiting

a	fat	ir	here	ou	out	zh	leisure
ā	ape	ī	bite, fire	u	up	ŋ	ring
ä	car, lot	ō	go	ʉr	fur		a *in* ago
e	ten	ô	law, horn	ch	chin		e *in* agent
er	care	oi	oil	sh	she	ə = i *in* unity
ē	even	oo	look	th	thin		o *in* collect
i	hit	o͞o	tool	th	then		u *in* focus

vogue (vōg) *n.* [Fr., a fashion, lit., a rowing] the accepted fashion at any particular time; often with *the*

W

W, W., w, w. 1. west **2.** western

wal·nut (wôl′nut′, -nət) *n.* [< OE. < *wealh,* foreign + *hnutu,* a nut] **1.** any of a number of related trees, valued for their nuts and wood **2.** their edible nut, having a hard, crinkled shell and a two-lobed seed **3.** their wood, used for furniture, paneling, etc.

waste (wāst) *v.* **wast′ed, wast′ing** [ONormFr. *waster* < L. *vastare,* to lay waste] to use up or spend without need or purpose [*waste* money]

waste·ful (-fəl) *adj.* using more than is necessary [a *wasteful* person] —**waste′ful·ly** *adv.*

Wed. Wednesday

weigh (wā) *v.* [OE. *wegan,* to carry] **1.** to find out the weight of by using a scale or balance **2.** to have a (specified) weight [It *weighs* ten pounds]

when·ev·er (hwen ev′ər, wen-, hwən, wən-) *conj.* at whatever time [visit us *whenever* you can]

whip (hwip, wip) *v.* **whipped, whip′ping** [MDu. *wippen,* to swing] **1.** to strike, as with a strap, rod, etc.; lash; beat **2.** to beat (eggs, cream, etc.) into a froth with a fork, whisk, mixer, etc.

whirl·pool (hwurl′ pool′, wurl′-) *n.* water whirling rapidly in a circle into which floating objects are drawn; eddy of water

whole (hôl) *adj.* [OE. hal] containing all the parts; complete [a *whole* set]

whose (hōōz) *pron.* [OE. *hwəes*] that or those belonging to whom [*whose* is this?] —*adj.* of, belonging to, made by whom or which [the woman *whose* car was stolen]

wor·ship (wur′ship) *v.* **-shiped** or **-shipped, -ship·ing** or **-ship·ping** to take part in a religious service [freedom to *worship* as they pleased] —**wor′ship·er, wor′ship·per** *n.*

would·'ve (wood′uv) would have

wrap (rap) *v.* **wrapped** or **wrapt, wrap′ping** [ME. *wrappen*] **1.** cover by winding or folding (something) around **2.** to enclose and fasten in a wrapper of paper, etc. [a box *wrapped* for mailing]

wreath (rēth) *n., pl.* **wreaths** (rē*th*z) [OE. *writha,* a ring < *writhan,* to twist] a twisted band or ring of leaves, flowers, etc.

writ·ten (rit′n) *pp. of* write —*adj.* put down in a form to be read; not spoken [a *written* message]

wrought (rôt) *alt. pt. & pp. of* work —*adj.* shaped by hammering or beating; said of metals [*wrought* silver]

wry (rī) *adj.* **wri′er, wri′est** [OE. *wrigian,* to turn] **1.** turned or bent to one side; twisted [a *wry* mouth] **2.** ironic or bitter [*wry* humor] —**wry′ly** *adv.*

a	fat	ir	here	ou	out	zh	leisure
ā	ape	ī	bite, fire	u	up	ŋ	ring
ä	car, lot	ō	go	ur	fur		a *in* ago
e	ten	ô	law, horn	ch	chin		e *in* agent
er	care	oi	oil	sh	she	ə = i *in* unity
ē	even	oo	look	th	thin		o *in* collect
i	hit	oo	tool	th	then		u *in* focus

ILLUSTRATIONS
B. J. Johnson: 8, 12, 16, 20, 24, 28, 32, 36, 125, 128, 129, 133, 135, 136, 144, 147, 148, 149
Ray Fredericks: 5
David Cunningham: 5, 45
Martucci Studio/Jerry Malone: 6
Richard Martin: 9, 10, 11, 13, 15, 17, 18, 19, 22, 25, 26, 31, 35, 38
Carol Stutz: 29
Don Sinks: 46, 50, 54, 58, 62, 66, 70, 74
Ed Aitchison: 47, 49, 52, 53, 56, 57, 63, 64, 68, 69, 72, 73
Troy Thomas: 83, 121
Larry Frederick: 84, 88, 92, 96, 100, 104, 108, 112
Yoshi Miyake: 85, 87, 90, 93, 94, 95, 97, 98, 105, 106, 107, 109, 110, 111
Jan Brett: 122, 126, 130, 134, 138, 142, 146, 150

Cover Photograph: M. P. Kahl/Photo Researchers
Cover Design: Martucci Studio

Editorial Credits

Executive Editor, Language Arts: Carolyn McConnell

Senior Editor: Sandra Corniels

Associate Editors: Lisa Maria DeSloover, Patricia King, Carol Kalas McMullen

Project Assistance: Brown Publishing Network, Inc.

Art and Design: Chestnut House, Martucci Studio